Christmas '95.

Marion J,
lots of love,
Angela & Jon.
xxx

# CHILDHOOD'S
## PATTERN

# CHILDHOOD'S PATTERN

*Christian Childhoods*
*Explored by*
## DAVID JARMAN

*and*

## CELIA VAN OSS

**FIRETHORN PRESS**

**Waterstone & Co. Limited**
**49 Hay's Mews**
**London W1X 7RT**

© 1985 Waterstone & Co. Limited

**FIRETHORN PRESS**
is an imprint of Waterstone & Co. Limited

Typeset by Concept Communications, Dartford, Kent.

Printed and bound by Whitstable Litho Ltd,
Whitstable, Kent.

ISBN: 0-947752-10-2 hardcover
ISBN: 0-947752-11-0 softcover

# CONTENTS

INTRODUCTION
pages ix – xiv

I
INTIMATIONS
pages 1 – 27

*Harold Owen*
*L P Hartley*
*Marcel Proust*
*A L Rowse*
*C S Lewis*

II
MISCHIEF
pages 29 – 43

*Edmund Gosse*
*Lord Berners*
*Charles Dickens*
*Flora Thompson*

III
THE SENSE OF UNFAIRNESS
pages 45 – 65

*St Augustine*
*Samuel Butler*
*Charles Dickens*
*Charlotte Brontë*

IV
THE DESIRE TO PLEASE
pages 67 – 96

*Mary McCarthy*
*Edwin Muir*
*E Nesbit*
*Louisa M Alcott*

## V
## QUESTIONING
pages 97 – 121

*W Somerset Maugham*
*Edmund Gosse*
*Lord Berners*
*James Joyce*

## VI
## ROLE PLAYING
pages 123 – 159

*Edmund Gosse*
*Flannery O'Connor*
*Mary McCarthy*

## VII
## ENCOUNTERING GOODNESS
pages 161 – 189

*Susan Hill*
*Christopher Milne*
*Maxim Gorki*
*Charlotte Brontë*
*Frank O'Connor*

## VIII
## THE AWAKENING CONSCIENCE
pages 191 – 210

*Juliana Horatia Ewing*
*Charles Lamb*
*Frances Hodgson Burnett*

# ACKNOWLEDGEMENTS

The publishers wish to thank the following for their kind permission to reprint copyright material.

Lord Berners from *First Childhood*. Reproduced by permission of Robert Heeber-Percy Esq.

Claud Cockburn from *Cockburn Sums Up*. Reproduced by permission of Quartet Books, London.

L P Hartley from *Eustace and Hilda*. Reproduced by permission of The Bodley Head Ltd.

James Joyce from *Portrait of the Artist as a Young Man*. Reproduced by permission of the Executors of the James Joyce Estate.

C S Lewis from *Surprised by Joy*. Reproduced by permission of William Collins & Co Ltd.

Mary McCarthy from *Memories of a Catholic Girlhood*. Reproduced by permission of the author.

W Somerset Maugham from *Of Human Bondage*. Reproduced by permission of the Executors of the Estate of W Somerset Maugham and William Heinemann Ltd.

Christopher Milne from *Enchanted Places*. Reproduced by permission of the author and Methuen, London.

Edwin Muir from *An Autobiography*. Reproduced by permission of the author's Estate and The Hogarth Press.

Flannery O'Connor, The River, from *A Good Man is Hard to Find*. Reproduced by permission of A D Peters and Co Ltd.

Frank O'Connor, *First Confession*. Reproduced by permission of A D Peters and Co Ltd.

Harold Owen from *Journey from Obscurity*, volume one © Oxford University Press (1963). Reproduced by permission of Oxford University Press.

Flora Thompson from *Lark Rise to Candleford* (1954). Reproduced by permission of Oxford University Press.

# INTRODUCTION

If there is any one thing which we all share it is a sense of the role of particular moments of childhood in determining our adulthood; such episodes may differ but their importance cannot. For the vast majority, too, our encounters as children with religious ideas, whether Christian or otherwise, have left their marks for good or ill. Let it be said at once then that both good and ill are represented here.

People may be wary of a collection such as this; the subtitle 'Christian Childhoods' might be expected to herald a collection of exhortations to childhood purity and piety. Thankfully, nothing could be further from the truth.

The appeal of a compilation such as this is multi-faceted and, as such, hard to define. For some, its literary qualitites will be enough, including as it does both the very well-known (Dickens, Charlotte Brontë, Somerset Maugham) and authors of great talent who have either been largely forgotten (Juliana Ewing, Edmund Gosse, Lord Berners) or have never been particularly widely read (Frank O'Connor, Flannery O'Connor). Others, it is hoped, will find it useful in attempting to assess their own experiences as children, for the sheer variety of the pieces ensures that some, if not all of it will strike a familiar chord. It may be that as a result it will promote a fresh consideration by parents of the way in which their own children are brought up. In a piece written for this collection, the British author and playwright Susan Hill sketches a kind of personal manifesto, assessing what is helpful and what is destructive in our encounters with religion as children, setting out the precepts and experiences by which her own family is guided, and examining and explaining these decisions. In a way, Ms Hill's piece is the kind of conclusion which any parent, indeed any adult, might come to having read the rest of the collection and learned from it, for the personal experience she draws on find many parallels here; while it is not 'a guide for parents' the book may have much to contribute in that way.

A great part of the book's effectiveness lies in its juxtaposition not only of pieces of widely different origin—St Augustine rubs shoulders with Flora Thompson and Samuel Butler—but from both books 'for children' and 'for adults'. Of course, none of the excerpts from children's books require the adult reader to plough through 'childish' writing; indeed there is a strong pleasure in rediscovering books as famous as Frances Hodgson Burnett's *The Little Princess*, Louisa M Alcott's *Little Women* and Edith Nesbit's *The Wouldbegoods*, all classics. That pleasure of rediscovery, and not simply the rediscovery of fine writing, can be described at least partially as 'nostalgia', and there is a strong sense of nostalgia elsewhere in the book, too, particularly in the passages by Harold Owen, L P Hartley and Mary McCarthy as well as in the more urgent self-investigation of Proust and Joyce. About this sense of nostalgia something perhaps needs to be said.

Today 'nostalgia' can be a dirty word; it is often used in a dis-paraging sense, carrying with it a series of concepts—sentimentality, escapism, distortion of the past, even reactionism. A collection such as this, then, even though barely half is contributors lived recently enough for the reader to look back at them with 'nostalgia' in the true sense, runs the risk of taking upon itself all these encumbering ideas, for childhood is more often in our cultural representations the object of nostalgic feeling than of distaste, and Christianity, it must be said, is more usually associated, at least by non-Christians (or lapsed ones come to that) with the past rather than the future. Childhood-in-the-past is nowadays very commonly thought of in terms of 'decency', 'discipline', 'respect' and so on—all 'barbed-wire' words today pre-cisely because they were often encouraged, as this collection shows, in grossly inhumanitarian ways. Nostalgia, then, is a two-edged sword, which needs to be tempered by a strong sense of the realities of the present; it becomes a useful, not just a simple, pleasure when it guides our thinking about the future.

Some of the pieces here are very well-known. The value of their inclusion lies not necessarily in that the experience they describe is forcefully communicated, not simply in that their words are arranged with great artistry. Passages like those from *Jane Eyre* and *Bleak House* are important here not only for those reasons but because they have become in a sense paradigmatic—so celebrated that they form the terms in which we now think about the whole subject of childhood in the past. No matter that Dickens' Reverend Chadband and street-sweeper Jo are 'over the top'; their exaggeration (as with all caricatures ensuring in the first place that the audience cannot possible misinter-pret what is being said) now informs our own conception of the Victorian era so strongly that we habitually think of it in terms of black-and-white, haves and have-nots, and of Christianity corrupted into a class weapon (and a schoolroom weapon). What is important here is not 'historical accuracy' but the relevance of the passage to ourselves and to *our* children; not whether these things happened, but whether they are possible.

Having said that, it should be stressed that by no means every piece has a didactic function here. The opening selection, from Harold Owen's vast history of his family *Journey from Obscurity*, leads us gently into the collection with an anecdote about the origin of one of his brother Wilfred's most famous couplets, from 'Spring Offensive';

> *And the far valley behind, where the buttercup*
> *Had blessed with gold their slow boots coming up.*

Owen creates a picture of rural England just before the Great War; a place and time widely recalled in literature but rarely more touchingly than this.

A story called *The River*, by the American writer Flannery O'Connor, is just as moving in its own way, but it is also disturbing and bizarre. During her short career Flannery O'Connor (1925–1964) published only two novels and two collections of stories, but her impact in the United States has been tremendous. An orthodox Catholic from the deeply Protestant South, her work, which often deals with people at the bottom of the social heap, is charged with religious, but personal and sometimes grotesque, inspiration.

In a completely different vein, but like Owen and O'Connor not strongly didactic, are the excerpts from the autobiography of Lord Berners, *First Childhood*. It was published in 1934, and preceded a series of successful novels. But Lord Berners, one of the most fascinating and colourful characters of his day, had already made a reputation for himself not only through distinct personal eccentricity but as a composer of ballet (his works were performed by Diaghilev's company and by Sadler's Wells), a painter who was close to the Futurist and Surrealist movements before such things had been heard of in England and, initially, as a diplomat. A friend of Stravinsky in the 'twenties and Firbank in the 'forties, the baleful influence of Emma Harriet, Baroness Berners, his grandmother, turned him into an 'unabashed hedonist', a process which he illustrates here, not entirely without affection. He composed his own epitaph;

> *Here lies Lord Berners*
> *One of the learners*

*His great love of learning*
*May earn him a burning*
*But, Praise the Lord*
*He was seldom bored.*

In the case of Sir Edmund Gosse (1849–1928) the bugbear was his father. A friend of Swinburne, R L Stevenson and Henry James, Gosse was a well-known critic—he introduced Ibsen to the British public—who became librarian of the House of Lords. In extracts which are alternately funny and tragic he traces the beginnings of what was to be a complete intellectual isolation from his puritanical father.

In contrast to the uneasy protestantism of Berners and Gosse, Mary McCarthy, an Irish-American, and Frank O'Connor, an Irishman who lived in the United States for a time, describe their struggles with Catholicism. McCarthy, a formidable critic, political essayist and novelist, was orphaned at an early age, and had amusing and affectionate memories of her convent education, as well as explaining seriously the nature of her belief. Frank O'Connor, best known as a poet and playwright, shows himself to be a master of prose in a hilarious and touching account of his 'encounter with goodness'.

The book is divided into eight sections, each of which is given a short introduction. Within each, the passages are related by theme yet the effect is not of repetition but of disparity. Thus, in the penultimate section, one would be hard put to imagine two more different childhoods than those of Maxim Gorki and Christopher Milne (better known as Christopher Robin, Pooh's friend). Gorki, an orphan (he chose his name deliberately—it means 'bitter') was born in 1868 in Nizhny Novgorod, now Gorki, and is one of the dominant figures of modern Russian literature. *My Childhood* was published in 1913, and recounts his early years with his grandparents and his subsequent wanderings all over southern Russia, more or less destitute, somehow managing to educate himself. His first books were published in the 1890s and his reputation grew until by the revolutionary era he was regarded as Russia's greatest living author and playwright. Christopher Milne, the author of *The Hollow on the Hill* and *The Path through the Trees* as well as *Enchanted Places* has, like Gorki, spent much of his adult life attempting to come to terms with his childhood, or at least A A Milne's version of it. Not a writer by profession, he has been a bookseller for over thirty years. They are both authors who conclude, in their different ways, that, unlike many of the other writers reproduced here, they were closer to God in childhood than at any time since;

*In those days my thoughts and feelings about God*
*were the chief nourishment of my soul and were the*
*most beautiful ones of my existence. (Gorki)*

*In those days of splendour and glory I certainly*
*. . . felt myself nearer to God—both the God that*
*Nanny was telling me about who lived up in the sky*
*and (A A Milne's) God who painted the buttercups—*
*than I do today.*

The great advantage of this book's design is that whilst it imposes a
'pattern' on the material it allows the reader to make comparisons
between different sections as well. Reading through Mary McCarthy's
account of her interview by a Jesuit priest one sees an immediate
connection with Samuel Butler's passage one hundred pages earlier;
Butler, in a way, satirising Mary McCarthy's priest:

*'You must accept what I tell you,' he said,*
*almost sharply. 'You are too young to understand*
*these things. You must have faith.' 'But you're*
*supposed to give me faith, Father.' . . . 'You*
*know your prayers,' he said, 'Say them.' (Mary McCarthy)*

*'I do say tum,' replied Ernest, meaning that he did*
*say 'come' . . . . Theobald noticed the fact that he was*
*being contradicted in a moment. He got up from his*
*arm-chair and went to the piano.*

*'Now, Ernest, you don't,' he said, 'you say nothing*
*of the kind, you say 'tum', not 'come'. Now say 'come'*
*after me, as I do.'*

*'Tum,' said Ernest, at once; 'Is that better?' I*
*have no doubt he thought it was, but it was not.*

*'Now, Ernest, you are not taking pains: you are not*
*trying as you ought to . . . There's no difficulty about*
*it, nor shadow of a difficulty. Now, take your time,*
*think about it, and say 'come' after me.'*

*The boy remained silent for a few minutes and*
*then said 'tum' again . . . . 'Now, Ernest, I will give*
*you one more chance, and if you don't say 'come', I*
*shall know that you are self-willed and naughty.'*

xiii

We live in an age, unlike the Victorians, when ordinary Christians are constantly re-assessing their faith, and one in which many who have no faith continuously turn their attention, in search of belief or guidance, not only towards Christianity but perhaps a greater variety of religions and creeds than at any other time. This uncertainty surely derives, in part, from the difficulty of understanding and retaining religious teachings while we are children, and from the difficulty of teaching children to understand not religion, but faith.

*Childhood's Pattern* will help to clarify this vexed subject, by providing an overview of literature in which writers have used their particular skills to illuminate a time which, for them and us, is paradoxically both vivid and clouded. When we reject the beliefs we held as children, and 'put away childish things', we too often forget as well their connection with the way we have come to see ourselves as individuals. These extracts may help us to uncover those connections. To read them is to discover an openness and an evident determination to provide amusement, stimulation and balance whilst allowing the reader a genuine freedom of interpretation.

# I
# INTIMATIONS

*Harold Owen*

*L P Hartley*

*Marcel Proust*

*A L Rowse*

*C S Lewis*

Harold Owen charts in the three volumes of *Journey from Obscurity* (1963–5) the life of his family until the death of his brother, the poet Wilfred Owen. For Harold, the country church at Uffington exudes an almost womb-like safety throughout his blissful childhood.

Although the setting is similar, L P Hartley's piece is startling in comparison, a *tour de force* by a writer with a penchant for the child's point of view, as in *The Go-Between*. The semi-autobiographical trilogy of which *Eustace and Hilda* (1947) is the final part never represents childish thoughts or belief as uncomplicated; here is an object-lesson in how words can get in the way of understanding (the guidebook/window/ religion train of thought) which is at the same time a celebration of the child's mind.

If 'The past is a foreign country' then Marcel Proust was its most diligent cartographer. *Remembrance of Things Past* occupied him continuously from 1910 until his death. For most of his life a semi-invalid, his reclusive and amazingly productive final years have become a legend and his work the focus of an enormous amount of critical attention. Like Owen and Hartley he evokes the church as a presence, a landmark in his childhood as much as in a geographical sense, in a passage which shows an author calling on his adult sensibilities (the influence of Ruskin, whom he translated, is clear) in order to revive, with infinite patience, the world of the child.

In contrast, the historian and poet A L Rowse (b. 1903) describes the 'naughty occupation' of the choirboy with a dry, distant wit and discusses the formative influence of that not particularly religious experience with persuasive clarity, whilst C S Lewis (1893–1963), best remembered for his para-Christian fables for children, the *Narnia* series, is alone here in attempting to describe his religious feelings, in a proper sense, as a child.

poor opinion of mere size: magnitude in any form appealed to him, and he wished that this kind of superiority, too, could have been claimed for Frontisham. But the book, which could not err, called the window the finest in the kingdom. That meant it was the best, the greatest, the grandest, the *ne plus* also of windows: the supreme window of the world. Eustace gazed at it in awe. It had entered for the architectural prize, and won; now it looked out upon the centuries, victorious, unchallenged, incomparable, a standard of absolute perfection to which all the homage due to merit naturally belonged.

It was not the window itself which fascinated him so much as the idea of its pre-eminence, just as it was not the guide-book's actual words (many of which he did not properly understand) that intoxicated him, so much as the tremendous, unqualified sense of eulogy they conveyed. He tried again, again not quite successfully, to see how the window differed from other church windows. But he could not see it through his own eyes, because he had so often visualised it through the eyes of the guide-book, nor could he describe it in words, because the author's eloquence came between him and his impressions. Feeling meant more to him than seeing, and the phrases of the panegyric, running like a tune in his mind, quickly started a train of feeling that impeded independent judgement.

Within the massive framework of the grey wall seven slender tapers of stone soared upwards. After that, it was as though the tapers had been lit and two people, standing one on either side, had blown the flames together. Curving, straining, interlocked, they flung themselves against the retaining arch in an ecstasy—or should we say an agony?—of petrification. But the builder had not been content with that. Higher still, in the gable above, was another window much smaller and with tracery much less involved, but similar in general effect. "An echo," the guide-book called it, "an earthly echo of a symphony which was made in heaven."

The word 'heaven', striking against his inner ear, released Eustace's visual eye from dwelling on the material structure of the mediaeval mason's masterpiece. The design with all its intricacy faded from his sight, to be replaced, in his mind's eye, by the window's abstract qualities, its beauty, its vigour, its originality, its pre-eminence, its perfection. With these, and not for the first time, he now began to feel as one. Disengaging himself from the tea-table he floated upwards. Out shot his left arm, caught by some force and twisted this way and that; he could feel his fingers, treble-jointed and unnaturally long, scraping against the masonry of the arch as they groped for the positions that had been assigned to them. Almost simultaneously his other limbs followed suit; even his hair, now long like Hilda's, rose from his head and, swaying like seaweed, strove up to reach the keystone. Splayed, spread-eagled, crucified (but for fear of blasphemy he must only think the shadow of that word) into a semblance of the writhing stonework, he seemed to be experiencing the ecstasy—or was it the agony?—of petrification.

Meanwhile the interstices, the spaces where he was not, began to fill with stained glass. Pictures of saints and angels, red, blue, and yellow, pressed against and into him, bruising him, cutting him, spilling their colours over him. The pain was exquisite, but there was rapture in it too. Another twitch, a final wriggle, and Eustace felt no more; he was immobilised, turned to stone. High and lifted up, he looked down from the church wall, perfect, pre-eminent, beyond criticism, not to be asked questions or to answer them, not to be added to or taken away from, but simply to be admired and worshipped by hundreds of visitors, many of the foreigners from Rome and elsewhere, coming miles to see him . . . Eustace, Eustace of Frontisham, Saint Eustace . . .

Eustace . . . the word seemed to be all round him.

"Eustace! Eustace!" His father's voice was raised in pretended indignation. "Stop day-dreaming! We want some more tea! You've forgotten to ring the bell!"

Coming to himself with a start, and avoiding the eyes of his family, Eustace glanced nervously left and right. Round about stood a few empty tables, on one of which a bold bird hopped perkily, looking for crumbs. He noticed with concern that the bird had been guilty of a misdemeanour more tangible than theft. Hoping to scare it away, he rang the bell more loudly than he meant to.

# *Marcel Proust*

*from:* Remembrance of Things Past

## COMBRAY

"That will be Mme. Sazerat's dog," Françoise would suggest, without any real conviction, but in the hope of peace, and so that my aunt should not 'split her head.'

"As if I didn't know Mme. Sazerat's dog!"—for my aunt's critical mind would not so easily admit any fresh fact.

"Ah, but that will be the new dog M. Galopin has brought her from Lisieux."

"Oh, if that's what it is!"

"It seems, it's a most engaging animal," Françoise would go on, having got the story from Théodore, "as clever as a Christian, always in a good temper, always friendly, always everything that's nice. It's not often you see an animal so well-behaved at that age. Mme. Octave, it's high time I left you; I can't afford to stay here amusing myself; look, it's nearly ten o'clock and my fire not lighted yet, and I've still to dress the asparagus."

"What, Françoise, more asparagus! It's a regular disease of asparagus you have got this year: you will make our Parisians sick of it."

"No, no, Mme. Octave, they like it well enough. They'll be coming back from church soon as hungry as hunters, and they won't turn their noses up at it, you'll see."

"Church! why, they must be there now; you'd better not lose any time. Go and look after your luncheon."

While my aunt gossiped on in this way with Françoise I would have accompanied my parents to mass. How I loved it: how clearly I can see it still, our church at Combray! The old porch by which we entered, black, and full of holes as a colander, was worn out of shape and deeply furrowed at the sides (as also was the holy water stoup to which it led us) just as if the gentle grazing touch of the cloaks of peasant-women going into the church, and of their fingers dipping into the water, had managed by agelong repetition to acquire a destructive force, to impress itself on the stone, to carve ruts in it like those made by cart-wheels upon stone gate-posts against which they are driven every day. Its memorial stones, beneath which the noble dust of the Abbots of Combray, who were buried there, furnished the choir with a sort of spiritual pavement, were themselves no longer hard and lifeless matter, for time had softened and sweetened them, and had made them melt like honey and flow beyond their proper margins, either surging out in a milky, frothing wave, washing from its place a florid gothic capital, drowning the white violets of the marble floor; or else reabsorbed into their limbs, contracting still further a crabbed Latin inscription, bringing a fresh touch of fantasy into the arrangement of its curtailed characters, closing together two letters of some word of which the rest were disproportionately scattered. Its windows were never so brilliant as on days when the sun scarcely shone, so that if it was dull outside you might be certain of fine weather in church. One of them was filled from top to bottom by a solitary figure, like the king on a playing-card, who lived up there beneath his canopy of stone, between earth and heaven; and in the blue light of its slanting shadow, on weekdays sometimes, at noon, when there was no service (at one of those rare moments when the airy, empty church, more human somehow and more luxurious with the sun showing off all its rich furnishings, seemed to have almost a habitable air, like the hall—all sculptured stone and painted glass—of some mediaeval mansion), you might see Mme. Sazerat kneel for an instant, laying down on the chair beside her own a neatly corded parcel of little cakes which she had just bought at the baker's and was taking home for her luncheon. In another, a mountain of rosy snow, at whose foot a battle was being fought, seemed to have frozen the window also, which it swelled and distorted with its cloudy sleet, like a pane to which snowflakes have drifted and clung, but flakes illumined by a sunrise—the same, doubtless, which purpled the reredos of the altar with tints so fresh that they seemed rather to be thrown on it for a moment by a light shining from outside and shortly to be extinguished than painted and permanently fastened on the stone. And all of them were so old that you could see, here and there, their silvery antiquity sparkling with the dust of centuries and shewing in its threadbare brilliance the very cords of their lovely tapestry of glass. There was one among them which was a tall panel composed of a hundred little rectangular windows, of blue principally, like a great game of patience of the kind planned to beguile King Charles VI; but, either because a ray of sunlight had gleamed through it or because my own shifting vision had sent across the window, whose colours died away and were rekindled by turns, a rare and transient fire—the next instant it had taken on all the iridescence of a peacock's tail, then shook and wavered in a flaming and fantastic shower, distilled and dropping from the groin of the dark and rocky vault down the moist walls, as though it were along the bed of some rainbow grotto of sinuous stalactites that I was following my parents, who walked in front of me, their prayer-books clasped in their hands; a moment later the little lozenge windows had taken on the deep transparency, the unbreakable hardness of sapphires clustered on some enormous breastplate; but beyond which could be distinguished, dearer than all such treasurers, a fleeting smile from the sun, which could be seen and felt as well here, in the blue and gentle flood: with which it washed the masonry, as on the pavement of the Square or the straw of the market-place; and even on our first Sundays, when we came down before Easter, it would console me for the blackness and bareness of the earth outside by making burst into blossom, as in some springtime in old history among the heirs of Saint Louis, this dazzling, gilded carpet of forget-me-nots in glass.

Two tapestries of high warp represented the coronation of Esther (in which tradition would have it that the weaver had given to Ahasuerus the features of one of the kings of France and to Esther those of a lady of Guermantes whose lover he had been); their colours had melted into one another, so as to add expression, relief, light to the pictures. A touch of red over the lips of Esther had strayed beyond their outline; the yellow on her dress was spread with such unctuous plumpness as to have acquired a kind of solidity, and stood boldly out against the receding background; while the green of the trees, which was still bright in silk and wool among the lower parts of the panel, but had quite 'gone' at the top, separated in a paler scheme, above the dark trunks, the yellowing upper branches, tanned and half-obliterated by the sharp though sidelong rays of an invisible sun. All these things and, still more than these, the treasures which had come to the church from personages who to me were almost legendary figures (such as the golden cross wrought, it was said, by Saint Eloi and presented by Dagobert, and the tomb of the sons of Louis the Germanic in porphyry and enamelled copper), because of which I used to go forward into the church when we were making our way to our chairs as into a fairy-haunted valley, where the rustic sees with amazement on a rock, a tree, a marsh, the tangible proofs of the little people's supernatural passage—all these things made the church something entirely different for me from the rest of the town; a building which occupied, so to speak, four dimensions of space—the name of the fourth being Time—which extending through the centuries with the old nave, which bay after bay, chapel after chapel seemed to stretch across and hold down and conquer not merely a few yards of soil, but each successive epoch from which the whole building had emerged triumphant, hiding the rugged barbarities of the eleventh century in the thickness of its walls, through which nothing could be seen of the heavy arches, long stopped and blinded with coarse blocks of ashlar, except where, near the porch, a deep groove was furrowed into one wall by the tower-stair; and even there the barbarity was veiled by the graceful gothic arcade which pressed coquettishly around it, like a row of grown-up sisters who, to hide him from the eyes of strangers, arrange themselves smilingly in front of a countrified, unmannerly and ill-dressed younger brother; raising up into the sky above the Square a tower which had looked down upon Saint Louis, and seemed to behold him still; and thrusting down with its crypt into the blackness of a Merovingian night, through which, guiding us with groping finger-tips beneath the shadowy vault, ribbed strongly like an immense bat's wing of stone, Théodore or his sister would light up for us with a candle the tomb of Sigebert's little daughter, in which a deep hole, like the bed of a fossil, had been bored, or so it was said, "by a crystal lamp which, on the night when the Frankish princess was murdered, had left, of its own accord, the golden chains by which it was suspended where the apse is today and with neither the crystal broken nor the light extinguished had buried itself in the stone, through which it had gently forced its way."

And then the apse of Combray: what am I to say of that? It was so coarse, so devoid of artistic beauty, even of the religious spirit. From outside, since the street crossing which it commanded was on a lower level, its great wall was thrust upwards from a basement of unfaced ashlar, jagged with flints, in all of which there was nothing particularly ecclesiastical; the windows seemed to have been pierced at an abnormal height, and its whole appearance was that of a prison wall rather than of a church. And certainly in later years, were I to recall all the glorious apses that I had seen, it would never enter my mind to compare with any one of them the apse of Combray. Only, one day, turning out of a little street in some country town, I came upon three alley-ways that converged, and facing them an old wall, rubbed, worn, crumbling, and unusually high; with windows pierced in it far overhead and the same asymmetrical appearance as the apse of Combray. And at that moment I did not say to myself, as at Chartres I might have done or at Rheims, with what strength the religious feeling had been expressed in its construction, but instinctively I exclaimed "The Church!"

The church! A dear, familiar friend; close up by the Rue Saint-Hilaire, upon which its north door opened, and by its two neighbours, Mme. Loiseau's house and the pharmacy of M. Rapin, against which its walls rested without interspace; a simple citizen of Combray, which might have had its number in the street had the streets of Combray borne numbers, and at whose door one felt that the postman ought to stop on his morning rounds, before going into Mme. Loiseau's and after leaving M. Rapin's, there existed, for all that, between the church and everything in Combray that was not the church a clear line of demarcation which I have never succeeded in eliminating from my mind. In vain might Mme. Loiseau deck her window-sills with fuchsias, which developed the bad habit of letting their branches trail at all times and in all directions, head downwards, and whose flowers had no more important business, when they were big enough to taste the joys of life, than to go and cool their purple, congested cheeks against the dark front of the church; to me such conduct sanctified the fuchsias not at all; between the flowers and the blackened stones towards which they leaned, if my eyes could discern no interval, my mind preserved the impression of an abyss.

From a long way off one could distinguish and identify the steeple of Saint-Hilaire inscribing its unforgettable form upon a horizon against which Combray had not yet appeared; when from the train which brought us down from Paris at Easter-time my father caught sight of it, as it slipped into every fold of the sky in turn, its little iron cock veering continually in all directions, he would say: "Come on, get your wraps together, we are here." And on one of the longest walks we ever took from Combray there was a spot where the narrow road emerged suddenly on to an immense plain, closed at the horizon by strips of forest over which rose and stood alone the fine point of Saint-Hilaire's steeple, but so sharpened and so pink that it seemed to be no more than sketched on the sky by the finger-nail of a painter anxious to give to such a landscape, to so pure a piece of 'nature,' this little sign of art, this single indication of human existence. As one drew near it and could make out the remains of the square tower, half in ruins, which still stood by its side, though without rivalling it in height, one was struck, first of all, by the tone, reddish and sombre, of its stones; and on a misty morning in autumn one would have called it, to see it rising above the violet thunder-cloud of the vineyards, a ruin of purple, almost the colour of the wild vine.

Often in the Square, as we came home, my grandmother would make me stop to look up at it. From the tower windows, placed two and two, one pair above another, with that right and original proportion in their spacing to which not only human faces owe their beauty and dignity, it released, it let fall at regular intervals flights of jackdaws which for a little while would wheel and caw, as though the ancient stones which allowed them to sport thus and never seemed to see them, becoming of a sudden uninhabitable and discharging some infinitely disturbing element, had struck them and driven them forth. Then after patterning everywhere the violet velvet of the evening air, they would return abruptly soothed and be absorbed in the tower, deadly no longer but benignant, some perching here and there (not seeming to move, but snapping, perhaps, and swallowing some passing insect) on the points of turrets, as a seagull perches, with an angler's immobility, on the crest of a wave. Without quite knowing why, my grandmother found in the steeple of Saint-Hilaire that absence of vulgarity, pretension, and meanness which made her love—and deem rich in beneficent influences—nature itself, when the hand of man had not, as did my great-aunt's gardener, trimmed it, and the works of genius. And certainly every part one saw of the church served to distinguish the whole from any other building by a kind of general feeling which pervaded it, but it was in the steeple that the church seemed to display a consciousness of itself, to affirm its individual and responsible existence. It was the steeple which spoke for the church. I think, too, that in a confused way my grandmother found in the steeple of Combray what she prized above anything else in the world, namely, a natural air and an air of distinction. Ignorant of architecture, she would say: "My dears, laugh at me if you like; it is not conventionally beautiful, but there is something in its quaint old face which pleases me. If it could play the piano, I am sure it would really *play*." And when she gazed on it, when her eyes followed the gentle tension, the fervent inclination of its stony slopes which drew together as they rose, like hands joined in prayer, she would absorb herself so utterly in the outpouring of the spire that her gaze seemed to leap upwards with it; her lips at the same time curving in a friendly smile for the worn old stones of which the setting sun now illumined no more than the topmost pinnacles, which, at the point where they entered that zone of sunlight and were softened and sweetened by it, seemed to have mounted suddenly far higher, to have become truly remote, like a song whose singer breaks into falsetto, an octave above the accompanying air.

It was the steeple of Saint-Hilaire which shaped and crowned and consecrated every occupation, every hour of the day, every point of view in the town. From my bedroom window I could discern no more than its base, which had been freshly covered with slates; but when on Sundays I saw these, in the hot light of a summer morning, blaze like a black sun I would say to myself: "Good heavens! Nine o'clock! I must get ready for mass at once if I am to have time to go in and kiss aunt

Léonie first," and I would know exactly what was the colour of the sunlight upon the Square, I could feel the heat and dust of the market, the shade behind the blinds of the shop into which Mamma would perhaps go on her way to mass, penetrating its odour of unbleached calico, to purchase a handkerchief or something; which the draper would let her look around while he, bowing from the waist, having made everything ready for shutting up, had just gone into the back shop to put on his Sunday coat and to wash his hands, which it was his habit, every few minutes and even on the saddest occasions, to rub one against the other with an air of enterprise, cunning, and success.

And again, after mass, when we looked in to tell Théodore to bring a larger loaf than usual because our cousins had taken advantage of the fine weather to come over from Thiberzy for luncheon, we had in front of us the steeple, which, baked and browned itself like a larger loaf still of 'holy bread,' with flakes and sticky drops on it of sunlight, thrust its sharp point into the blue sky. And in the evening, as I came in from my walk and thought of the approaching moment when I must say good night to my mother and see her no more, the steeple was by contrast so gentle, here at the close of day, that I would imagine it as being thrust like a brown velvet cushion, against—into the pallid sky which had yielded beneath its pressure, had hollowed slightly so as to make room for it, and had correspondingly risen on either side; while the cries of the birds wheeling to and fro about it seemed to intensify its silence, to elongate its spire still further, and to invest it with some quality beyond the power of words.

Even when our errands lay in places behind the church, from which it could not be seen, the view seemed always to have been composed with reference to the steeple, which would stand up, now here, now there, among the houses, and was perhaps even more affecting when it appeared thus without the church. And, indeed, there are many others which look best when seen in this way, and I can call to mind vignettes of housetops with surmounting steeples in quite another category of art than those formed by the dreary streets of Combray. I shall never forget, in a quaint Norman town not far from Balbec, two charming eighteenth-century houses, dear to me and venerable for many reasons, between which, when one looks up at them from a fine garden which descends in terraces to the river, the gothic spire of a church (itself hidden by the houses) soars into the sky with the effect of crowning and completing their fronts, but in a material so different, so precious, so beringed, so rosy, so polished, that it is at once seen to be no more a part of them than would be a part of two pretty pebbles lying side by side, between which it had been washed on the beach, the purple, crinkled spire of some sea-shell spun out into a turret and gay with glossy colour. Even in Paris, in one of the ugliest parts of the town, I know a window from which one can see across a first, a second, and even a third layer of jumbled roofs, street beyond street, a violet bell, sometimes ruddy, sometimes too, in the finest 'prints' which the atmosphere makes of it, of an ashy solution of black; which is, in fact, nothing else than the dome of Saint-Augustin, and which imparts to this view of Paris the character of some of the Piranesi views of Rome. But since into none of these little etchings, whatever the taste my memory may have been able to bring to their execution, was it able to contribute an element I have long lost, the feeling which makes us not merely regard a thing as a spectacle, but believe in it as in a creature without parallel, so none of them keeps in dependence on it a whole section of my inmost life as does the memory of those aspects of the steeple of Combray from the streets behind the church. Whether one saw it at five o'clock when going to call for letters at the post-office, some doors away, on the left, raising abruptly with its isolated peak the ridge of housetops; or again, when one had to go in and ask for news of Mme. Sazerat, one's eyes followed the line where it ran low again beyond the farther, descending slope, and one knew that it would be the second turning after the steeple; or yet again, if pressing further afield one went to the station, one saw it obliquely, shewing in profile fresh angles and surfaces, like a solid body surprised at some unknown points in its revolution; or, from the banks of the Vivonne, the apse, drawn muscularly together and heightened in perspective, seemed to spring upward with the effort which the steeple made to hurl its spire-point into the heart of heaven: it was always to the steeple that one must return, always it which dominated everything else, summing up the houses with an unexpected pinnacle, raised before me like the Finger of God, Whose Body might have been concealed below among the crowd of human without fear of my confusing It with them. And so even to-day in any large provincial town, or in a quarter of Paris which I do not know well, if a passer-by who is 'putting me on the right road' shews me from afar, as a point to aim at, some belfry of a hospital, or a convent of the street which I am to take, my memory need only find in it some dim resemblance to that dear and vanished outline, and the passer-by, should he turn round to make sure that I have not gone astray, would see me, to his astonishment, oblivious to the walk that I had planned to take or the place where I was obliged to call, standing still on the spot, before that steeple, for hours on end, motionless, trying to remember, feeling deep within myself a tract of soil reclaimed from the waters of Lethe slowly drying until the buildings rise on it again; and then no doubt, and then more uneasily than when, just now, I asked him for a direction, I will seek my way again, I will turn a corner . . . but . . . the goal is in my heart . .

# A L Rowse

*from:* A Cornish Childhood

## CHURCH

The reader will gather the deep impression made by Church upon my infant mind when I say that my firm intention from five onwards was to become Archbishop of Canterbury, until I found that grown-ups would ask me what I was going to become in order to laugh at the expected answer. But that did not make me relinquish the intention; it only taught me to keep quiet about it. For a time I deserted that ambition for the more compassable objective of church organist: my heart was seduced by the great variety of noises you could make with a church organ: so that the court was rendered almost uninhabitable by my attempts to reproduce these noises, sitting ensconced in the tree with various convenient branches as pedals and stops to pull in and out, and roaring like Tregeagle. After that I went back to my earlier ambition, and I don't think I wavered until I went to Oxford and saw for myself how impossible was the intellectual foundation which supported that precarious (and in these days unsatisfactory) eminence.

My imagination was stimulated by, and in turn fed upon, the ritual of the Church. There were occasional visits of the Bishop, all purple or scarlet, with white lawn sleeves and pectoral cross, and complete with chaplain to carry his pastoral staff. I remember once seeing Stubbs, the successor of dear Bishop Gott, whom I have portrayed in my poem *Invocation for a Cornish House:* Stubbs had a wonderful appearance with his noble profile and silver-white hair and beard, every inch a bishop, as you might say, looking at the portrait of him turned out with his opulent astrakhan collar. Burrows was less exciting: a heavy scholar and somewhat constipated athlete who had taken too many Firsts at the University to be very human. What I chiefly remember about him was the unexpectedly heavy weight of his hands upon my head at Confirmation—'Defend, O Lord, this thy child', etc.—I wriggled a little, it felt so very committal and might, I thought, give one a headache. He was succeeded by Warman, kind but unimpressive and regrettably Low Church: a good preacher to C.E.M.S. gatherings.

Then came Frere, who was my ideal of a bishop in every way: a scholar, an artist, a saint, a prince of the Church but very unaffected and easy to talk to; a monk but also a man of the world, who knew Europe from one end to the other, who knew Russian; a musician, an ascetic who appreciated the good things of life; a man who looked even more the part than Stubbs had done (that was a trifle too opulent for a Christian Socialist). Very important that people should look their part. Frere was unpopular with the people who didn't know him, especially with the Nonconformists, who could not have appreciated such a man. And as for the Protestant *canaille* who made his last years at Truro unhappy—well, it is wonderful what professed Christians can do for each other. But this is rushing on years ahead: Frere was too late for me. By the time he came I was already away at Oxford. And wonderfully persuasive as his personality was—I used to dream about him and think that if anybody could persuade one it was he—not even Frere could have retained me once I had begun to think out my position clearly for myself, and with whatever emotional regrets, 'hoping it might be so'.

By now you may have guessed that I had become a choirboy, like those distinguished contemporaries, Noel Coward, William Walton, Laurence Olivier. It is a naughty occupation, and choirboys are liable to turn out to be 'no good' because of their too early familiarity with the holy of holies. It was a bright idea of mine one choir-practice night, when the organist was late, that we should all make for different quarters of the dark church and when he arrived converge crawling upon him from the various aisles, from the south door, Lady Chapel door, vestry and west door. I gave myself the last post, because it was farthest and so arrived on the scene last, having seen and heard all the fun. On another occasion I was one of the ringleaders, and certainly the most obstinate, in a strike we declared. We considered that we were unfairly treated in being watched and reported on by the head-boy, whose voice had broken and who was paid a higher rate than we were. We middle-boys did all the effective singing and we weren't going to have it. We arranged not to sing the Sunday evening service, which happened to be the appalling Stanford in B flat, that begins with two screeching notes, top F and top G. There are a good many high notes in that service, which was one of our star-turns. But that evening there was nobody to sing them: the top-boys whose voices had broken were helpless, the very junior were inaudible and morally browbeaten. It had a disintegrating effect on the service: the men didn't know what was happening, the curate (now Canon Shaw of Penzance) didn't know what was happening; they thought we had lost our voices and sang all the louder to make up for us. That made the effect all the more obvious. It was deliciously enjoyable—even the reckoning was when it came. We felt we had been in the right. Nothing gives one a better appetite; and though some of our pay was stopped, I felt that I had rather scored in the discussion with the organist at the next choir-practice, and in the end we won the substance of our claim: the useless top-boys went; we took their places.

Mine was on the Cantoris side, beginning with the lowest, at the altar end, and gradually progressing up the seat until I was promoted to the top pew, very grand on my own, immediately under the curate's reading-desk. This was a crucial strategic position to occupy in church, a very conspicuous and favoured one; and, to tell the truth, after my voice broke and I had in the end to evacuate what I had come to consider as my special and privileged place in church in the choir, and after so many years, I had no heart for (and no intention of) taking an ordinary back seat with the rest of the congregation; so I ceased to go. My brother, who was in the choir for a short while with me and then left, sat always on the Decani side. There was as much rivalry between Cantoris and Decani as between two houses at a school. Which was superior to which? The fact that the vicar's pew was on the Decani side might have been taken to end the argument in their favour had it not been that, when a special chair was installed in the sactuary for the bishop, it was placed on ours. Very childish; very human: lesser matters have caused civil wars in the past.

. . . Of singing as experience, and what it meant to me, there is little enough that I can say; and I daresay it is the same with other people who have been singers. All I can say is that it was my one talent, a very remarkable gift, to judge from the impression it made on people who heard me and from the memories of it that remain in the district. My subsequent *réclame*, what with politics, books, broadcasting, lectures, scholarships, the University—all dates back really to that. What I do

19

know is that, when my voice went, it was utter misery to me. I experienced all the anguish of a *prima donna* whose powers are failing and who is eclipsed by a rival. I never said anything at the time: it was a very lonely time for me and there was no one to confide in. I should have been too proud to anyway. And it was a slow process: my voice didn't break all at once; it rather subsided gradually into a lower register—like the central tower of Chichester Cathedral, a story which has always amused me. The celebrated Dean Hook was at work in his study one day, and happening to look up at the window, his astonished gaze saw the Cathedral tower slowly give way and subside upon its haunches. It was a disintegrating moment. The good Victorian Dean knew what to do, however: he flung himself upon his knees in prayer.

In my case, too, I resorted rather more to prayer: not to arrest my voice—I knew that was hopeless anyway, short of the drastic steps which, I recalled, were resorted to with the papal choir of Renaissance times, but which would have been out of place in Georgian (V) England. Not so: it happened that this coincided, as is often the case, with my Anglo-Catholic phase. So religion became more important. More important still—it was a blessing it was so—my work at school was gathering momentum; I was on the way to trying for scholarships at the University. Without that I should have been lost. Even as it was I was let down lightly; for, a year or two after my voice began to break, I continued to sing in the choir, being promoted for a while to sing alto with the men. Though this was less satisfactory, and may ultimately have been rather damaging to the proper development of my man's voice, it was better than nothing.

While as a boy my voice was at the height of its power, there is little to say—singing was so natural to me. I sang like a bird, and didn't think much about it. True, I did what I could with the gift. We were well trained by the organist, who taught us to produce our voices naturally and well. Mine was not especially remarkable in range—though it went up to B flat easily enough—but in quality, a rich mezzo-soprano, and in expression, which was that of a boy of exceptional intelligence and emotional capacity. It was from some cheap book, which impressed me greatly—I think *The Rosary*—that I learnt something important, that in singing you should throw yourself into the part, forget yourself, so far as you can, in what you are singing. This, though obvious enough now, was a great discovery for a boy of twelve.

What did I sing? I can remember little enough, though the name comes back to me of the anthem in which I sang my first solo: 'O for a closer walk with God', a very sentimental piece of work which plucked at the heartstrings and became a favourite with me. We prided ourselves on adhering to a Cathedral standard, and so it was, a rather small Victorian Catheral in the provinces, which sang Stainer and Stanford, J.B. Dykes and Berthold Tours. We occasionally tackled something better and bigger, Haydn's *Creation* or a chorus from Brahms's *Requiem:* 'All Flesh is as the Grass'. We always sang an oratorio on Good Friday, in which I took all the soprano solos and recitative. My favourite pieces where Mendelssohn's 'I waited for the Lord' from *Elijah,* and the lovely pastoral 'He shall feed his flock' from Handel's *Messiah.* The last I had been taught to sing for a recital after the church service. This was very popular, and there came a request that I should sing it one Sunday evening after service at the Baptist chapel. I sang it, and to my astonishment there broke out a round of applause. I had to sing it again. There followed a request from another chapel, where I sang. Then it was stopped. The organist said that I was a member of the church choir and that I shouldn't sing outside. No demur on my part. But if they had had any sense of responsibility they would have sent me off to a Cathedral choir-school and given me a good education. A younger namesake of mine, with a much less good voice and more intelligent parents, went into the choir of Winchester Cathedral. I rather think I must have been too good a proposition to lose. Between one and the other of them, at home and in the choir, they never even had me taught the piano. What I learnt I picked up for myself; naturally I learnt to read music pretty well. My one regret was that I never sang 'I know that my Redeemer liveth'; it was suggested that I might one Easter, but it was put off and I never did. If I had done, I should have made it something to remember.

At these organ recitals after church on Sunday evenings I would steal alone in my cassock into a pew in the darkened Lady Chapel and give myself up to an exquisite wandering dream, induced by the music. I did not follow it intellectually, and in those days I did not like Bach Fugues; I just sat in the darkling and thought my own thoughts, while the music ebbed and flowed among the pillars of the lighted church, and came and went in my heart and along my nerves. The walls of the little chapel were filled with the memorials of the Sawles of Penrice; here a fine big decorated monument of the time of Queen Anne, the gilt upon the arms gleaming out of the darkness above the aumbry; here a black, draped urn of the Georges; there a marble relief of a lady in Greek draperies mourning over a bier, very Regency; the plainer slabs of the Victorians. The dream was a period-dream, of the quintessence of the eighteenth century: one could not lay one's finger upon its core, for it was only a succession of images, in which the 'white gate on the road to Trenarren' always appeared, and the young heir returning from service at sea from some Portobello or Louisburg or Lagos. I saw him in his three-cornered hat, his tie-wig, the formal pose, the gestures of the time. Or there was a moon through the flickering trees along the path of childhood that led by Gewing's Wood to Penrice. Or it was summer-time and I saw the lovely lateral lights of the wood within, the shadowed light upon the silver boles of vanished beeches, the romance and mystery of the house in the wood. Or there was grief and mourning in the great house—a young man killed before his time, and I remembered that it was war-time, the young heir to all these monuments indeed dead. The music came to an end, and with it my ecstasy.

I do not know why Mr. Symons in his *Quest for Corvo* speaks of 'that nostalgia of the past which, of all temptations of the mind, is the most destructive of contentment'. There is a sense indeed in which it is hopeless, like so much of the ideal life of the mind, or of the activity of the passions, of love as much as of grief, for two can never be one, as love of its very nature demands. But this nostalgia is not more destructive of contentment than any other; and in so far as it encourages unrest of the mind, it is a stimulant to creation, a greater source of joy than anything else in life. Cyril Connolly begins his autobiography with the clever, too clever, sentence: 'I have always disliked myself at any given moment; the sum of these moments is my life.' Smart, but pathetic. When I think of my life as a whole, I do not in the end think of myself, but of the sum of those moments of ecstasy which is my real inner life. They constitute my revealed religion—a revelation of the world as beauty.

There are similar moments all along the way, which I can resort to at will and which have nourished me in anguish of body and mind, in misery and extreme disillusionment about human beings, and when I have lain at death's door. I have in fact a technique of resorting to them: hearing the rooks cawing round Mrs. Arthur's trees, that most nostalgic of sounds, on bright Sunday mornings of summer in child-hood, or calling up the rich glow of the setting sun making a coloured pathway up the aisle from the western window in the tower till at last it rested a blood-red gleam upon the altar, on those Wednesday night

Intercession services which we held all through the War, hearing the list of the dead lads from our parish grow longer, while we prayed in the intensity of silence (I know that I prayed) that it might not reach our loved ones and that the War might end; or coming home from choir-practice and up the hill-side to where, turning the corner by the school, you suddenly felt the pure keen air of the uplands coming down from the moors and ran the remaining way, frightened of the shadows that lurked in the hedges, with a keener appetite for supper round that lighted table in the kitchen, the family circle unbroken then, undispersed, the nest warm, complete, the fledglings unflown, and with no thought for what would come next.

# C S Lewis

*from:* Surprised by Joy

## THE FIRST YEARS

It will be clear that at this time—at the age of six, seven, and eight—I was living almost entirely in my imagination; or at least that the imaginative experience of those years now seems to me more important than anything else. Thus I pass over a holiday in Normandy (of which, nevertheless, I retain very clear memories) as a thing of no account; if it could be cut out of my past I should still be almost exactly the man I am. But imagination is a vague word and I must make some distinctions. It may mean the word of reverie, day-dream, wish-fulfilling fantasy. Of that I knew more than enough. I often pictured myself cutting a fine figure. But I must insist that this was a totally different activity from the invention of Animal-Land. Animal-Land was not (in that sense) a fantasy at all. I was not one of the characters it contained. I was its creator, not a candidate for admission to it. Invention is essentially different from reverie; if some fail to recognise the difference that is because they have not themselves experienced both. Anyone who has will understand me. In my day-dreams I was training myself to be a fool; in mapping and chronicling Animal-Land I was training myself to be a novelist. Note well, a novelist; not a poet. My invented world was full (for me) of interest, bustle, humour, and character; but there was no poetry, even no romance, in it. It was almost astonishingly prosaic. Thus if we use the word imagination in a third sense, and the highest sense of all, this invented world was not imaginative. But certain other experiences were, and I will now try to record them. The thing has been much better done by Traherne and Wordsworth, but every man must tell his own tale.

The first is itself the memory of a memory. As I stood beside a flowering currant bush on a summer day there suddenly arose in me without warning, and as if from a depth not of years but of centuries, the memory of that earlier morning at the Old House when my brother had brought his toy garden into the nursery. It is difficult to find words strong enough for the sensation which came over me; Milton's "enormous bliss" of Eden (giving the full, ancient meaning to "enormous") comes somewhere near it. It was a sensation, of course, of desire; but desire for what? not, certainly, for a biscuit-tin filled with moss, nor even (though that came into it) for my own past. Ἰουλίαν ποθῶ—and before I knew what I desired, the desire itself was gone, the whole glimpse withdrawn, the world turned commonplace again, or only stirred by a longing for the longing that had just ceased. It had taken only a moment of time; and in a certain sense everything else that had ever happened to me was insignificant in comparison.

The second glimpse came through *Squirrel Nutkin;* through it only, though I loved all the Beatrix Potter books. But the rest of them were merely entertaining; it administered the shock, it was a trouble. It troubled me with what I can only describe as the Idea of Autumn. It sounds fantastic to say that one can be enamoured of a season, but that is something like what happened; and, as before, the experience was one of intense desire. And one went back to the book, not to gratify the desire (that was impossible—how can one *possess* Autumn?) but to re-awake it. And in this experience also there was the same surprise and the same sense of incalculable importance. It was something quite different from ordinary life and even from ordinary pleasure; something, as they would now say, "in another dimension".

The third glimpse came through poetry. I had become fond of Longfellow's *Saga of King Olaf*: fond of it in a casual, shallow way for its story and its vigorous rhythms. But then, and quite different from such pleasures, and like a voice from far more distant regions, there came a moment when I idly turned the pages of the book and found the unrhymed translation of *Tegner's Drapa* and read

*I heard a voice that cried,*

> *Balder the beautiful*
> *Is dead, is dead——*

I knew nothing about Balder; but instantly I was uplifted into huge regions of northern sky, I desired with almost sickening intensity something never to be described (except that it is cold, spacious, severe, pale, and remote) and then, as in the other examples, found myself at the very same moment already falling out of that desire and wishing I were back in it.

The reader who finds these three episodes of no interest need read this book no further, for in a sense the central story of my life is about nothing else. For those who are still disposed to proceed I will only underline the quality common to the three experiences; it is that of an unsatisfied desire which is itself more desirable than any other satisfaction. I call it Joy, which is here a technical term and must be sharply distinguished both from Happiness and from Pleasure. Joy (in my sense) has indeed one characteristic, and one only, in common with them; the fact that anyone who has experienced it will want it again. Apart from that, and considered only in its quality, it might almost equally well be called a particular kind of unhappiness or grief. But then it is a kind we want. I doubt whether anyone who has tasted it would ever, if both were in his power, exchange it for all the pleasures in the world. But then Joy is never in our power and pleasure often is.

I cannot be absolutely sure whether the things I have just been speaking of happened before or after the great loss which befell our family and to which I must now turn. There came a night when I was ill and crying both with headache and toothache and distressed because my mother did not come to me. That was because she was ill too; and what was odd was that there were several doctors in her room, and voices and comings and goings all over the house and doors shutting and opening. It seemed to last for hours. And then my father, in tears, came into my room and began to try to convey to my terrified mind things it had never conceived before. It was in fact cancer and followed the usual course; an operation (they operated in the patient's house in those days), an apparent convalescence, a return of the disease, increasing pain, and death. My father never fully recovered from this loss.

Children suffer not (I think) less than their elders, but differently. For us boys the real bereavement had happened before our mother died. We lost her gradually as she was gradually withdrawn from our life into the hands of nurses and delirium and morphia, and as our whole existence changed into something alien and menacing, as the house became full of strange smells and midnight noises and sinister whispered conversations. This had two further results, one very evil and one very good. It divided us from our father as well as our mother. They say that a shared sorrow draws people closer together; I can hardly believe that it often has that effect when those who share it are of widely different ages. If I may trust my own experience, the sight of adult misery and adult terror has an effect on children which is merely paralysing and alienating. Perhaps it was our fault. Perhaps if we had been better children we might have lightened our father's sufferings at this time. We certainly did not. His nerves had never been of the steadiest and his emotions had always been uncontrolled. Under the pressure of anxiety his temper became incalculable; he spoke wildly and acted unjustly. Thus by a peculiar cruelty of fate, during those months the unfortunate man, had he but known it, was really losing his sons as well as his wife. We were coming, my brother and I, to rely more and more exclusively on each other. I expect that we (or at any rate I) were already learning to lie to him. Everything that had made the house a home had failed us; everything except one another. We drew daily closer together (that was the good result)—two frightened urchins huddled for warmth in a bleak world.

Grief in childhood is complicated with many other miseries. I was taken into the bedroom where my mother lay dead; as they said, "to see her", in reality, as I at once knew, "to see it". There was nothing that a grown-up would call disfigurement—except for that total disfigurement which is death itself. Grief was overwhelmed in terror. To this day I do not know what they mean when they call dead bodies beautiful. The ugliest man alive is an angel of beauty compared with the loveliest of the dead. Against all the subsequent paraphernalia of coffin, flowers, hearse, and funeral I reacted with horror. I even lectured one of my aunts on the absurdity of mourning clothes in a style which would have seemed to most adults both heartless and precocious; but this was our dear Aunt Annie, my maternal uncle's Canadian wife, a woman almost as sensible and sunny as my mother herself. To my hatred for what I already felt to be all the fuss and flummery of the funeral I may perhaps trace something in me which I now recognise as a defect but which I have never fully overcome—a distaste for all that is public, all that belongs to the collective; a boorish inaptitude for formality.

My mother's death was the occasion of what some (but not I) might regard as my first religious experience. When her case was pronounced hopeless I remembered what I had been taught; that prayers offered in faith would be granted. I accordingly set myself to produce by will-power a firm belief that my prayers for her recovery would be successful; and, as I thought, I achieved it. When nevertheless she died I shifted my ground and worked myself into a belief that there was to be a miracle. The interesting thing is that my disappointment produced no results beyond itself. The thing hadn't worked, but I was used to things not working, and I thought no more about it. I think the truth is that the belief into which I had hypnotised myself was itself too irreligious for its failure to cause any religious revolution. I had approached God, or my idea of God, without love, without awe, even without fear. He was, in my mental picture of this miracle, to appear neither as Saviour nor as Judge, but merely as a magician; and when He had done what was required of Him I supposed He would simply—well, go away. It never crossed my mind that the tremendous contact which I solicited should have any consequences beyond restoring the *status quo*. I imagine that a "faith" of this kind is often generated in children and that its disappointment is of no religious importance; just as the things believed in, if they could happen and be only as the child pictured them, would be of no religious importance either.

With my mother's death all settled happiness, all that was tranquil and reliable, disappeared from my life. There was to be much fun, many pleasures, many stabs of Joy; but no more of the old security. It was sea and islands now; the great continent had sunk like Atlantis.

# II
# MISCHIEF

Edmund Gosse
Lord Berners
Charles Dickens
Flora Thompson

The four extracts here are each amusing in their own way, but none is simply that. Edmund Gosse, whose father was a distinguished zoologist and a member of the Plymouth Brethren, draws an entertaining sketch in *Father and Son* (1907) of the child's confusion of divine and paternal authority and his subversion of them.

Lord Berners recounts, with tongue firmly in cheek, his encounters with his grandmother, Lady Bourchier, the kind of terrifying Victorian matron whose ideas of piety show Christianity at the nadir of its usefulness—a type which occurs over and again in literature from Dickens and the Brontës to John Fowles's Mrs Poulteney in *The French Lieutenant's Woman*.

In a short excerpt from *David Copperfield* Dickens, whether drawing on imagination or his own appalling childhood, reveals through the eyes of the child the source of much 'mischief'; only tedium exists for the boy here; no meaning in the ritual, no communication in the words.

*Lark Rise to Candleford* (1937) has become perhaps the most widely-read work of English social history, a frequent set-book for schools. Yet it is much more than 'social history'; it is an insider's account of the transformation of the agrarian working-class and an affectionate but hard-headed memorial to a vanished world too often described in terms of cosy, idyllic simplicity. As our own society knows only too well, children are extremely susceptible to the prejudices of their parents and have an unquestioning capacity for cruelty which may exist alongside a sophisticated moral sense. Here, however, unlike the passage from *David Copperfield*, the children make a futile effort to understand.

# Edmund Gosse

### *from:* Father and Son

About this time there was a great flow of tea-table hospitality in the village, and my friends and their friends used to be asked out, by respective parents and by more than one amiable spinster, to faint little entertainments where those sang who were ambitious to sing, and where all played post and forfeits after a rich tea. My Father was constantly exercised in mind as to whether I should or should not accept these glittering invitations. There hovered before him a painful sense of danger in resigning the soul to pleasures which savoured of 'the world'. These, though apparently innocent in themselves, might give an appetite for yet more subversive dissipations.

I remember, on one occasion, — when the Browns, a family of Baptists who kept a large haberdashery shop in the neighbourhood town, asked for the pleasure of my company 'to tea and games', and carried complacency so far as to offer to send that local vehicle, 'the midge', to fetch me and bring me back, — my Father's conscience was so painfully perplexed, that he desired me to come up with him to the now-deserted 'boudoir' of the departed Marks, that we might 'lay the matter before the Lord'. We did so, kneeling side by side, with our backs to the window and our foreheads pressed upon the horsehair cover of the small, coffin-like sofa. My Father prayed aloud, with great fervour, that it might be revealed to me, by the voice of God, whether it was or was not the Lord's will that I should attend the Browns' party. My Father's attitude seemed to me to be hardly fair, since he did not scruple to remind the Deity of various objections to a life of pleasure and of the snakes that lie hidden in the grass of evening parties. It would have been more scrupulous, I thought, to give no sort of hint of the kind of answer he desired and expected.

It will be justly said that my life was made up of very trifling things, since I have to confess that this incident of the Browns' invitation was one of its landmarks. As I knelt, feeling very small, by the immense bulk of my Father, there gushed through my veins like a wine the determination to rebel. Never before, in all these years of my vocation, had I felt my resistance take precisely this definite form. We rose presently from the sofa, my forehead and the backs of my hands still chafed by the texture of the horsehair, and we faced one another in the dreary light. My Father, perfectly confident in the success of what had really been a sort of incantation, asked me in a loud wheedling voice, 'Well, and what is the answer which our Lord vouchsafes?' I said nothing, and so my Father, more sharply, continued, 'We have asked Him to direct you to a true knowledge of His will. We have desired Him to let you know whether it is, or is not, in accordance with His wishes that you should accept this invitation from the Browns.' He positively beamed down at me; he had no doubt of the reply. He was already, I believe, planning some little treat to make up to me for the material deprivation. But my answer came, in the high-piping accents of despair: 'The Lord says I may go to the Browns.' My Father gazed at me in speechless horror. He was caught in his own trap, and though he was certain that the Lord had said nothing of the kind, there was no road open for him but just sheer retreat. Yet surely it was an error in tactics to slam the door.

# Lord Berners

*from:* First Childhood

## LADY BOURCHIER

My paternal grandmother, Lady Bourchier, was a very different person to the kindly, angelic-featured Mrs Farmer. She was actually one of the most forbidding, awe-inspiring women I have ever known, and my two grandmothers might have served as twin allegorical figures representing the brighter and darker aspects of Divine Charity.

Lady Bourchier was intensely and violently low-church. She went so far as to have herself described in *Who's Who* as 'distinctly low,' an epithet which must have caused some surprise to those who were unaware of its sectarian significance.

While quite a young woman she became acquainted with Lord Radstock and was 'converted' by him. I was told that, in the unregenerate period before her conversion, she had, like Saint Augustine, led a frivolous and mundane life, had enjoyed dancing and social festivities. But I am inclined to doubt this legend. I feel sure that she must have been born with the seeds of a baleful asceticism in her heart, for not even conversion could have succeeded in so permanently embittering any human being.

Lady Bourchier lived at a place called Stackwell about three miles from Arley on the other side of the river. It was a gloomy, unattractive house. Originally Elizabethan in style, it had been deformed by later additions out of all recognition. It was surrounded by a moat which was generally half-dry and always rather smelly, and the house was shut in on all sides by tall fir trees. Even under a blue sky and when the sun shone its brightest Stackwell looked as grim as an ogre's castle. I was always thankful that I never had to stay there often, and never for any length of time.

Lady Bourchier had brought up her children on the principle that respect is preferable to love. As a precept of education this may perhaps be valuable, but in her particular case she succeeded in obtaining neither; her children merely came to regard her with a sullen aversion. Anyone so bigoted could hardly inspire respect and she was lacking in any single lovable quality. On the other hand, she had a forcible personality and a will of iron. She dominated and repressed all those with whom she came into contact. There was something a little tragic about all this waste of energy. You felt that, if only some interest had possessed her, other than this narrow intolerant religion which cramped and stultified her whole being, she might have been quite a remarkable woman. Even with her total lack of amenity, she might have distinguished herself in some capacity for which amenity is not an absolute necessity. She might have become a Florence Nightingale, a Lady Astor.

Somebody once asked my father if Lady Bourchier were not a Baroness in her own right. He replied, 'Yes, but she is everything else in her own wrong.'

In appearance Lady Bourchier was not unlike Holbein's portrait of Bloody Mary with just a touch of Charley's Aunt. In fact her coiffure might have been modelled upon that of the latter, and she wore a lace cap with two large, melancholy black bows on it, which always made me think of a couple of crows perching on the roof of a Methodist chapel. There was indeed something very peculiar about all her clothes. Though she usually wore a simple costume of black silk resembling in style the dresses worn by Queen Victoria in her later years, the garment was not as simple as it looked. It appeared to possess the faculty of increasing or diminishing in volume like the sails of a ship. It was rumoured that, concealed beneath her skirts, there was an elaborate system of strings and pulleys for raising her petticoats off the ground whenever she walked in the garden. Whether this was the case or not I imagine nobody had ever ventured to prove. It is certain that, whenever she went out of doors, her clothes used to assume a curious bunched-up appearance behind, which made her look like an emu.

In fact my cousins and I always used to refer to her among ourselves as 'The Emu,' and I remembered that once, when she took us to visit the Zoo, we contrived to confront her with the bird itself. Our little joke was not particularly successful, because she guessed immediately what we were up to and said with a sour smile, 'I suppose you imagine it looks like me.' It was among her many alarming characteristics that she seemed to be able to read your inmost thoughts and to be endowed with the same sort of inquisitorial omniscience as the dour God she worshipped and with whom she gave one the impression of being on terms of exclusive amity.

My grandfather, a pleasant easy-going individual with the air of a Paterfamilias out of one of John Leech's drawings in *Punch*, was completely under her thumb. He had a mild liking for politics in which, however, he was never permitted to indulge. The only subjects Lady Bourchier allowed to be discussed in her presence were the less sensational items of general news and those preferably of a theological nature. It must be confessed she sometimes appeared to take an interest in local scandals. She seemed to derive a certain pleasure from hearing instances of other people's godlessness. It gave her satisfaction, no doubt, to hear of yet another of God's creatures obviously destined for Hell.

Whenever conversation strayed into one of the many paths of which she disapproved, my grandmother had a remarkable faculty of making her disapproval felt. Without saying a single word she managed to radiate disapproval. The air seemed to grow heavy with it, and the most audacious, the most garrulous talker would wilt and be silent. You may imagine that conversation under such circumstances was not likely to attain a very high level of interest.

There was, however, one note of humanity in Lady Bourchier's nature, and that was her fondness for birds. She used to encourage robins, tits, nuthatches and sparrows to come to her windows and be fed. She had succeeded in taming a pair of blue-tits, so that they would come on to the window-sill and take food out of her hands. At least that was what she said. We had to take her word for it because nobody had ever seen them do it. She used to say rather pointedly that this famous pair of blue-tits would never come to her if a stranger were present. In fact she always referred to them in a mysterious, exclusive fashion rather in the manner in which Elijah might have spoken of his ravens. However, one day I was privileged to catch a glimpse of the birds, and I remember causing a mild sensation by rushing into the drawing-room where several members of the family were sitting, and crying out excitedly, 'I say! I've just seen Grandmother's tits!'

Lady Bourchier spent a good deal of her time in paying minatory visits to the sick and the poor. She would set out on these charitable raids, in a small pony-chaise which she used to drive herself, armed with soup and propaganda. The rest of the day she passed in meditation in her grim little study overlooking the moat. There was always an immense pile of cheap, ill-bound Bibles on the table and these she would give away whenever she got a chance. 'Let me see, child, have I given you a Bible?' 'Yes, Grandmother,' one would hastily reply. But you never managed to get out of the room without having one of them thrust into your hand. Disposing of a Bible was no easy matter. It would, of course, be sacrilegious to burn it. If deliberately left behind or lost it would invariably be returned because she always took the precaution of writing one's name and address on the title-page. I remember once when I dropped one of them into the moat being horrified to find that it refused to sink and continued to bob up and down on the surface like a life-buoy. Even this contigency, I felt, must have been foreseen by my grandmother and in consequence she had had it lined with cork.

Before I take leave of Stackwell and its grim *châtelaine* I must speak of the dreary rite that took place twice a day and was known as Family Prayers. I imagine that in 1930 there are very few households where this practice still lingers. In those days it was customary in nearly every home. But at Stackwell, family prayers took on a peculiarly drastic form and the institution seemed to be resented equally by the family and by the servants. I remember, as a child, being impressed by the annoyance and ill-feeling it caused among the domestics, who were obliged to quit whatever work they were engaged upon, dress themselves in tidy clothes and troop into the dining-room in order to sit upon hard benches for twenty minutes or more, listening to my grandmother declaiming scriptural exhortations in a voice that seemed to hold out very little hope of salvation for the lower classes.

Samuel Butler, in *The Way of All Flesh*, likens the family prayers of the Pontifex household to a swarm of bees he saw fruitlessly attacking the painted bunches of flowers on the wall-paper, 'so many of the associated ideas present but the main idea hopelessly lacking.' Of the family prayers at Stackwell one could not even say that there was a question of associated ideas. The ceremony appeared to be devised solely for my grandmother's benefit. It was a sort of daily rite to emphasise her own intimacy with God at the expense of her audience.

I think that my grandmother and I were the only two people who got any real pleasure out of the Stackwell family prayers, but for vastly different reasons. I have always taken an almost intoxicating delight in 'perilous laughter,' that is to say laughter which, either from good manners or fear, has to be controlled at all costs. The kind of laughter which, on solemn occasions or in the presence of the great, sometimes wells up within one with such violence that the human frame is nearly shattered in the course of its suppression. The vision of that grave row of domestics sitting bolt upright on the benches opposite to me was irresistible. I used to try to disturb their deadly seriousness by making surreptitious grimaces at them, and on one occasion I scored a memorable triumph by laying on the place occupied by the butler a notice bearing the words 'Stand for one donkey.' This masterpiece of humour was successful in producing an explosion of muffled snorts, and one of the footmen was obliged to leave the room with his handkerchief to his face.

Towards the end of her life my grandmother's reading of family prayers developed into a sort of macabre farce. With the gradual failing of her intellect, the collects and lessons became more and more seasoned with spoonerisms and every form of ludicrous mistake. I remember her starting off one morning with the alarming request, 'Oh, Lord, bear down upon us from on high!' and on another occasion she got horribly mixed up in the prayer in which the words 'true joys' occur, and kept on referring to 'Jew's toys.' But it was really more pathetic than funny. Poor Lady Bourchier! What a dreary, unprofitable existence! If only her religion had proved some sort of consolation to her instead of merely serving to fill her soul with bitterness. How different were my two grandmothers! The one brimming over with the milk of human kindness, the other soured by the vinegar and gall of a cramped Protestant intolerance.

# Charles Dickens

*from:* David Copperfield

Here is our pew in the church. What a high-backed pew! With a window near it, out of which our house can be seen, and *is* seen many times during the morning service, by Peggotty, who likes to make herself as sure as she can that it's not being robbed, or is not in flames. But though Peggotty's eye wanders, she is much offended if mine does, and frowns to me, as I stand upon the seat, that I am to look at the clergyman. But I can't always look at him — I know him without that white thing on, and I am afraid of his wondering why I stare so, and perhaps stopping the service to enquire — and what am I to do? It's a dreadful thing to gape, but I must do something. I look at my mother, but *she* pretends not to see me. I look at a boy in the aisle, and *he* makes faces at me. I look at the sunlight coming in at the open door through the porch, and there I see a stray sheep — I don't mean a sinner, but mutton — half making up his mind to come into the church. I feel that if I looked at him any longer, I might be tempted to say something out loud; and what would become of me then! I look up at the monumental tablets on the wall, and try to think of Mr. Bodgers late of this parish, and what the feelings of Mrs. Bodgers must have been, when affliction sore, long time Mr. Bodgers bore, and physicians were in vain. I wonder whether they called in Mr. Chillip, and he was in vain; and if so, how he likes to be reminded of it once a week. I look from Mr. Chillip, in his Sunday neckcloth, to the pulpit; and think what a good place it would be to play in, and what a castle it would make, with another boy coming up the stairs to attack it, and having the velvet cushion with the tassels thrown down on his head. In time my eyes gradually shut up; and, from seeming to hear the clergyman singing a drowsy song in the heat, I hear nothing, until I fall off the seat with a crash, and am taken out, more dead than alive, by Peggotty.

# Flora Thompson

*from:* Lark Rise to Candleford

## TO CHURCH ON SUNDAY

If the Lark Rise people had been asked their religion, the answer of
nine out of ten would have been 'Church of England', for practically
all of them were christened, married and buried as such, although, in
adult life, few went to church between the baptisms of their offspring.
The children were shepherded there after Sunday school and about a
dozen of their elders attended regularly; the rest stayed at home, the
women cooking and nursing, and the men, after an elaborate Sunday
toilet, which included shaving and cutting each other's hair and much
puffing and splashing with buckets of water, but stopped short before
lacing up boots or putting on a collar and tie, spent the rest of the day
eating, sleeping, reading the newspaper, and strolling round to see
how their neighbours' pigs and gardens were looking.

There were a few keener spirits. The family at the inn was Catholic
and was up and off to early Mass in the next village before others had
turned over in bed for an extra Sunday morning snooze. There were
also three Methodist families which met in one of their cottages on
Sunday evenings for prayer and praise; but most of these attended
church as well, thus earning for themselves the name of 'Devil dodgers'.

Every Sunday, morning and afternoon, the two cracked, flat-toned
bells at the church in the mother village called the faithful to worship.
*Ding-dong, Ding-dong, Ding-dong,* they went, and, when they heard
them, the hamlet churchgoers hurried across fields and over stiles, for
the Parish Clerk was always threatening to lock the church door when
the bells stopped and those outside might stop outside for all he cared.

With the Fordlow cottagers, the Squire's and farmer's families and
maids, the Rectory people and the hamlet contingent, the congregation
averaged about thirty. Even with this small number, the church was
fairly well filled, for it was a tiny place, about the size of a barn, with
nave and chancel only, no side aisles. The interior was almost as bare
as a barn, with its grey roughcast walls, plain-glass windows, and
flagstone floor. The cold, damp, earthy odour common to old and
unheated churches pervaded the atmosphere, with occasional whiffs
of a more unpleasant nature said to proceed from the stacks of

mouldering bones in the vault beneath. Who had been buried there, or when, was unknown, for, excepting one ancient and mutilated brass in the wall by the font, there were but two memorial tablets, both of comparatively recent date. The church, like the village, was old and forgotten, and those buried in the vault, who must have once been people of importance, had not left even a name. Only the stained glass window over the altar, glowing jewel-like amidst the cold greyness, the broken piscina within the altar rails, and a tall broken shaft of what had been a cross in the churchyard, remained to witness mutely to what once had been.

The Squire's and clergyman's families had pews in the chancel, with backs to the wall on either side, and between them stood two long benches for the schoolchildren, well under the eyes of authority. Below the steps down into the nave stood the harmonium, played by the clergyman's daughter, and round it was ranged the choir of small schoolgirls. Then came the rank and file of the congregation, nicely graded, with the farmer's family in the front row, then the Squire's gardener and coachman, the schoolmistress, the maidservants and the cottagers, with the Parish Clerk at the back to keep order.

'Clerk Tom', as he was called, was an important man in the parish. Not only did he dig the graves, record the banns of marriage, take the chill off the water for winter baptisms, and stoke the coke stove which stood in the nave at the end of his seat; but he also took an active and official part in the service. It was his duty to lead the congregation in the responses and to intone the 'Amens'. The psalms were not sung or chanted, but read, verse and verse about, by the Rector and people, and in these especially Tom's voice so drowned the subdued murmur of his fellow worshippers that it sounded like a duet between him and the clergyman — a duet in which Tom won easily, for his much louder voice would often trip up the Rector before he had quite finished his portion, while he prolonged his own final syllables at will.

The afternoon service, with not a prayer left out or a creed spared, seemed to the children everlasting. The schoolchildren, under the stern eye of the Manor House, dared not so much as wriggle; they sat in their stiff, stuffy, best clothes, their stomachs lined with heavy Sunday dinner, in a kind of waking doze, through which Tom's 'Amens' rang like a bell and the Rector's voice buzzed beelike. Only on the rare occasions when a bat fluttered down from the roof, or a butterfly drifted in at a window, or the Rector's little fox terrier looked in at the door and sidled up the nave, was the tedium lightened.

39

Edmund and Laura, alone in their grandfather's seat, modestly situated exactly half-way down the nave, were more fortunate, for they sat opposite the church door and, in summer, when it was left open, they could at least watch the birds and the bees and the butterflies crossing the opening and the breezes shaking the boughs of the trees and ruffling the long grass on the graves. It was interesting, too, to observe some woman in the congregation fussing with her back hair, or a man easing his tight collar, or old Dave Pridham, who had a bad bunion, shuffling off a shoe before the sermon began, with one eye all the time upon the clergyman; or to note how closely together some newly married couple were sitting, or to see Clerk Tom's young wife suckling her baby. She wore a fur tippet in winter and her breast hung like a white heather bell between the soft blackness until it was covered up with a white handkerchief, 'for modesty'.

Mr Ellison in the pulpit was the Mr Ellison of the Scripture lessons, plus a white surplice. To him, his congregation were but children of a larger growth, and he preached as he taught. A favourite theme was the duty of regular churchgoing. He would hammer away at that for forty-five minutes, never seeming to realize that he was preaching to the absent, that all those present were regular attendants, and that the stray sheep of his flock were snoring upon their beds a mile and a half away.

Another favourite subject was the supreme rightness of the social order as it then existed. God, in His infinite wisdom, had appointed a place for every man, woman, and child on this earth and it was their bounden duty to remain contentedly in their niches. A gentleman might seem to some of his listeners to have a pleasant, easy life, compared to theirs at field labour; but he had his duties and responsibilities, which would be far beyond their capabilities. He had to pay taxes, sit on the Bench of Magistrates, oversee his estate, and keep up his position by entertaining. Could they do these things? No. Of course they could not; and he did not suppose that a gentleman could cut as straight a furrow or mow or thatch a rick as expertly as they could. So let them be thankful and rejoice in their physical strength and the bounty of the farmer, who found them work on his land and paid them wages with his money.

Less frequently, he would preach eternal punishment for sin, and touch, more lightly, upon the bliss reserved for those who worked hard, were contented with their lot and showed proper respect to their superiors. The Holy Name was seldom mentioned, nor were human griefs or joys, or the kindly human feelings which bind a man to man. It was not religion he preached, but a narrow code of ethics, imposed from above upon the lower orders, which, even in those days, was out of date.

Once and once only did inspiration move him. It was the Sunday after the polling for the General Election of 1886, and he had begun preaching one of his usual sermons on the duty to social superiors, when suddenly something, perhaps the memory of the events of the past week, seemed to boil up within him. Flushed with anger— 'righteous anger', he would have called it — and his frosty blue eyes flashing like swords, he cast himself forward across the ledge of his pulpit and roared: 'There are some among you who have lately forgotten that duty, and we know the cause, the *bloody* cause!'

Laura shivered. Bad language in church! And from the Rector! But, later in life, she liked to think that she had lived early enough to have heard a mild and orthodox Liberalism denounced from the pulpit as 'a bloody cause'. It lent her the dignity of an historical survival.

The sermon over, the people sprang to their feet like Jacks-in-a-box. With what gusto they sang the evening hymn, and how their lungs expanded and their tongues wagged as they poured out of the church-yard! Not that they resented anything that was said in the Rector's sermons. They did not listen to them. After the Bloody Cause sermon Laura tried to find out how her elders had reacted to it; but all she could learn was: 'I seems to have lost the thread just then,' or, more frankly, 'I must've been nodding'; the most she could get was one woman's, 'My! didn't th' old parson get worked up today!'

Some of them went to church to show off their best clothes and to see and criticize those of their neighbours; some because they loved to hear their own voices raised in the hymns, or because churchgoing qualified them for the Christmas blankets and coals; and a few to worship. There was at least one saint and mystic in that parish and there were several good Christian men and women, but the majority regarded religion as something proper to extreme old age, for which they themselves had as yet no use.

'About time he wer' thinkin' about his latter end,' they would say of one who showed levity when his head and beard were white, or of anybody who was ill and afflicted. Once a hunchback from another village came to a pig feast and distinguished himself by getting drunk and using bad language; and, because he was a cripple, his conduct was looked upon with horror. Laura's mother was distressed when she

41

heard about it. 'To think of a poor afflicted creature like that cursing and swearing,' she sighed. 'Terrible! Terrible!' And when Edmund, then about ten, looked up from his book and said calmly, 'I should think if anybody's got a right to swear it's a man with a back like that,' she told him he was nearly as bad to say such a thing.

The Catholic minority at the inn was treated with respect, for a landlord could do no wrong, especially the landlord of a free house where such excellent beer was on tap. On Catholicism at large, the Lark Rise people looked with contemptuous intolerance, for they regarded it as a kind of heathenism, and what excuse could there be for that in a Christian country? When, early in life, the end house children asked what Roman Catholics were, they were told they were 'folks as prays to images', and further inquiries elicited the information that they also worshipped the Pope, a bad old man, some said in league with the Devil. Their genuflexions in church and their 'playin' wi' beads' were described as 'monkey tricks'. People who openly said they had no use for religion themselves became quite heated when the Catholics were mentioned. Yet the children's grandfather, when the sound of the Angelus bell was borne on the wind from the chapel in the next village, would take off his hat and, after a moment's silence, murmur, 'In my Father's house are many mansions.' It was all very puzzling.

Later on, when they came to associate more with the other children, on the way to Sunday school they would see horses and traps loaded with families from many miles around on their way to the Catholic church in the next village. 'There go the old Catholics!' the children would cry, and run after the vehicles shouting: 'Old Catholics! Old lick the cats!' until they had to fall behind for want of breath. Sometimes a lady in one of the high dogcarts would smile at them forbearingly, otherwise no notice was taken.

The horses and traps were followed at a distance by the young men and big boys of the families on foot. Always late in starting, yet always in time for the service, how they legged it! The children took good care not to call out after them, for they knew whatever their haste, the boy Catholics would have time to turn back and cuff them. It had happened before. So they let them get on for quite a distance before they started to mock their gait and recite in a snuffling sing-song:

> 'O dear Father, I've come to confess.'
> 'Well, my child, and what have you done?'

'O dear Father, I've killed the cat.'
'Well, my child, and what about that?'
'O dear Father, what shall I do?'
'You kiss me and I'll kiss you.'

a gem which had probably a political origin, for the seeds of their ignorant bigotry must have been sown at some time. Yet, strange to say, some of those very children still said by way of a prayer when they went to bed:

Matthew, Mark, Luke and John,
Bless the bed where I lie on.
Four corners have I to my bed;
At them four angels nightly spread.
One to watch and one to pray
And two to take my soul away.

# III
# THE SENSE OF UNFAIRNESS

*St Augustine*

*Samuel Butler*

*Charles Dickens*

*Charlotte Brontë*

St Augustine, a man noted in his own lifetime (354–430) for his tolerance and loyalty makes a plea for "children's business' to be tolerated in the same way as the often less godly and more destructive business of adults. As is often noted, in this collection, he comments on the futility of attempting to impose an adult order, and adult ideas, on the very young, and is indignant even in adulthood at the punishments he suffered as a consequence of an incapacity to understand—a feeling we all know.

Samuel Butler's sense of outrage at his own bitter and traumatic childhood in *The Way of All Flesh* (pub. 1903) is glossed with poker-faced, sarcastic wit. The kind of gentle ridicule displayed by Gosse and Berners becomes an eloquent lesson, revealing an underlying hollowness in his adult characters, an incapacity to love, for which religion becomes at once a screen, a channel by which self-hatred can be transferred to others and a blunt instrument with which to punish.

Dickens, too, manages deep irony, but was never one to be anything but straightforward when chastising the middle-class hand that fed him. The fatuous Chadband and the waif Jo may be sketchily-drawn, and the motif of the cross of St Paul's simple and direct, but it must not be forgotten that they lie within a novel of great length and subtlety.

Charlotte Brontë's life, and that of her family, is well-known enough; suffice it to say that *Jane Eyre's* childhood, albeit depressing, was tolerable in comparison with her own. This piece must be one of the best portrayals of a child's feelings in the English language.

# St Augustine

*from:* The Confessions of St Augustine

## IX

1. O God, my God, what misery did I then endure, what deception! For it was held up to me, as the whole duty of a boy, to obey those who exhorted me to get on in this world, and make a name in wordy arts, which minister to the glory of man and deceitful riches. Then was I sent to school to learn letters. Alas, I knew not what profit they were, and yet I was flogged, if I was slow to learn. For this was the good old way. Those who have lived this life before us laid out thorny paths which we were compelled to tread, so sorely are labour and pain multiplied for the sons of Adam.

2. Yet we met with men who prayed to Thee, O Lord, and from them we learned to feel (as well as boys could feel), that Thou art some great One, that Thou couldst hear us and help, though we could not see Thee. For, even as a boy, I began to pray to Thee, my Help and my Refuge; to call upon Thee I burst the bonds of my tongue, and prayed to Thee — child as I was, how passionately! — that I might not be flogged at school. Thou didst not hear me, yet countedst it not for folly unto me; but my elders, and even my parents, who wished me nothing but good, laughed at my stripes, my great and grievous ill. Is there anyone, O Lord, so high in spirit, so bound to Thee by lofty devotion — is there anyone at all, for even want of feeling may give courage — is there a man who by filial adhesion to Thee is made so stout of heart, that he despises racks and hooks and the whole arsenal of torture, which all men shrink from with horror and prayers for deliverance, and laughs at the cruel executioner, as our own parents laughed at the torments inflicted on their children by the school-master? Certainly we feared them as much, and prayed as earnestly that we might escape them. And yet we were sinning, when we wrote less, or read less, or thought less about our lessons than was expected of us.

3. For I had no want, O Lord, of memory or capacity — these Thou gavest me in full measure for that age — but we loved play, and for this we were punished, by those who surely were doing the same thing. But the follies of elders are called business, while the business of

47

children is punished by grown men; and no one pities boy or man or both. Can any reasonable person think it is right that a boy should be flogged for playing at ball, because play hinders him in the acquisition of knowledge, with which he is only to play a baser game in after years? Or was there anything to choose between me and the master who flogged me? For he, if his fellow-teacher worsted him in some pedantic dispute, was more disordered by rage and envy, than I, when beaten by my playmate in a game of catch.

# Samuel Butler

*from:* The Way of all Flesh

The birth of his son opened Theobald's eyes to a good deal which he had but faintly realised hitherto. He had had no idea how great a nuisance a baby was. Babies come into the world so suddenly at the end, and upset everything so terribly when they do come: why cannot they steal in upon us with less of a shock to the domestic system? His wife, too, did not recover rapidly from her confinement; she remained an invalid for months; here was another nuisance and an expensive one, which interfered with the amount which Theobald liked to put by out of his income against, as he said, a rainy day, or to make provision for his family if he should have one. Now he was getting a family, so that it became all the more necessary to put money by, and here was the baby hindering him. Theorists may say what they like about a man's children being a continuation of his own identity, but it will generally be found that those who talk this way have no children of their own. Practical family men know better.

About twelve months after the birth of Ernest there came a second, also a boy, who was christened Joseph, and in less than twelve months afterwards, a girl, to whom was given the name of Charlotte. A few months before this girl was born Christina paid a visit to the John Pontifexes in London, and, knowing her condition, passed a good deal of time at the Royal Academy exhibition looking at the types of female beauty portrayed by the Academicians, for she had made up her mind that the child this time was to be a girl. Alethea warned her not to do this, but she persisted, and certainly the child turned out plain, but whether the pictures caused this or no I cannot say.

Theobald had never liked children. He had always got away from them as soon as he could, and so had they from him; oh, why, he was inclined to ask himself, could not children be born into the world grown-up? If Christina could have given birth to a few full-grown clergymen in priest's orders — of moderate views, but inclining rather to Evangelicalism, with comfortable livings and in all respects facsimiles of Theobald himself — why, there might have been more sense it it; or if people could buy ready-made children at a shop of whatever age and sex they liked, instead of always having to make them at home and to begin at the beginning with them — that might do better, but as it was he did not like it. He felt as he had felt when he had been required to come and be married to Christina — that he had been going on for a long time quite nicely, and would much rather continue things on their present footing. In the matter of getting married he had been obliged to pretend he liked it; but times were changed, and if he did not like a thing now, he could find a hundred unexceptionable ways of making his dislike apparent.

It might have been better if Theobald in his younger days had kicked more against his father: the fact that he had not done so encouraged him to expect the most implicit obedience from his own children. He could trust himself, he said (and so did Christina), to be more lenient than perhaps his father had been to himself; his danger, he said (and so again did Christina), would be rather in the direction of being too indulgent; he must be on his guard against this, for no duty could be more important than that of teaching a child to obey its parents in all things.

He had read not long since of an Eastern traveller, who, while exploring somewhere in the more remote parts of Arabia and Asia Minor, had come upon a remarkably hardy, sober, industrious little Christian community — all of them in the best of health — who had turned out to be the actual living descendants of Jonadab, the son of Rechab; and two men in European costume, indeed, but speaking English with a broken accent, and by their colour evidently Oriental, had come begging to Battersby soon afterwards, and represented themselves as belonging to this people; they had said they were collecting funds to promote the conversion of their fellow tribesmen to the English church of the Christian religion. True, they turned out to be imposters, for when he gave them a pound and Christina five shillings from her private purse, they went and got drunk with it in the next village but one to Battersby; still, this did not invalidate the story of the Eastern traveller. Then there were the Romans — whose greatness was probably due to the wholesome authority exercised by the head of a family over all its members. Some Romans had even killed their children; this was going too far, but then the Romans were not Christians, and knew no better.

The practical outcome of the foregoing was a conviction in Theobald's mind, and if in his, then in Christina's, that it was their duty to begin training up their children in the way they should go, even from their earliest infancy. The first signs of self-will must be carefully looked for, and plucked up by the roots at once before they had time to grow. Theobald picked up this dumb serpent of a metaphor and cherished it in his bosom.

Before Ernest could well crawl he was taught to kneel; before he could well speak he was taught to lisp the Lord's prayer, and the general confession. How was it possible that these things could be taught too early? If his attention flagged or his memory failed him, here was an ill weed which would grow apace, unless it were plucked out immediately, and the only way to pluck it out was to whip him, or shut him up in a cupboard, or dock him of some of the small pleasures of childhood. Before he was three years old he could read and, after a fashion, write. Before he was four he was learning Latin, and could do rule of three sums.

As for the child himself, he was naturally of an even temper, he doted upon his nurse, on kittens and puppies, and on all things that would do him the kindness of allowing him to be fond of them. He was fond of his mother, too, but as regards his father, he has told me in later life he could remember no feeling but fear and shrinking. Christina did not remonstrate with Theobald concerning the severity of the tasks imposed upon their boy, nor yet as to the continual whippings that were found necessary at lesson times. Indeed, when during any absence of Theobald's the lessons were entrusted to her, she found to her sorrow that it was the only thing to do, and she did it no less effectually than Theobald himself; nevertheless she was fond of her boy, which Theobald never was, and it was long before she could destroy all affection for herself in the mind of her first-born. But she persevered.

. . . I was there on a Sunday, and observed the rigour with which the young people were taught to observe the Sabbath; they might not cut out things, nor use their paint-box on a Sunday, and this they thought rather hard, because their cousins the John Pontifexes might do these things. Their cousins might play with their toy train on Sunday, but though they had promised that they would run none but Sunday trains, all traffic had been prohibited. One treat only was allowed them — on Sunday evenings they might choose their own hymns.

In the course of the evening they came into the drawing-room, and, as an especial treat, were to sing some of their hymns to me, instead of saying them, so that I might hear how nicely they sang. Ernest was to choose the first hymn, and he chose one about some people who were to come to the sunset tree. I am no botanist, and do not know what kind of tree a sunset tree is, but the words began, 'Come, come, come; come to the sunset tree for the day is past and gone.' The tune was rather pretty and had taken Ernest's fancy, for he was unusually fond of music and had a sweet little child's voice which he liked using.

He was, however, very late in being able to sound a hard 'c' or 'k', and, instead of saying 'Come,' he said 'Tum, tum, tum.'

'Ernest,' said Theobald, from the arm-chair in front of the fire, where he was sitting with his hands folded before him, 'don't you think it would be very nice if you were to say "come" like other people, instead of "tum"?'

'I do say tum,' replied Ernest, meaning that he had said 'come'.

Theobald was always in a bad temper on Sunday evening. Whether it is that they are as much bored with the day as their neighbours, or whether they are tired, or whatever the cause may be, clergymen are seldom at their best on Sunday evening; I had already seen signs that evening that my host was cross, and was a little nervous at hearing Ernest say so promptly 'I do say tum', when his papa had said he did not say it as he should.

Theobald noticed the fact that he was being contradicted in a moment. He got up from his arm-chair and went to the piano.

'No, Ernest, you don't,' he said, 'you say nothing of the kind, you say "tum," not "come." Now say "come" after me, as I do.'

'Tum,' said Ernest, at once; 'Is that better?' I have no doubt he thought it was, but it was not.

'Now, Ernest, you are not taking pains: you are not trying as you ought to. It is high time you learned to say "come," why, Joey can say "come," can't you, Joey?'

'Yeth, I can,' replied Joey, and he said something which was not far off 'come.'

'There Ernest, do you hear that? There's no difficulty about it, nor shadow of difficulty. Now, take your own time, think about it, and say "come" after me.'

The boy remained silent for a few seconds and then said 'tum' again.

I laughed, but Theobald turned to me impatiently and said, 'Please do not laugh, Overton; it will make the boy think it does not matter, and it matters a great deal;' then turning to Ernest, he said, 'Now, Ernest, I will give you one more chance, and if you don't say "come," I shall know that you are self-willed and naughty.

He looked very angry, and a shade came over Ernest's face, like that which comes upon the face of a puppy when it is being scolded without understanding why. The child saw well what was coming now, was frightened, and, of course, said 'tum' once more.

'Very well, Ernest,' said his father, catching him angrily by the shoulder, 'I have done my best to save you, but if you will have it so, you will,' and lugged the little wretch, crying by anticipation, out of the room. A few minutes more and we could hear screams coming from the dining-room, across the hall which separated the drawing-room from the dining-room, and knew that poor Ernest was being beaten.

'I have sent him to bed,' said Theobald, as he returned to the drawing-room, 'and now, Christina, I think we will have the servants in to prayers,' and he rang the bell for them, red-handed as he was.

# *Charles Dickens*

*from:* Bleak House

## MOVING ON

Mr Chadband is a large yellow man, with a fat smile, and a general appearance of having a good deal of train oil in his system. Mrs Chadband is a stern, severe-looking, silent woman. Mr Chadband moves softly and cumbrously, not unlike a bear who has been taught to walk upright. He is very much embarrassed about the arms, as if they were inconvenient to him, and he wanted to grovel; is very much in a perspiration about the head; and never speaks without first putting up his great hand, as delivering a token to his bearers that he is going to edify them.

'My friends,' says Mr Chadband, 'Peace be on this house! On the master thereof, on the mistress thereof, on the young maidens, and on the younger men! My friends, why do I wish for peace? What is peace? Is it war? No. Is it strife? No. Is it lovely, and gentle, and beautiful, and pleasant, and serene, and joyful? O yes! Therefore, my friends, I wish for peace, upon you and upon yours.'

In consequence of Mrs Snagsby looking deeply edified, Mr Snagsby thinks it expedient on the whole to say Amen, which is well received.

'Now, my friends,' proceeds Mr Chadband, 'since I am upon this theme—'

Guster presents herself. Mrs Snagsby, in a spectral bass voice, and without removing her eyes from Chadband, says, with dread distinctness, 'Go away!'

'Now, my friends,' says Chadband, 'since I am upon this theme, and in my lowly path improving it—'

Guster is heard unaccountably to murmur 'one thousing seven hunderd and eighty-two.' The spectral voice repeats more solemnly, 'Go away!'

'Now, my friends,' says Mr Chadband, 'we will inquire in a spirit of love—'

Still Guster reiterates 'one thousing seven hunderd and eighty-two.'

Mr Chadband, pausing with the resignation of a man accustomed to be persecuted, and languidly folding up his chin into his fat smile, says, 'Let us hear the maiden! Speak, maiden!'

'One thousing seven hunderd and eighty-two, if you please, sir. Which he wish to know what the shilling ware for,' says Guster, breathless.

'For?' returns Mrs Chadband. 'For his fare!'

Guster replied that 'he insists on one and eightpence, or on summonsizzing the party.' Mrs Snagsby and Mrs Chadband are proceeding to grow shrill in indignation when Mr Chadband quiets the tumult by lifting up his hand.

'My friends,' says he, 'I remember a duty unfulfilled yesterday. It is right that I should be chastened in some penalty. I ought not to murmur. Racheal, pay the eightpence!'

While Mrs Snagsby, drawing her breath, looks hard at Mr Snagsby, as who should say, 'You hear this Apostle!' and while Mr Chadband glows with humility and train oil, Mrs Chadband pays the money. It is Mr Chadband's habit—it is the head and front of his pretensions indeed—to keep this sort of debtor and creditor account in the

53

smallest items, and to post it publicly on the most trivial occasions.

'My friends,' says Chadband, 'eightpence is not much; it might justly have been one and fourpence; it might justly have been half a crown. O let us be joyful, joyful! O let us be joyful!'

With which remark, which appears from its sound to be an extract in verse, Mr Chadband stalks to the table, and, before taking a chair, lifts up his admonitory hand.

'My friends,' says he, 'what is this which we now behold as being spread before us? Refreshment. Do we need refreshment then, my friends? We do. And why do we need refreshment, my friends? Because we are but mortal, because we are but sinful, because we are but of the earth, because we are not of the air. Can we fly, my friends? We cannot. Why can we not fly, my friends?'

Mr Snagsby, presuming on the success of his last point, ventures to observe in a cheerful and rather knowing tone, 'No wings.' But, is immediately frowned down by Mrs Snagsby.

'I say, my friends,' pursues Mr Chadband, utterly rejecting and obliterating Mr Snagsby's suggestion, 'why can we not fly? Is it because we are calculated to walk? It is. Could we walk, my friends, without strength? We could not. What should we do without strength, my friends? Our legs would refuse to bear us, our knees would double up, our ankles would turn over, and we should come to the ground. Then from whence, my friends, in a human point of view, do we derive the strength that is necessary to our limbs? Is it,' says Chadband, glancing over the table, 'from bread in various forms, from butter which is churned from the milk which is yielded unto us by the cow, from the eggs which are laid by the fowl, from ham, from tongue, from sausage, and from such like? It is. Then let us partake of the good things which are set before us!'

The persecutors denied that there was any particular gift in Mr Chadband's piling verbose flights of stairs, one upon another, after this fashion. But this can only be received as a proof of their determination to persecute, since it must be within everybody's experience, that the Chadband style of oratory is widely received and much admired.

Mr Chadband, however, having concluded for the present, sits down at Mr Snagsby's table, and lays about him prodigiously. The conversion of nutriment of any sort into oil of the quality already mentioned, appears to be a process so inseparable from the constitution of this exemplary vessel, that in beginning to eat and drink, he may be described as always becoming a kind of considerable Oil Mill, or other large factory for the production of that article on a wholesale scale. On the present evening of the long vacation, in Cook's Court, Cursitor Street, he does such a powerful stroke of business, that the warehouse appears to be quite full when the works cease.

At this period of the entertainment, Guster, who has never recovered her first failure, but has neglected no possible or impossible means of bringing the establishment and herself into contempt—among which may be briefly enumerated her unexpectedly performing clashing military music on Mr Chadband's head with plates, and afterwards crowning that gentleman with muffins—at which period of the entertainment, Guster whispers Mr Snagsby that he is wanted.

'And being wanted in the—not to put too fine a point upon it—in the shop!' says Mr Snagsby rising, 'perhaps this good company will excuse me for half a minute.'

Mr Snagsby descends, and finds the two 'prentices intently contemplating a police constable, who holds a ragged boy by the arm.

'Why bless my heart,' says Mr Snagsby, 'what's the matter!'

'This boy,' says the constable, 'although he's repeatedly told to, won't move on—'

'I'm always a-moving on, sir,' cries the boy, wiping away his grimy tears with his arm. 'I've always been a-moving and a-moving on, ever since I was born. Where can I possibly move to, sir, more nor I do move!'

'He won't move on,' says the constable, calmly, with a slight professional hitch of his neck involving its better settlement in his stiff stock, 'although he has been repeatedly cautioned, and therefore I am obliged to take him into custody. He's as obstinate a young gonoph as I know. He WON'T move on.'

'O my eye! Where can I move to!' cries the boy, clutching quite desperately at his hair, and beating his bare feet upon the floor of Mr Snagsby's passage.

'Don't you come none of that, or I shall make blessed short work of you!' says the constable, giving him a passionless shake. 'My instructions are, that you are to move on. I have told you so five hundred times.'

'But where?' cries the boy.

'Well! Really, constable, you know,' says Mr Snagsby wistfully, and coughing behind his hand his cough of great perplexity and doubt;

'really, that does seem a question. Where, you know?'

'My instructions don't go to that,' replies the constable. 'My instructions are that this boy is to move on.'

Do you hear, Jo? It is nothing to you or to any one else, that the great lights of the parliamentary sky have failed for some few years, in this business, to set you the example of moving on. The grand recipe remains for you—the profound philosophical prescription—the be-all and the end-all of your strange existence upon earth. Move on! You are by no means to move off, Jo, for the great lights can't at all agree about that. Move on!

Mr Snagsby says nothing to this effect; says nothing at all, indeed; but coughs his forlornest cough, expressive of no thoroughfare in any direction. By this time Mr and Mrs Chadband, and Mrs Snagsby, hearing the altercation, have appeared upon the stairs. Guster having never left the end of the passage, the whole household are assembled.

'The simple question is, sir,' says the constable, 'whether you know this boy. He says you do.'

Mrs Snagsby, from her elevation, instantly cries out, 'No he don't!'

'My lit-tle woman!' says Mr Snagsby, looking up the staircase. 'My love, permit me! Pray have a moment's patience, my dear. I do know something of this lad, and in what I know of him, I can't say that there's any harm; perhaps on the contrary, constable.' To whom the law-stationer relates his Joful and woful experience, suppressing the half-crown fact.

'Well!' says the constable, 'so far, it seems, he had grounds for what he said. When I took him into custody up in Holborn, he said you knew him. Upon that, a young man who was in the crowd said he was acquainted with you, and you were a respectable housekeeper, and if I'd call and make the inquiry, he'd appear. The young man don't seem inclined to keep his word, but—Oh! Here *is* the young man!'

Enter Mr Guppy, who nods to Mr Snagsby, and touches his hat with the chivalry of clerkship to the ladies on the stairs.

'I was strolling away from the office just now, when I found this row going on,' says Mr Guppy to the law-stationer; 'and as your name was mentioned, I thought it was right the thing should be looked into.'

'It was very good-natured of you sir,' says Mr Snagsby, 'and I am obliged to you.' And Mr Snagsby again relates his experience, again suppressing the half-crown fact.

'Now, I know where you live,' says the constable, then, to Jo. 'You live down in Tom-all-Alone's. That's a nice innocent place to live in, ain't it?'

'I can't go and live in no nicer place, sir', replies Jo. 'They wouldn't have nothing to say to me if I wos to go to a nice innocent place fur to live. Who ud go and let a nice innocent lodging to such a reg'lar one as me!'

'You are very poor, ain't you?' says the constable.

'Yes, I am indeed, sir, wery poor in gin'ral,' replies Jo.

'I leave you to judge now! I shook these two half-crowns out of him,' says the constable, producing them to the company, 'in only putting my hand upon him!'

'They're wot's left, Mr Snagsby', says Jo, 'out of a sov-ring as wos give me by a lady in a wale as sed she wos a servant and as come to my crossin one night and asked to be showd this 'ere ouse and the ouse wot him as you giv the writin to died at, and the berrin-ground, wot he's berrid in. She ses to me she ses "are you the boy at the Inkwhich?" she ses. I ses "yes" I ses. She ses to me she ses "can you show me all them places?" I ses "yes I can" I ses. And she ses to me "do it" and I dun it and she giv me a sov'ring and hooked it. And I an't had much of the sov'ring neither,' says Jo, with dirty tears, 'fur I had to pay five bob, down in Tom-all-Alone's, afore they'd square it fur to give me change, and then a young man he thieved another five while I was asleep and another boy thieved ninepence and the landlord he stood drains round with a lot more on it.'

'You don't expect anybody to believe this, about the lady and the sovereign, do you?' says the constable, eyeing him aside with ineffable disdain.

'I don't know as I do, sir,' replies Jo. 'I don't expect nothing at all, sir, much, but that's the true hist'ry on it.'

'You see what he is!' the constable observes to the audience. 'Well, Mr Snagsby, if I don't lock him up this time, will you engage for his moving on?'

'No!' cries Mrs Snagsby from the stairs.

'My little woman!' pleads her husband. 'Constable, I have no doubt he'll move on. You know you really must do it,' says Mr Snagsby.

'I'm everyways agreeable, sir,' says the hapless Jo.

'Do it, then,' observes the constable. 'You know what you have got to do. Do it! And recollect you won't get off so easy next time. Catch hold of your money. Now, the sooner you're five mile off, the better for all parties.'

With this farewell hint, and pointing generally to the setting sun, as a likely place to move on to, the constable bids his auditors good afternoon; and makes the echoes of Cook's Court perform slow music for him as he walks away on the shady side, carrying his iron-bound hat in his hand for a little ventilation.

Now, Jo's improbable story concerning the lady and the sovereign has awakened more or less the curiosity of all the company. Mr Guppy, who has an inquiring mind in matters of evidence, and who has been suffering severely from the lassitude of the long vacation, takes that interest in the case, that he enters on a regular cross-examination of the witness, which is found so interesting by the ladies that Mrs Snagsby politely invites him to step upstairs, and drink a cup of tea, if he will excuse the disarranged state of the tea-table, consequent on their previous exertions. Mr Guppy yielding his assent to this proposal, Jo is requested to follow into the drawing-room doorway, where Mr Guppy takes him in hand as a witness, patting him into this shape, and the other shape, like a butterman dealing with so much butter, and worrying him according to the best models. Nor is the examination unlike many such model displays, both in respect of its eliciting nothing, and of its being lengthy; for, Mr Guppy is sensible of his talent, and Mrs Snagsby feels, not only that it gratifies her inquisitive disposition, but that it lifts her husband's establishment higher up in the law. During the progress of this keen encounter, the vessel Chadband, being merely engaged in the oil trade, gets aground, and waits to be floated off.

'Well!' says Mr Guppy, 'either this boy sticks to it like cobbler's-wax, or there is something out of the common here that beats anything that ever came into my way at Kenge and Carboy's.'

Mrs Chadband whispers to Mrs Snagsby, who exclaims, 'You don't say so!'

'For years!' replied Mrs Chadband.

'Has known Kenge and Carboy's office for years,' Mrs Snagsby triumphantly explains to Mr Guppy. 'Mrs Chadband—this gentleman's wife—Reverend Mr Chadband.'

'Oh, indeed!' says Mr Guppy.

'Before I married my present husband,' says Mrs Chadband.

'Was you a party in anything, ma'am?' says Mr Guppy, transferring his cross-examination.

'No.'

'*Not* a party to anything, ma'am?' says Mr Guppy.

Mrs Chadband shakes her head.

'Perhaps you were acquainted with somebody who was a party in something, ma'am?' says Mr Guppy, who likes nothing better than to model his conversation on forensic principles.

'Not exactly that, either,' replies Mrs Chadbland, humouring the joke with a hard-favoured smile.

'Not exactly that, either!' repeats Mr Guppy. 'Very good. Pray ma'am, was it a lady of your acquaintance who had some transactions (we will not at present say what transactions) with Kenge and Carboy's office, or was it a gentleman of your acquaintance? Take time, ma'am. We shall come to it presently. Man or woman, ma'am?'

'Neither,' says Mrs Chadband, as before.

'Oh! A child!' says Mr Guppy, throwing on the admiring Mrs Snagsby the regular acute professional eye which is thrown on British jurymen. 'Now, ma'am, perhaps you'll have the kindness to tell us *what* child.'

'You have got it at last, sir,' says Mrs Chadband, with another hard-favoured smile. 'Well, sir, it was before your time, most likely, judging from your appearance. I was left in charge of a child named Esther Summerson, who was put out in life by Messrs Kenge and Carboy.'

'Miss Summerson, ma'am!' cries Mr Guppy, excited.

'*I* call her Esther Summerson,' says Mrs Chadband, with austerity. 'There was no Miss-ing of the girl in my time. It was Esther. "Esther, do this! Esther, do that!" and she was made to do it.'

'My dear ma'am,' returns Mr Guppy, moving across the small apartment, 'the humble individual who now addresses you received that young lady in London, when she first came here from the establishment to which you have alluded. Allow me to have the pleasure of taking you by the hand.'

Mr Chadband, at last seeing his opportunity, makes his accustomed signal, and rises with a smoking head, which he dabs with his pocket-handkerchief. Mrs Snagsby whispers 'Hush!'

'My friends,' says Chadband, 'we have partaken in moderation' (which was certainly not the case so far as he was concerned), 'of the comforts which have been provided for us. May this house live upon the fatness of the land; may corn and wine be plentiful therein; may it grow, may it thrive, may it prosper, may it advance, may it proceed, may it press forward! But, my friends, have we partaken of anything else? We have. My friends, of what else have we partaken? Of spiritual profit? Yes. From whence have we derived that spiritual profit? My young friend, stand forth!'

Jo, thus apostrophized, gives a slouch backward, and another slouch forward, and another slouch to each side, and confronts the eloquent Chadband, with evident doubts of his intentions.

'My young friend,' says Chadband, 'you are to us a pearl, you are to us a diamond, you are to us a gem, you are to us a jewel. And why, my young friend?'

'*I* don't know,' replies Jo. 'I don't know nothink.'

'My young friend,' says Chadband, 'it is because you know nothing that you are to us a gem and jewel. For what are you, my young friend? Are you a beast of the field? No. A bird of the air? No. A fish of the sea or river? No. You are a human boy, my young friend. A human boy. O glorious to be a human boy! And why glorious, my young friend? Because you are capable of receiving the lessons of wisdom, because you are capable of profiting by the discourse which I now deliver for your good, because you are not a stick, or a staff, or a stock, or a stone, or a post, or a pillar.

> O running stream of sparkling joy
> To be a roaring human boy!

And do you cool yourself in that stream now, my young friend? No. Why do you not cool yourself in that stream now? Because you are in a state of darkness, because you are in a state of obscurity, because you are in a state of sinfulness, because you are in a state of bondage. My young friend, what *is* bondage? Let us, in a spirit of love, inquire.'

At this threatening stage of discourse, Jo, who seems to have been gradually going out of his mind, smears his right arm over his face, and gives a terrible yawn. Mrs Snagsby indignantly expresses her belief that he is a limb of the arch-fiend.

'My friends,' says Mr Chadband, with his persecuted chin folding itself into its fat smile again as he looks round, 'it is right that I should be humbled, it is right that I should be tried, it is right that I should be mortified, it is right that I should be corrected. I stumbled, on Sabbath last, when I thought with pride of my three hours' improving. The account is now favourably balanced: my creditor has accepted a composition. O let us be joyful! O let us be joyful!'

Great sensation on the part of Mrs Snagsby.

'My friends,' says Chadband, looking round him in conclusion, 'I will not proceed with my young friend now. Will you come tomorrow, my young friend, and inquire of this good lady where I am to be found to deliver a discourse unto you, and will you come like the thirsty swallow upon the next day, and upon the day after that, and upon the day after that, and upon many pleasant days, to hear discourses?' (This, with a cow-like lightness.)

Jo, whose immediate object seems to be to get away on any terms, gives a shuffling nod. Mr Guppy then throws him a penny, and Mrs Snagsby calls to Guster to see him safely out of the house. But, before he goes dowstairs, Mr Snagsby loads him with some broken meats from the table, which he carries away, hugging in his arms.

So, Mr Chadband—of whom the persecutors say that it is no wonder he should go on for any length of time uttering such abominable nonsense, but that the wonder rather is that he should ever leave off, having once the audacity to begin—retires into private life until he invests a little capital of supper in the oil-trade. Jo moves on, through the long vacation, down to Blackfriars Bridge, where he finds a baking stony corner, wherein to settle to his repast.

And there he sits munching, and gnawing, and looking up at the great Cross on the summit of St Paul's Cathedral, glittering above a red and violet-tinted cloud of smoke. From the boy's face one might suppose that sacred emblem to be, in his eyes, the crowning confusion of the great, confused city;—so golden, so high up, so far out of his reach. There he sits, the sun going down, the river running fast, the crowd flowing by him in two streams—everything moving on to some purpose and to one end—until he is stirred up, and told to 'move on' too.

# Charlotte Brontë

*from:* Jane Eyre

'Who could want me?' I asked inwardly, as with both hands I turned the stiff door-handle which, for a second or two, resisted my efforts. 'What should I see besides Aunt Reed in the apartment? — a man or a woman?' The handle turned, the door unclosed, and passing through and curtseying low, I looked up at — a black pillar! — such, at least, appeared to me, at first sight, the straight, narrow, sable-clad shape standing erect on the rug; the grim face at the top was like a carved mask, placed above the shaft by way of a capital.

Mrs Reed occupied her usual seat by the fireside; she made a signal to me to approach; I did so, and she introduced me to the stony stranger with the words —

'This is the little girl respecting whom I applied to you.'

*He* — for it was a man — turned his head slowly towards where I stood, and having examined me with the two inquisitive looking gray eyes which twinkled under a pair of bushy brows, said solemnly, and in a bass voice —

'Her size is small; what is her age?'

'Ten years.'

'So much?' was the doubtful answer; and he prolonged his scrutiny for some minutes. Presently he addressed me —

'Your name, little girl?'

'Jane Eyre, sir.'

In uttering these words I looked up: he seemed to me a tall gentleman, but then I was very little; his features were large, and they and all the lines of his frame were equally harsh and prim.

'Well, Jane Eyre, and are you a good child?'

Impossible to reply to this in the affirmative: my little world held a contrary opinion: I was silent. Mrs Reed answered for me by an expressive shake of the head, adding soon, 'Perhaps the less said on that subject the better, Mr Brocklehurst.'

'Sorry indeed to hear it! She and I must have some talk;' and bending from the perpendicular, he installed his person in the armchair, opposite Mrs Reed's. 'Come here,' he said.

I stepped across the rug: he placed me square and straight before him. What a face he had, now that it was almost on a level with mine! what a great nose! and what a mouth! and what large, prominent teeth!

'No sight so sad as that of a naughty child,' he began, 'especially a naughty little girl. Do you know where the wicked go after death?'

'They go to hell,' was my ready and orthodox answer.

'And what is hell? Can you tell me that?'

'A pit full of fire.'

'And should you like to fall into that pit, and to be burning there for ever?'

'No, sir.'

'What must you do to avoid it?'

I deliberated a moment: my answer, when it did come, was objectionable: 'I must keep in good health, and not die.'

'How can you keep in good health? Children younger than you die daily. I buried a little child of five years old only a day or two since — a good little child, whose soul is in heaven. It is to be feared the same could not be said of you, were you to be called thence.'

Not being in a condition to remove his doubt, I only cast my eyes down on the two large feet planted on the rug, and sighed, wishing myself far enough away.

'I hope that sigh is from the heart, and that you repent of ever having been the occasion of discomfort to your excellent benefactress.'

'Benefactress! benefactress!' said I inwardly: 'they all call Mrs Reed my benefactress; if so, a benefactress is a disagreeable thing.'

'Do you say your prayers night and morning?' continued my interrogator.

'Yes, sir.'

'Do you read your Bible?'

'Sometimes.'

'With pleasure? Are you fond of it?'

'I like Revelations, and the Book of Daniel, and Genesis, and Samuel, and a little bit of Exodus, and some parts of Kings and Chronicles, and Job and Jonah.'

'And the Psalms? I hope you like them?'

'No, sir.'

'No? Oh, shocking! I have a little boy, younger than you, who knows six Psalms by heart: and when you ask him which he would rather have, a ginger-bread-nut to eat, or a verse of a Psalm to learn, he says: "Oh! the verse of a Psalm! angels sing Psalms," says he; "I wish to be a little angel here below." He then gets two nuts in recompense for his infant piety.'

'Psalms are not interesting,' I remarked.

'That proves you to have a wicked heart; and you must pray to God to change it: to give you a new and clean one: to take away your heart of stone and give you a heart of flesh.'

I was about to propound a question, touching the manner in which that operation of changing my heart was to be performed, when Mrs Reed interposed, telling me to sit down; she then proceeded to carry on the conversation herself.

'Mr Brocklehurst, I believe I intimated in the letter which I wrote to you three weeks ago, that this little girl has not quite the character and disposition I could wish: should you admit her into Lowood school, I should be glad if the superintendent and teachers were requested to keep a strict eye on her, and, above all, to guard against her worst fault, a tendency to deceit. I mention this in your hearing, Jane, that you may not attempt to impose on Mr Brocklehurst.'

Well might I dread, well might I dislike Mrs Reed; for it was her nature to wound me cruelly: never was I happy in her presence. However carefully I obeyed, however strenuously I strove to please her, my efforts were still repulsed, and repaid by such sentences as the above. Now, uttered before a stranger, the accusation cut me to the heart: I dimly perceived that she was already obliterating hope from the new phase of existence which she destined me to enter. I felt, though I could not have expressed the feeling, that she was sowing aversion and unkindness along my future path: I saw myself transformed, under Mr Brocklehurst's eye, into an artful, noxious child, and what could I do to remedy the injury?

'Nothing, indeed,' thought I, as I struggled to repress a sob, and hastily wiped away some tears, the impotent evidences of my anguish.

'Deceit is, indeed, a sad fault in a child,' said Mr Brocklehurst; 'it is akin to falsehood, and all liars will have their portion in the lake burning with fire and brimstone; she shall, however, be watched, Mrs Reed. I will speak to Miss Temple and the teachers.'

'I should wish her to be brought up in a manner suiting her prospects,' continued my benefactress; 'to be made useful, to be kept humble. As for the vacations she will, with your permission, spend them always at Lowood.'

'Your decisions are perfectly judicious, madam,' returned Mr Brocklehurst. 'Humility is a Christian grace, and one peculiarly appropriate to the pupils of Lowood; I, therefore, direct that special care shall be bestowed on its cultivation amongst them. I have studied how best to mortify in them the worldly sentiment of pride, and, only the other day, I had a pleasing proof of my success. My second daughter, Augusta, went with her mamma to visit the school, and on her return she exclaimed, "Oh, dear papa, how quiet and plain all the girls at Lowood look; with their hair combed behind their ears, and their long pinafores, and those little holland pockets outside their frocks, they are almost like poor people's children! and," said she, "they looked at my dress and mamma's, as if they had never seen a silk gown before".'

'This is the state of things I quite approve,' returned Mrs Reed. 'Had I sought all England over, I could scarcely have found a system more exactly fitting a child like Jane Eyre. Consistency, my dear Mr Brocklehurst — I advocate consistency in all things.'

'Consistency, madam, is the first of Christian duties, and it has been observed in every arrangement connected wih the establishment of Lowood: plain fare, simple attire, unsophisticated accommodations, hardy and active habits: such is the order of the day in the house and its inhabitants.'

'Quite right, sir. I may then depend upon this child being received as a pupil at Lowood, and there being trained in conformity to her position and prospects?'

'Madam, you may: she shall be placed in that nursery of chosen plants, and I trust she will show herself grateful for the inestimable privilege of her election.'

'I will send her, then, as soon as possible, Mr Brocklehurst; for, I assure you, I feel anxious to be relieved of a responsibility that was becoming too irksome.'

'No doubt, no doubt, madam. And now I wish you good-morning. I shall return to Brocklehurst Hall in the course of a week or two; my good friend, the Archdeacon, will not permit me to leave him sooner. I shall send Miss Temple notice that she is to expect a new girl, so that there will be no difficulty about receiving her. Good-bye.'

'Good-bye, Mr Brocklehurst; remember me to Mrs and Miss Brocklehurst, and to Augusta and Theodore, and Master Broughton Brocklehurst.'

'I will, madam.—Little girl, here is a book entitled the *Child's Guide;* read it with prayer, especially that part containing "an account of the awfully sudden death of Martha G—, a naughty child addicted to falsehood and deceit".'

With these words Mr Brocklehurst put into my hand a thin pamphlet, sewn in a cover, and, having rung for his carriage, he departed.

# IV
# THE DESIRE TO PLEASE

*Mary McCarthy*

*Edwin Muir*

*E Nesbit*

*Louisa M Alcott*

It is refreshing to find an account of a convent school as a happy and liberal place. Mary McCarthy was orphaned at the age of six and after attending several Catholic schools in her native Seattle, studied at Vassar, an experience which forms the basis of her best-known novel, *The Group* (1963). This account of the attempt to save her grandfather's soul is really charming.

The poet Edwin Muir (1887–1959), a native of Orkney, spent his teens in the Glasgow slums, and educated himself. He argues that the kind of Revivalist experience which he details here is nothing to do with Christianity *per se* but a communal, 'orgiastic' cleansing. Revivalism, itself strongly reviving in the 1980's, seems to appeal very successfully to teenagers; Muir attempts to provide some explanation for this.

*The Wouldbegoods* (1901) is one of the extraordinary series of children's books produced by E Nesbit between 1899 *(The Treasure Seekers)* and 1924, the best known of which is *The Railway Children* (1906), and few of which have ever gone out of print. Edith Nesbit's work for children is more accessible today than that of almost anyone else of her era and a good many since; her middle-class children are never priggish and her working-class ones never sentimentalized. The 'Wouldbegoods' solemnity and the malleability of their 'Rules' ring very true.

*Little Women* (1869) seems stilted by comparison and is too saccharine for some. Yet it remains extremely popular because its honesty, and that of its author, are quite irreproachable, despite all that we know in retrospect about the times which produced it.

# Mary McCarthy

*from:* Memories of a Catholic Girlhood

## THE BLACKGUARD

Were he living today, my Protestant grandfather would be displeased to hear that the fate of his soul had once been the occasion of intense theological anxiety with the Ladies of the Sacred Heart. While his mortal part, all unaware, went about its eighteen holes of golf, its rubber of bridge before dinner at the club, his immortal part lay in jeopardy with us, the nuns and pupils of a strict convent school set on a wooded hill quite near a piece of worthless real estate he had bought under the impression that Seattle was expanding in a northerly direction. A sermon delivered at the convent by an enthusiastic Jesuit had disclosed to us his danger. Up to this point, the disparity in religion between my grandfather and myself had given me no serious concern. The death of my parents, while it had drawn us together in many senses, including the legal one (for I became his ward), had at the same time left the gulf of a generation between us, and my grandfather's Protestantism presented itself as a natural part of the grand, granite scenery on the other side. But the Jesuit's sermon destroyed this ordered view in a single thunderclap of doctrine.

As the priest would have it, this honest and upright man, a great favourite with the Mother Superior, was condemned to eternal torment by the accident of having been baptized. Had he been a Mohammedan, a Jew, a pagan, or the child of civilized unbelievers, a place in Limbo would have been assured him; Cicero and Aristotle and Cyrus the Persian might have been his companions, and the harmless souls of unbaptized children might have frolicked about his feet. But if the Jesuit were right, all baptized Protestants went straight to Hell. A good life did not count in their favour. The baptismal rite, by conferring on them God's grace, made them also liable to His organizational displeasure. That is, baptism turned them Catholic whether they liked it or not, and their persistence in the Protestant ritual was a kind of asseverated apostasy. Thus my poor grandfather, sixty years behind in his Easter duty, actually reduced his prospects of salvation every time he sat down in the Presbyterian church.

The Mother Superior's sweet frown acknowledged me, an hour

after the sermon, as I curtsied, all agitation, in her office doorway. Plainly, she had been expecting me. Madame MacIllvra, an able administrator, must have been resignedly ticking off the names of the Protestant pupils and parents all during the concluding parts of the morning's service. She had a faint worried air, when the conversation began, of depreciating the sermon: doctrinally, perhaps, correct, it had been wanting in delicacy; the fiery Jesuit, a missionary celebrity, had lived too long among the Eskimos. This disengaged attitude encouraged me to hope. Surely this lady, the highest authority I knew, could find a way out for my grandfather. She could see that he was a special case, outside the brutal rule of thumb laid down by the Jesuit. It was she, after all, in the convent, from whom all exemptions flowed, who created arbitrary holidays (called *congés* by the order's French tradition); it was she who permitted us to get forbidden books from the librarian and occasionally to receive letters unread by the convent censor. (As a rule, all slang expressions, violations of syntax, errors of spelling, as well as improper sentiments, were blacked out of our friends' communications; so, unless we moved in a circle of young Addisons or Burkes, the letters we longed for came to us as fragments from which the original text could only be conjectured.) To my twelve-year-old mind, it appeared probable that Madame MacIllvra, our Mother Superior, had the power to give my grandfather *congé*, and I threw myself on her sympathies.

How could it be that my grandfather, the most virtuous person I knew, whose name was a byword among his friends and colleagues for a kind of rigid and fantastic probity — how could it be that this man should be lost, while I, the object of his admonition, the despair of his example — I, who yielded to every impulse, lied, boasted, betrayed — should, by virtue of regular attendance at the sacraments and the habit of easy penitence, be saved?

Madame MacIllvra's full white brow wrinkled; her childlike blue eyes clouded. Like many headmistresses, she loved a good cry, and she clasped me to her plump, quivering, middle-aged bosom. She understood; she was crying for my grandfather and the injustice of it too. She and my grandfather had, as a matter of fact, established a very amiable relation, in which both took pleasure. The masculine line and firmness of his character made an aesthetic appeal to her, and the billowy softness and depth of the Mother Superior struck him favourably, but, above all, it was their difference in religion that salted their conversations. Each of them enjoyed, whenever they met in her straight, black-and-white little office, a sense of broadness, of enlightenment, of trascendent superiority to petty prejudice. My grandfather would remember that he wrote a cheque every Christmas for two Sisters of Charity who visited his office; Madame MacIllvra would perhaps recall her graduate studies and Hume. They had long, liberal talks which had the tone of *performances;* virtuoso feats of magnanimity were achieved on both sides. Afterward, they spoke of each other in nearly identical terms: 'A very fine woman,' 'A very fine man.'

All this (and possibly the suspicion that her verdict might be repeated at home) made Madame MacIllvra's answer slow. 'Perhaps God,' she murmured at last, 'in His infinite mercy . . .' Yet this formulation satisfied neither of us. God's infinite mercy we believed in, but its manifestations were problematical. Sacred history showed up that it was more likely to fall on the Good Thief or the Woman Taken in Adultery than on persons of daily virtue and regular habits, like my grandfather. Our Catholic thoughts journeyed and met in a glance of alarmed recognition. Madame MacIllvra pondered. There were, of course, she said finally, other loopholes. If he had been improperly baptized . . . a careless clergyman . . . I considered this suggestion and shook my head. My grandfather was not the kind of man who, even as an infant, would have been guilty of a slovenly baptism.

It was a measure of Madame MacIllvra's intelligence, or of her knowledge of the world, that she did not, even then, when my grandfather's soul hung, as it were, pleadingly between us, suggest the obvious, the orthodox solution. It would have been ridiculous for me to try to convert my grandfather. Indeed, as it turned out later, I might have dropped him into the pit with my innocent traps (the religious books left open beside his cigar cutter, or 'Grandpa, won't you take me to Mass this Sunday? I am so tired of going alone'). 'Pray for him, my dear,' said Madame MacIllvra, sighing, 'and I will speak to Madame Barclay. The point may be open to interpretation. She may remember something in the Fathers of the Church. . .'

A few days later, Madame MacIllvra summoned me to her office. Not only Madame Barclay, the learned prefect of studies, but the librarian and even the convent chaplain had been called in. The Benedictine view, it seemed, differed sharply from the Dominican, but a key passage in Saint Athanasius seemed to point to my grandfather's safety. The unbeliever, according to this generous authority, was not to be damned unless he rejected the true Church with sufficient knowledge and full consent of the will. Madame MacIllvra handed me the book, and I read the passage over. Clearly, he was saved. Sufficient knowledge he had not. The Church was foreign to him; he knew it only distantly, only by repute, like the heathen Hiawatha, who had heard strange stories of missionaries, white men in black robes who bore a Cross. Flinging my arms about Madame MacIllvra, I blessed for the first time the insularity of my grandfather's character, the long-jawed, shut face it turned towards ideas and customs not its own. I resolved to dismantle at once the little altar in my bedroom at home, to leave off grace before meals, elaborate fasting, and all ostentatious practices of devotion, lest the light of my example shine upon him too powerfully and burn him with sufficient knowledge to a crisp.

Since I was a five-day boarder, this project had no time to grow stale, and the next Sunday, at home, my grandfather remarked on the change in me, which my feeling for the dramatic had made far from unobtrusive. 'I hope,' he said in a rather stern and ironical voice, 'that you aren't using the *irreligious* atmosphere of this house as an excuse for backsliding. There will be time enough when you are older to change your beliefs if you want to.' The unfairness of this rebuke delighted me. It put me solidly in the tradition of the saints and martyrs; Our Lord had known something like it, and so had Elsie Dinsmore at the piano. Nevertheless, I felt quite angry and slammed the door of my room behind me as I went in to sulk. I almost wished that my grandfather would die at once, so that God could furnish him with the explanation of my behaviour — certainly he would have to wait till the next life to get it; in this one he would only have seen in it an invasion of his personal liberties.

As though to reward me for my silence, the following Wednesday brought me the happiest moment of my life. In order to understand my happiness, which might otherwise seem perverse, the reader must yield himself to the spiritual atmosphere of the convent. If he imagines that the life we led behind those walls was bare, thin, cold, austere, sectarian, he will have to revise his views; our days were a tumult of emotion. In the first place, we ate, studied, and slept in that atmosphere of intrigue, rivalry, scandal, favouritism, tyranny, and revolt that is common to all girls' boarding-schools and that makes 'real' life afterward seem a long and improbable armistice, a cessation of the true anguish of activity. But above the tinkling of this girlish operetta, with its clink-clink of changing friendships, its plot of smuggled letters, notes passed from desk to desk, secrets, there sounded in the Sacred Heart convent heavier, more solemn strains, notes of a great religious drama, which was also all passion and caprice, in which salvation was the issue and God's rather sultan-like and elusive favour was besought, scorned, despaired of, connived for, importuned. It was the paradoxical element in Catholic doctrine that lent this drama its suspense. The Divine Despot we courted could not be bought, like a piece of merchandise, by long hours at the *prie-dieu*, faithful attendance at the sacraments, obedience, reverence towards one's superior. These solicitations helped, but it might well turn out that the worst girl in the school, whose pretty, haughty face wore rouge and a calm, closed look that advertised even to us younger ones some secret knowledge of men, was in the dark of her heart another Mary of Egypt, the strumpet saint in our midst. Such notions furnished a strange counterpoint to discipline; surely the Mother Superior never could have expelled a girl without recalling, with a shade of perplexity, the profligate youth of Saint Augustine and of Saint Ignatius of Loyola.

This dark-horse doctrine of salvation, with all its worldly wisdom and riddling charm, was deep in the idiom of the convent. The merest lay sister could have sustained with spiritual poise her end of a conversation on the purification through sin with Mr Auden, Herr Kafka, or *Gospodin* Dostoevski; and Madame MacIllvra, while she would have held it bad taste to bow down, like Father Zossima, before the murder in Dmitri Karamazov's heart, would certainly have had him in for a series of long, interesting talks in her office.

Like all truly intellectual women, these were in spirit romantic desperadoes. They despised organizational heretics of the stamp of Luther and Calvin, but the great atheists and sinners were the heroes of the costume picture they taught as a subject called history. Marlowe, Baudelaire — above all, Byron — glowered like terrible stars above their literature courses. Little girls of ten were reciting 'The Prisoner of Chillon' and hearing stories of Claire Clairmont, Caroline Lamb, the Segatti, and the swim across the Hellespont. Even M. Voltaire enjoyed a left-handed popularity. The nuns spoke of him with horror and admiration mingled: 'A great mind, an unconquerable spirit — and what fearful use they were put to.' In Rousseau, an unbuttoned, middle-class figure, they had no interest whatever.

The infatuations, shared by the pupils, were brought into line with official Catholic opinion by a variety of stratagems. The more highly educated nuns were able to accept the damnation of these great

73

Luciferian spirits. A simple young nun, on the other hand, who played baseball and taught arithmetic to the sixth and seventh grades, used to tell her pupils that she personally was convinced that Lord Byron in his last hours must have made an act of contrition.

# Edwin Muir

*from:* An Autobiography

## GARTH

At Garth for the first time beggars came about the house. There was one in particular, an old man called John Simpson, half lay-preacher and half vagrant, who came often and ate enormously each time: these beggars were always taken in and given food. John Simpson had a black beard and a resonant voice; he wore a frock-coat very much soiled by food, and battered black hat, but no collar: he always carried a Bible with him, and at the least encouragement would flop down on his knees in the kitchen and burst into prolonged prayer, pulling us down with him — a habit which embarrassed us, for we knew that he was not right in the mind. My father once, out of kindness, offered him work on the farm as a potato-picker, but John Simpson groaned so loudly over his job, saying that he felt very ill — actually he was a big, strong man — that my father told him he could stop. He went away in a few days, after eating his fill. I saw him once or twice afterwards in Kirkwall, pursued by a crowd of jeering boys, and I felt sorry and ashamed for him. He preached whenever the children would let him, but his words were quite without sense.

I had often heard my mother talking about another beggar who had come regularly to the Folly in the old days, bringing his own tea and food to be cooked over the fire, and sleeping in the barn. His name was Fred Spence, and he was a man of education and breeding who had lost his money and his wits, but still kept his fine manners. He sometimes told a story of how he had strangled his wife, concluding in a well-bred, finicking voice, "Her neck was very tough." I met him one summer day as I was returning from school. He was a good-looking man with a high forehead and a pointed beard; very elegant and very dirty, like a grimy version of Cunninghame Graham. With great condescension he asked me my name, which I gave him somewhat fearfully, for I recognized him at once from my mother's description. His extreme courtesy, being half mad, was frightening; but I stood my ground, for I was curious. Fred was wearing a swallow-tail coat and a soft black hat on his matted grey hair, which fell down over his shoulders. As if he were some noble patron he inquired into my progress at school, saying at intervals, "Latin! Latin is very important!" And then, with a royal, absent-mindedness, he abruptly dismissed me, asking me, however, to remember him to my father and mother. He was a harmless madman, but as I stood listening to him on the deserted road I could not help thinking of his wife, whose neck had been so tough. I never saw him again.

When I was thirteen my father gave up the farm, sold off his stock and farm implements, and went to live in a small house in Kirkwall. My Aunt Maggie went to stay with a sister. A relative of Sutherland in America had died and left him some money, and he sailed to join his cousins in Leith, where we lost sight of him for a while. Only my father and mother, my sister Clara and myself, remained.

Except for my reading, which went on still more eagerly, my year in Kirkwall was drab and sordid. I had reached the stage when boys stick together to hide the shame of their inexperience, and turn without knowing it against their parents and the laws of the house. My rough friendships were an indirect challenge to my father and mother, a hidden gesture of rebellion. I played a great deal of football; it was as if my body demanded explosive action. The place where we played was called the Craftie; it was a little field of grass, worn bare in patches, close by the slaughter-house. To us in our raw and unhappy state the slaughter-house had an abominable attraction, and the strong stench and sordid colours of blood and intestines seemed to follow us in our play. Our language and manners grew rough; even our friendship had an acrid flavour. There were savage fights in the Craftie, and the boys, crying with rage, would have killed each other if they could; yet behind their fury there was a sort of sad shame and frustration.

I do not know why boys of this age, the age of awakening puberty, should turn against everything that was pleasant in their lives before and rend it in a fit of crude cynicism. Perhaps it comes from their first distorted knowledge of the actual world, which is not the world of childhood, and a divination that all their childish games in which they played at being grown-up were of no use, something sterner being needed. Or it may be merely that I was unlucky in my friends, for I had far less worldly knowledge at the time than town boys of my age, and I was always perfectly prepared to be friendly with anyone who was friendly with me. I remember one fine summer day spent with another boy wandering along the Wideford Burn, picking flowers and looking at birds' nests, without a single rough word. Why did I not have more days like that one in which I was perfectly happy, instead of all those days in the Craftie, when I was really miserable, though I did not know it? The Craftie seemed to hypnotize us; we kicked the football in hatred; there was a deep enmity in the bond between us.

All this was in the year before we left for Glasgow. That winter a revivalist preacher, a thin, tense young man called Macpherson, came to Kirkwall and began to make converts. While we were at Garth the famous John McNeill, a large-scale evangelist, had made a short visit to Orkney, and had preached in the church we attended in Kirkwall. I can remember him dimly; a big, stout, genial man with a black beard, who greatly embarrassed the congregation by keeping them laughing during the whole service, for he was a great wit. He did not make any converts; our people refused to be chaffed into salvation. Later two other revivalists appeared together: one of them, thin, small, and tense, preached hell fire, and the other, tall, stout, and expansive, radiated the love of God. We all went in to hear them one Sunday evening; many people at the end of the service rose from their seats when the preachers summoned them to Christ: I looked on with excitement, but did not understand the glad perturbation of the people round me. As we left the church the two preachers, standing at the door, shook hands with the congregation. It was the big, benevolent preacher who was at our side of the door, and as he took my hand in his large, comforting one, he looked down at me and said to my father, "Will not this little fellow come to Christ?" My father, to shield me, murmured something to the effect that perhaps I was too young and tender yet. "What! Too young and tender to come to gentle Jesus!" the preacher said in a shocked voice. My father was much impressed by this answer, and often repeated it afterwards; but I felt that the preacher was not really so shocked as he appeared to be.

This must have happened when I was ten or eleven; I was now fourteen, and, except when I was reading, very unhappy. I paid no attention to the visit of Mr Macpherson; the boys I went about with jeered at his converts whenever they met them; some of their acquaintances had already been saved. Then my sister Clara was converted, and my mother in her delight drew closer to her. I felt alone in the house; but I was reading *Les Misérables*, and consoled myself with the thought that I too was capable of loving noble things. Yet gradually, by a power independent of myself, I felt impelled toward the only act which would make me one with my family again; for my father and mother and sister were saved, and I was outside, separated from them by an invisible wall. A tremor of the fear which had cut me off in a world of my own at Helye returned, and I began to listen to Mr Macpherson's outdoor services at the head of the pier, standing well back in the crowd so as not to be seen by my friends. Then one dark cold night — how it happened I do not know — I found myself in the crowd which marched after the preacher, all the length of Kirkwall, to the mission hall. As we passed through the narrow streets groups standing there turned round and stared at us: the unredeemed, whom I still feared so much that I slipped for safety deeper into the heart of the crowd. The people round me marched on side by side, ignoring one another in a sort of embarrassment at still being lost sinners, their eyes fixed straight before them. At last we reached the hall; after the darkness outside the white-washed walls and the yellow benches were so bright that they dazzled me; the worshippers entered, ordinary men and women and children now, smiling at one another as if in secret understanding; the doors were shut; the service began. I remember nothing of it; I probably did not listen, for I was filled with an impatience which did not have anything to do with the words the preacher was saying; all round me people were bursting into sobs and loud cries, as if they too felt the same agonized anticipation and could wait no longer for redemption; and when Mr Macpherson stopped at last and asked those who had accepted Christ to rise in their places the whole audience rose, lifting me with them, and I found myself on my feet with a wild sense of relief. But the great majority of the audience had accepted Christ already, and the difficult moment came now, for when we had all sat down again the new converts, a mere handful, were asked to walk up to the platform and kneel down at the penitent form, a long wooden bench set there in full view. I hesitated; I was appalled by this naked exposure before people whom I did not know; but when a small group — men, women, boys, and girls — had risen, I rose too and followed them and knelt down. The preacher went along the bench where we were kneeling and asked each of us in turn, "Do you accept Jesus Christ as your personal Saviour?" and when my turn came and I replied, "I do," I felt that these words, which were the seal of my salvation, yet were uttered deliberately, not torn from me, must bring with them an overwhelming assurance; and I was deeply disappointed when they did not, for they seemed merely to be two words. The preacher asked me to offer up a prayer, but I could not think of one, and felt that it would be presumptuous of me, so newly converted, to address God out of my own invention. Beside me was kneeling a red-haired, spectacled young man who served in a shop. He had been the most conspicuous groaner during the service, exclaiming so emphatically that people had looked round at him with surprise and respect; he now burst into a loud and rapid prayer, as if he were already resolved to make a record in the world of the saved. My exaltation did not keep me from feeling slightly annoyed with him for his forwardness; but I suppressed the feeling, telling myself that I must love him. When I got up at last, dazzled, an involuntary smile of joy on my face, and returned to my seat with the others, all the faces of the congregation melted into one great maternal face filled with welcome and wonder, and I felt I was walking straight into a gigantic pair of loving arms.

I went home and told my mother, and returned with a sense of absolute security to *Les Misérables*, which now seemed a new and holy book, with meanings which I had never guessed at before. But a doubtful look came into my mother's face when she saw me returning so eagerly to a profane story; she stood and thought for a moment, then smiled whimsically, glancing at the book and then at me. I felt she doubted that my conversion was real, and was deeply offended.

What was the nature of my experience that night? For some time afterwards I certainly felt a change within myself; coarse thoughts and words to which I had become hardened during the last year became unendurable to me; I was perpetually happy, and found it easy to reply gently to insults and sneers. The slightest suggestion of evil pierced me to the heart; yet I remained unaffected in some part of myself, as if I were invulnerable. At the same time I found myself often reflecting with relief that I should be leaving Kirkwall in a fortnight, so that I should not have to testify for long before those who had known me: in Glasgow, I told myself, I should associate with the saved from the start; they would be all round me. At times I actually felt ashamed of my new state, belittling it to my friends instead of proclaiming it loudly like the ardent, red-haired shop assistant. I made friends with the Kirkwall boys of my own age who had been saved, and avoided my old companions. Among the saved were some of the roughest boys at the school; they were now incapable of speaking a rude word, and their faces shone with grace. A sort of purification had taken place in us, and it washed away the poisonous stuff which had gathered in me during that year; but it was more a natural than a spiritual cleansing, and more a communal than a personal experience, for it is certain that if the whole audience had not risen that night I should not have risen. To pretend that it was a genuine religious conversion would be ridiculous; I did not know what I was doing; I had no clear knowledge of sin or of the need for salvation; at most I wished to be rescued from the companions among whom I had fallen and to be with the good, with my father and my mother and my sister. Yet the change itself was so undeniable that it astonished me. I was not trying to be changed; I was changed quite beyond my expectation; but the change did not last long.

Though they were glad at the conversion of my sister and myself, my father and mother had doubts of the virtue of these revivals which periodically swept over the country. Much later I remember someone telling me that each revival was followed by a great increase in the number of illegitimate children. In one of them which took place when my mother was a young girl people fell down in fits in the church and rolled on the floor. How these orgiastic movements were set going I do not know; their effect while they lasted was probably good in some ways; they made people forget their narrow concerns and open their hearts to one another. But the wave passed, and people returned to their private concerns again and became more sparing of love. These revivals were communal orgies such as were probably known long before Christianity came to these islands, and they cleansed people's hearts for the time being; but they had very little to do with religion, and, like most orgies, they often left behind them a feeling of shame.

Later on, in Glasgow, I was flung among the violently converted just as I had wished to be, and though I experienced a second dubious conversion before I was finished with that kind of religion, I came to know so much about the way in which revivals are organized that I was soon disillusioned with them. I was in Glasgow during the famous Torry and Alexander campaign, and a pious second cousin kept begging me so often to go with him that at last I went. The meetings were held in an enormous hall. Alexander, a willowy, sleek, slightly bald young man, kept the audience cheerful with catchy hymns:

> We're marching to Zion,
> Beautiful, beautiful Zion,

We're marching onward to Zion,
That beautiful city of God.

After he had prepared the way Dr Torry, a burly, grey-haired club-man, got up and fired off a number of wisecracks on salvation, which he made out to be a good business proposition. The time came to summon the saved to rise in their places; everybody round me rose, and to my great astonishment I found myself getting up too, although I had had no intention of doing so: it is very hard to remain sitting when everybody else has risen. I did not go up to the penitent form, of course, but my rising greatly pleased my second cousin, who probably fancied he had won a soul.

A friend of mine who attended a Baptist church in Glasgow which I also attended for a while disillusioned me finally with revivals. He had himself taken part in one, and one night after a meeting, the minister having asked him how many had been saved, he said somewhat shortly, "Five." "What, a mere wretched five!" the minister replied, whereupon my friend retorted, "I think you should remember, Mr X, that they're precious in God's sight!" He came away in a rage, and after that refused to have anything more to do with revivals.

# *E Nesbit*

*from:* The Wouldbegoods

When we were sent down into the country to learn to be good we felt it was rather good business, because we knew our being sent there was really only to get us out of the way for a little while, and we knew right enough that it wasn't a punishment, though Mrs Blake said it was, because we had been punished thoroughly for taking the stuffed animals out and making a jungle on the lawn with them, and the garden hose. And you cannot be punished twice for the same offence. This is the English law; at least I think so. And at any rate no one would punish you three times, and we had had the Malacca cane and the solitary confinement; and the uncle had kindly explained to us that all ill-feeling between him and us was wiped out entirely by the bread and water we had endured. And what with the bread and water and being prisoners, and not being able to tame any mice in our prisons, I quite feel that we had suffered it up thoroughly, and now we could start fair.

I think myself that descriptions of places are generally dull, but I have sometimes thought that was because the authors do not tell you what you truly want to know. However, dull or not, here goes—because you won't understand anything unless I tell you what the place was like.

The Moat House was the one we went to stay at. There has been a house there since Saxon times. It is a manor, and a manor goes on having a house on it whatever happens. The Moat House was burnt down once or twice in ancient centuries—I don't remember which—but they always built a new one, and Cromwell's soldiers smashed it about, but it was patched up again. It is a very odd house: the front door opens straight into the dining-room, and there are red curtains and a black-and-white marble floor like a chess-board, and there is a secret staircase, only it is not secret now—only rather rickety. It is not very big, but there is a watery moat all round it with a brick bridge that leads to the front door. Then, on the other side of the moat there is the farm, with barns and oast-houses and stables, or things like that. And the other way the garden lawn goes on till it comes to the churchyard. The churchyard is not divided from the garden at all except by a little grass bank. In the front of the house there is more garden, and the big fruit garden is at the back.

The man the house belongs to likes new houses, so he built a big one with conservatories and a stable with a clock in a turret on the top, and he left the Moat House. And Albert's uncle took it, and my father was to come down sometimes from Saturday to Monday, and Albert's uncle was to live with us all the time, and he would be writing a book, and we were not to bother him, but he would give an eye to us. I hope all this is plain. I have said it as short as I can.

We got down rather late, but there was still light enough to see the big bell hanging at the top of the house. The rope belonging to it went right down the house, through our bedroom to the dining-room. H.O. saw the rope and pulled it while he was washing his hands for supper, and Dicky and I let him, and the bell tolled solemnly. Father shouted to him not to, and we went down to supper. But presently there were many feet trampling on the gravel, and Father went out to see. When he came back he said—

'The whole village, or half of it, has come up to see why the bell rang. It's only rung for fire or burglars. Why can't you kids let things alone?' Albert's uncle said—

'Bed follows supper as the fruit follows the flower. They'll do no more mischief to-night, sir. To-morrow I will point out a few of the things to be avoided in this bucolic retreat.'

So it was bed directly after supper, and that was why we did not see much that night.

But in the morning we were all up rather early, and we seemed to have awakened in a new world rich in surprises beyond the dreams of anybody, as it says in the quotation.

We went everywhere we could in the time, but when it was break-fast-time we felt we had not seen half or a quarter. The room we had breakfast in was exactly like in a story—black oak panels and china in corner cupboards with glass doors. These doors were locked. There were green curtains, and honeycomb for breakfast. Afterwards my father went back to town, and Albert's uncle went too, to see publishers. We saw them to the station, and Father gave us a long list of what we weren't to do. It began with 'Don't pull ropes unless you're quite sure what will happen at the other end,' and it finished with 'For goodness sake, try to keep out of mischief till I come down on Saturday'. There were lots of other things in between.

We all promised we would. And we saw them off, and waved till the train was quite out of sight. Then we started to walk home. Daisy was tired so Oswald carried her home on his back. When we got home she said—

'I do like you Oswald.'

She is not a bad little kid; and Oswald felt it was his duty to be nice to her because she was a visitor. Then we looked all over everything. It was a glorious place. You did not know where to begin.

We were all a little tired before we found the hayloft, but we pulled ourselves together to make a fort with the trusses of hay—great square things—and we were having a jolly good time, all of us, when suddenly a trap-door opened and a head bobbed up with a straw in its mouth. We knew nothing about the country then, and the head really did scare us rather, though, of course, we found out directly that the feet belonging to it were standing on the bar of the loose-box underneath. The head said—

'Don't you let the governor catch you a-spoiling of that there hay, that's all.' And it spoke thickly because of the straw.

It is strange to think how ignorant you were in the past. We can hardly believe now that once we really did not know that it spoiled hay to mess about with it. Horses don't like to eat it afterwards. Always remember this.

When the head had explained a little more it went away, and we turned the handle of the chaff-cutting machine, and nobody got hurt, though the head *had* said we should cut our fingers off if we touched it.

And then we sat down on the floor, which is dirty with the nice clean dirt that is more than half chopped hay, and those there was room for hung their legs down out of the top door, and we looked down at the farm-yard, which is very slushy when you get down into it, but most interesting.

Then Alice said—

'Now we're all here, and the boys are tired enough to sit still for a minute, I want to have a council.'

We said what about? And she said, 'I'll tell you. H.O., don't wriggle so; sit on my frock if the straws tickle your legs.'

You see he wears socks, and so he can never be quite as comfortable as anyone else.

'Promise not to laugh,' Alice said, getting very red, and looking at Dora, who got red too.

We did, and then she said: 'Dora and I have talked this over, and Daisy too, and we have written it down because it is easier than saying it. Shall I read it? or will you, Dora?'

Dora said it didn't matter; Alice might. So Alice read it, and though she gabbled a bit we all heard it. I copied it afterwards. This is what she read:

## 'NEW SOCIETY FOR BEING GOOD IN

'I, Dora Bastable, and Alice Bastable, my sister, being of sound mind and body, when we were shut up with bread and water on that jungle day, we thought a great deal about our naughty sins, and we made our minds up to be good for ever after. And we talked to Daisy about it, and she had an idea. So we want to start a society for being good in. It is Daisy's idea, but we think so too.'

'You know,' Dora interrupted, 'when people want to do good things they always make a society. There are thousands—there's the Missionary Society.'

'Yes,' Alice said, 'and the Society for the Prevention of something or

other, and the Young Men's Mutual Improvement Society, and the
S.P.G.'

'What's S.P.G.?' Oswald asked.

'Society for the Propagation of the Jews, of course,' said Noël, who
cannot always spell.

'No, it isn't; but do let me go on.'

Alice did go on.

'We propose to get up a society, with a chairman and a treasurer
and secretary, and keep a journal-book saying what we've done. If that
doesn't make us good it won't be my fault.

'The aim of the society is nobleness and goodness, and great and
unselfish deeds. We wish not to be such a nuisance to grown-up people
and to perform prodigies of real goodness. We wish to spread our
wings'—here Alice read very fast. She told me afterwards Daisy had
helped her with that part, and she thought when she came to the wings
they sounded rather silly—'to spread our wings and rise above the
kind of interesting things that you ought not to do, but to do kind-
nesses to all, however low and mean.'

Denny was listening carefully. Now he nodded three or four times.

> *'Little words of kindness'* (he said),
> *'Little deeds of love,*
> *Make this earth an eagle*
> *Like the one above.'*

This did not sound right, but we let it pass, because an eagle *does* have
wings, and we wanted to hear the rest of what the girls had written.
But there was no rest.

'That's all,' said Alice, and Daisy said—

'Don't you think it's a good idea?'

'That depends,' Oswald answered, 'who is president and what you
mean by being good.' Oswald did not care very much for the idea
himself, because being good is not the sort of thing he thinks it is
proper to talk about, especially before strangers. But the girls and
Denny seemed to like it, so Oswald did not say exactly what he
thought, especially as it was Daisy's idea. This was true politeness.

'I think it would be nice,' Noël said, 'if we made it a sort of play.
Let's do the *Pilgrim's Progress*.'

We talked about that for some time, but it did not come to anything, because we all wanted to be Mr Greatheart, except H.O., who wanted to be the lions, and you could not have lions in a Society for Goodness.

Dicky said he did not wish to play if it meant reading books about children who die; he really felt just as Oswald did about it, he told me afterwards. But the girls were looking as if they were in Sunday school, and we did not wish to be unkind.

At last Oswald said, 'Well, let's draw up the rules of the society, and choose the president and settle the name.'

Dora said Oswald should be president, and he modestly consented. She was secretary, and Denny treasurer if we ever had any money.

Making the rules took us all the afternoon. They were these:

## RULES

1. Every member is to be as good as possible.
2. There is to be no more jaw than necessary about being good. (Oswald and Dicky put that rule in.)
3. No day must pass without our doing some kind action to a suffering fellow-creature.
4. We are to meet every day, or as often as we like.
5. We are to do good to people we don't like as often as we can.
6. No one is to leave the Society without the consent of all the rest of us.
7. The Society is to be kept a profound secret from all the world except us.
8. The name of our Society is—

And when we got as far as that we all began to talk at once. Dora wanted it called the Society for Humane Improvement; Denny said the Society for Reformed Outcast Children; but Dicky said, No, we really were not so bad as all that. Then H.O. said, 'Call it the Good Society.'

'Or the Society for Being Good In,' said Daisy.

'Or the Society of Goods,' said Noël.

'That's priggish,' said Oswald; 'besides, we don't know whether we shall be so very.'

'You see,' Alice explained, 'we only said if we *could* we would be good.'

'Well, then,' Dicky said, getting up and beginning to dust the chopped hay off himself, 'call it the Society of the Wouldbegoods and have done with it.'

Oswald thinks Dicky was getting sick of it and wanted to make himself a little disagreeable. If so, he was doomed to disappointment. For everyone else clapped hands and called out, 'That's the very thing!' Then the girls went off to write out the rules, and took H. O. with them, and Noël went to write some poetry to put in the minute book. That's what you call the book that a society's secretary writes what it does in. Denny went with him to help. He knows a lot of poetry. I think he went to a lady's school where they taught nothing but that. He was rather shy of us, but he took to Noël. I can't think why. Dicky and Oswald walked round the garden and told each other what they thought of the new society.

'I'm not sure we oughtn't to have put our foot down at the beginning,' Dicky said. 'I don't see much in it, anyhow.'

'It pleases the girls,' Oswald said, for he is a kind brother.

'But we're not going to stand jaw, and "words in season", and "loving sisterly warnings". I tell you what it is, Oswald, we'll have to run this thing our way, or it'll be jolly beastly for everybody.'

Oswald saw this plainly.

'We must do something,' Dicky said; 'it's very very hard, though. Still, there must be *some* interesting things that are not wrong.'

'I suppose so,' Oswald said, 'but being good is so much like being a muff, generally. Anyhow I'm not going to smooth the pillows of the sick, or read to the aged poor, or any rot out of *Ministering Children.*'

'No more am I,' Dicky said. He was chewing a straw like the head had in its mouth, 'but I suppose we must play the game fair. Let's begin by looking out for something useful to do—something like mending things or cleaning them, not just showing off.'

'The boys in books chop kindling wood and save their pennies to buy tea and tracts.'

'Little beasts!' said Dicky. 'I say, let's talk about something else.' And Oswald was glad to, for he was beginning to feel jolly uncomfortable.

We were all rather quiet at tea, and afterwards Oswald played draughts with Daisy and the others yawned. I don't know when we've had such a gloomy evening. And everyone was horribly polite, and said 'Please' and 'Thank you' far more than requisite.

Albert's uncle came home after tea. He was jolly, and told us stories, but he noticed us being a little dull, and asked what blight had fallen on our young lives. Oswald could have answered and said, 'It is the Society of the Wouldbegoods that is the blight,' but of course he didn't; and Albert's uncle said no more, but he went up and kissed the girls when they were in bed, and asked them if there was anything wrong. And they told him no, on their honour.


# Louisa M Alcott

*from:* Little Women

## PLAYING PILGRIMS

'Christmas won't be Christmas without any presents,' grumbled Jo, lying on the rug.

'It's so dreadful to be poor!' sighed Meg, looking down at her old dress.

'I don't think it's fair for some girls to have plenty of pretty things, and other girls nothing at all,' added little Amy, with an injured sniff.

'We've got father and mother and each other,' said Beth, contentedly, from her corner.

The four faces on which the firelight shone brightened at the cheerful words, but darkened again as Jo said sadly:

'We haven't got father, and shall not have him for a long time.' She didn't say 'perhaps never', but each silently added it, thinking of father far away, where the fighting was.

Nobody spoke for a minute; then Meg said in an altered tone:

'You know the reason mother proposed not having any presents this Christmas was because it is going to be a hard winter for everyone; and she thinks we ought not to spend money for pleasure when our men are suffering so in the army. We can't do much, but we can make our little sacrifices, and ought to do it gladly. But I am afraid I don't'; and Meg shook her head, and she thought regretfully of all the pretty things she wanted.

'But I don't think the little we should spend would do any good. We've each got a dollar, and the army wouldn't be much helped by our giving that. I agree not to expect anything from mother or you, but I do want to buy *Undine and Sintram* for myself; I've wanted it *so* long,' said Jo, who was a bookworm.

'I planned to spend mine on new music,' said Beth, with a little sigh, which no one heard but the hearth-brush and kettle-holder.

'I shall get a nice box of Faber's drawing pencils; I really need them,' said Amy, decidedly.

'Mother didn't say anything about our money, and she won't wish us to give up everything. Let's each buy what we want, and have a little fun; I'm sure we work hard enough to earn it,' cried Jo, examining the heels of her shoes in a gentlemanly manner.

'I know *I* do — teaching those tiresome children nearly all day when I am longing to enjoy myself at home,' began Meg, in the complaining tone again.

'You don't have half such a hard time as I do,' said Jo. 'How would you like to be shut up for hours with a nervous fussy old lady, who keeps you trotting, is never satisfied, and worries you till you're ready to fly out of the window or cry?'

'It's naughty to fret; but I do think washing dishes and keeping things tidy is the worst work in the world. It makes me cross; and my hands get so stiff, I can't practise well at all'; and Beth looked at her rough hands with a sigh that anyone could hear that time.

'I don't believe any of you suffer as I do,' cried Amy; 'for you don't have to go to school with impertinent girls, who plague you if you don't know your lessons, and laugh at your dresses, and label your father if he isn't rich, and insult you when your nose isn't nice.'

'If you mean *libel*, I'd say so, and not talk about *labels*, as if papa was a pickle-bottle,' advised Jo, laughing.

'I know what I mean, and you needn't be *statirical* about it. It's proper to use good words, and improve your *vocabulary*,' returned Amy, with dignity.

'Don't peck at one another, children. Don't you wish we had the money papa lost when we were little, Jo? Dear me! how happy and good we'd be, if we had no worries!' said Meg, who could remember better times.

'You said, the other day, you thought we were a deal happier than the King children, for they were fighting and fretting all the time, in spite of their money.'

'So I did, Beth. Well, I think we are; for, though we do have to work, we make fun for ourselves, and are a pretty jolly set, as Jo would say.'

'Jo does use such slang words!' observed Amy, with a reproving look at the long figure stretched on the rug. Jo immediately sat up, put her hands in her pockets, and began to whistle.

'Don't, Jo; it's so boyish!'

'That's why I do it.'

'I detest rude, unladylike girls!'

'I hate affected, niminy-piminy chits!'

'"Birds in their little nests agree,"' sang Beth, the peacemaker, with such a funny face that both sharp voices softened to a laugh, and the 'pecking' ended for that time.

'Really, girls, you are both to be blamed,' said Meg, beginning to lecture in her elder-sisterly fashion. 'You are old enough to leave off boyish tricks, and to behave better, Josephine. It didn't matter so much when you were a little girl; but now you are so tall, and turn up your hair, you should remember that you are a young lady.'

'I'm not! and if turning up my hair makes me one, I'll wear it in two tails till I'm twenty,' cried Jo, pulling off her net, and shaking down her chestnut mane. 'I hate to think I've got to grow up, and be Miss March, and wear long gowns, and look as prim as a China-aster! It's bad enough to be a girl, anyway, when I like boys' games and work and manners! I can't get over my disappointment in not being a boy; and it's worse than ever now, for I'm dying to go and fight with papa, and I can only stay at home and knit, like a poky old woman!' And Jo shook the blue army sock till the needles rattled like castanets, and her ball bounded across the room.

'Poor Jo! It's too bad, but it can't be helped; so you must try to be contented with making your name boyish, and playing brother to us girls,' said Beth, stroking the rough head at her knee with a hand that all the dish-washing and dusting in the world could not make ungentle in its touch.

'As for you, Amy,' continued Meg, 'you are altogether too particular and prim. Your airs are funny now; but you'll grow up an affected little goose, if you don't take care. I like your nice manners and refined ways of speaking when you don't try to be elegant; but your absurd words are as bad as Jo's slang.'

'If Jo is a tomboy and Amy a goose, what am I, please?' asked Beth, ready to share the lecture.

'You're a dear, and nothing else,' answered Meg, warmly; and no one contradicted her, for the 'Mouse' was the pet of the family.

As young readers like to know 'how people look', we will take this moment to give them a little sketch of the four sisters, who sat knitting away in the twilight, while the December snow fell quietly without, and the fire crackled cheerfully within. It was a comfortable old room, though the carpet was faded and the furniture very plain; for a good picture or two hung on the walls, books filled the recesses, chrysanthemums and Christmas roses bloomed in the windows, and a pleasant atmosphere of home-peace pervaded it.

Margaret, the eldest of the four, was sixteen, and very pretty, being plump and fair, with large eyes, plenty of soft, brown hair, a sweet mouth, and white hands, of which she was rather vain. Fifteen-year-old Jo was very tall, thin, and brown, and reminded one of a colt; for she never seemed to know what to do with her long limbs, which were very much in her way. She had a decided mouth, a comical nose, and sharp, grey eyes, which appeared to see everything, and were by turns fierce, funny, or thoughtful. Her long, thick hair was her one beauty; but it was usually bundled in a net, to be out of her way. Round shoulders had Jo, big hands and feet, a fly-away look to her clothes, and the uncomfortable appearance of a girl who was rapidly shooting up into a woman, and didn't like it. Elizabeth—or Beth, as everyone called her—was a rosy, smooth-haired, bright-eyed girl of thirteen, with a shy manner, a timid voice, and a peaceful expression, which was seldom disturbed. Her father called her 'Little Tranquillity', and the name suited her excellently; for she seemed to live in a happy world of her own, only venturing out to meet the few whom she trusted and loved. Amy, though the youngest, was a most important person — in her own opinion at least. A regular snow-maiden, with blue eyes, and yellow hair, curling on her shoulders, pale and slender, and always carrying herself like a young lady mindful of her manners. What the characters of the four sisters were we will leave to be found out.

The clock struck six; and, having swept up the hearth, Beth put a pair of slippers down to warm. Somehow the sight of the old shoes had a good effect upon the girls; for mother was coming, and everyone brightened to welcome her. Meg stopped lecturing, and lighted the lamp, Amy got out of the easy-chair without being asked, and Jo forgot how tired she was as she sat up to hold the slippers nearer to the blaze.

'They are quite worn out; Marmee must have a new pair.'

'I thought I'd get her some with my dollar,' said Beth.

'No, I shall!' cried Amy.

'I'm the oldest,' began Meg, but Jo cut in with a decided:

'I'm the man of the family now papa is away, and *I* shall provide the slippers, for he told me to take special care of mother while he was gone.'

'I'll tell you what we'll do,' said Beth; 'let's each get her something for Christmas, and not get anything for ourselves.'

'That's like you, dear! What will we get?' exclaimed Jo.

Everyone thought soberly for a minute; then Meg announced as if the idea was suggested by the sight of her own pretty hands, 'I shall give her a nice pair of gloves.'

'Army shoes, best to be had,' cried Jo.

'Some handkerchiefs, all hemmed,' said Beth.

'I'll get a little bottle of cologne; she likes it, and it won't cost much, so I'll have some left to buy my pencils,' added Amy.

'How will we give the things?' asked Meg.

'Put them on the table, and bring her in and see her open the bundles. Don't you remember how we used to do on our birthdays?' answered Jo.

'I used to be *so* frightened when it was my turn to sit in the big chair with the crown on, and see you all come marching round to give the presents, with a kiss. I liked the things and the kisses, but it was dreadful to have you sit looking at me while I opened the bundles,' said Beth, who was toasting her face and the bread for tea, at the same time.

'Let Marmee think we are getting things for ourselves, and then surprise her. We must go shopping tomorrow afternoon, Meg; there is so much to do about the play for Christmas night,' said Jo, marching up and down, with her hands behind her back and her nose in the air.

'I don't mean to act any more after this time; I'm getting too old for such things,' observed Meg, who was as much a child as ever about 'dressing-up' frolics.

'You won't stop, I know, as long as you can trail round in a white gown with your hair down, and wear gold-paper jewellery. You are the best actress we've got, and there'll be an end of everything if you quit the boards,' said Jo. 'We ought to rehearse tonight. Come here, Amy, and do the fainting scene, for you are as stiff as a poker in that.'

'I can't help it; I never saw anyone faint, and I don't choose to make myself all black and blue, tumbling flat as you do. If I can go down easily, I'll drop; if I can't, I shall fall into a chair and be graceful; I don't care if Hugo does come at me with a pistol,' returned Amy, who was not gifted with dramatic power, but was chosen because she was small enough to be borne out shrieking by the villain of the piece.

'Do it this way; clasp your hands so, and stagger across the room, crying frantically, "Roderigo! save me! save me!"' and away went Jo, with a melodramatic scream which was truly thrilling.

Amy followed, but she poked her hands out stiffly before her, and jerked herself along as if she went by machinery; and her 'Ow!' was more suggestive of pins being run into her than of fear and anguish. Jo gave a despairing groan, and Meg laughed outright, while Beth let her bread burn as she watched the fun with interest.

'It's no use! Do the best you can when the time comes, and if the audience laugh, don't blame me. Come on, Meg.'

Then things went smoothly, for Don Pedro defied the world in a speech of two pages without a single break; Hagar, the witch, chanted an awful incantation over her kettleful of simmering toads, with weird effect; Roderigo rent his chains asunder manfully, and Hugo died in agonies of remorse and arsenic, with a wild 'Ha! ha!'

'It's the best we've had yet,' said Meg, as the dead villain sat up and rubbed his elbows.

'I don't see how you can write and act such splendid things, Jo. You're a regular Shakespeare!' exclaimed Beth, who firmly believed that her sisters were gifted with wonderful genius in all things.

'Not quite,' replied Jo modestly. 'I do think "*The Witch's Curse*, an Operatic Tragedy", is rather a nice thing; but I'd like to try *Macbeth*, if we only had a trap-door for Banquo. I always wanted to do the killing part. "Is that a dagger I see before me?"' muttered Jo, rolling her eyes and clutching at the air, as she had seen a famous tragedian do.

'No, it's the toasting fork, with mother's shoe on it instead of the bread. Beth's stage-struck!' cried Meg, and the rehearsal ended in a general burst of laughter.

'Glad to find you so merry, my girls,' said a cheery voice at the door, and actors and audience turned to welcome a tall, motherly lady, with a 'can-I-help-you' look about her which was truly delightful. She was not elegantly dressed, but a noble-looking woman, and the girls thought the grey cloak and unfashionable bonnet covered the most splendid mother in the world.

'Well, dearies, how have you got on today? There was so much to do, getting the boxes ready to go tomorrow, that I didn't come home to dinner. Has anyone called, Beth? How is your cold, Meg? Jo, you look tired to death. Come and kiss me, baby.'

While making these maternal inquiries, Mrs March got her wet things off, her warm slippers on, and sitting down in the easy-chair, drew Amy to her lap, preparing to enjoy the happiest hour of her busy day. The girls flew about, trying to make things comfortable, each in her own way. Meg arranged the tea-table; Jo brought wood and set chairs, dropping, overturning, and clattering everything she touched; Beth trotted to and fro between parlour and kitchen, quiet and busy; while Amy gave directions to everyone, as she sat with her hands folded.

As they gathered about the table, Mrs March said, with a particularly happy face, 'I've got a treat for you after supper.'

A quick, bright smile went round like a streak of sunshine. Beth clapped her hands, regardless of the biscuit she held, and Jo tossed up her napkin, crying, 'A letter! a letter! Three cheers for father!'

'Yes, a nice long letter. He is well, and thinks he shall get through the cold season better than we feared. He sends all sorts of loving wishes for Christmas, and an especial message to you girls,' said Mrs March, patting her pocket as if she had got a treasure there.

'Hurry and get done! Don't stop to quirk your little finger, and simper over your plate, Amy,' cried Jo, choking in her tea, and dropping her bread, butter side down, on the carpet in her haste to get at the treat.

Beth ate no more, but crept away, to sit in her shadowy corner and brood over the delight to come, till the others were ready.

'I think it was so splendid of father to go as chaplain when he was too old to be drafted, and not strong enough for a soldier,' said Meg, warmly.

'Don't I wish I could go as a drummer, a *vivan* — what's its name? or a nurse, so I could be near him and help him,' exclaimed Jo, with a groan.

'It must be very disagreeable to sleep in a tent, and eat all sorts of bad-tasting things, and drink out of a tin mug,' sighed Amy.

'When will he come home, Marmee?' asked Beth, with a little quiver in her voice.

'Not for many months, dear, unless he is sick. He will stay and do his work faithfully as long as he can, and we won't ask for him back a minute sooner than he can be spared. Now come and hear the letter.'

They all drew to the fire, mother in the big chair, with Beth at her feet, Meg and Amy perched on either arm of the chair, and Jo leaning on the back, where no one would see any sign of emotion if the letter should happen to be touching. Very few letters were written in those hard times that were not touching, especially those which fathers sent home. In this one little was said of the hardship endured, the dangers faced, or the home-sickness conquered; it was a cheerful, hopeful letter, full of lively descriptions of camp life, marches, and military news; and only at the end did the writer's heart overflow with fatherly love and longing for the little girls at home.

'Give them all my dear love and a kiss. Tell them I think of them by day, pray for them by night, and find my best comfort in their affection at all times. A year seems very long to wait before I see them, but remind them, that while we wait we may all work, so that these hard days need not be wasted. I know they will remember all I said to them, that they will be loving children to you, will do their duty faithfully, fight their bosom enemies bravely, and conquer themselves so beautifully, that when I come back to them I may be fonder and prouder than ever of my little women.'

Everybody sniffed when they came to that part; Jo wasn't ashamed of the great tear that dropped off the end of her nose, and Amy never minded the rumpling of her curls as she hid her face on her mother's shoulder and sobbed out, 'I *am* a selfish girl! but I'll truly try to be better, so he mayn't be disappointed in me by and by.'

'We all will!' cried Meg. 'I think too much of my looks, and hate to work, but won't any more, if I can help it.'

'I'll try and be what he loves to call me, "a little woman", and not be rough and wild; but do my duty here instead of wanting to be somewhere else,' said Jo, thinking that keeping her temper at home was a much harder task than facing a rebel or two down South.

Beth said nothing, but wiped away her tears with the blue army sock, and began to knit with all her might, losing no time in doing her duty that lay nearest her, while she resolved in her quiet little soul to be all that father hoped to find her when the year brought round the happy coming home.

Mrs March broke the silence that followed Jo's words, by saying in her cheery voice, 'Do you remember how you used to play *Pilgrim's Progress* when you were little things? Nothing delighted you more than to have me tie my piece-bags on your backs for burdens, give you hats and sticks and rolls of paper, and let you travel through the house from the cellar, which was the City of Destruction, up, up, to the housetop, where you had all the lovely things you could collect to make a Celestial City.'

'What fun it was, especially going by the lions, fighting Apollyon, and passing through the Valley where the hobgoblins were!' said Jo.

'I liked the place where the bundles fell off and tumbled downstairs,' said Meg.

'My favourite part was when we came out on the flat roof where our flowers and arbours and pretty things were, and all stood and sang for joy up there in the sunshine,' said Beth, smiling, as if that pleasant moment had come back to her.

'I don't remember much about it, except I was afraid of the cellar and the dark entry, and always liked the cake and milk we had up at the top. If I wasn't too old for such things, I'd rather like to play it over again,' said Amy, who began to talk of renouncing childish things at the mature age of twelve.

'We never are too old for this, my dear, because it is a play we are playing all the time in one way or another. Our burdens are here, our road is before us, and the longing for goodness and happiness is the guide that leads us through many troubles and mistakes to the peace which is a true Celestial City. Now, my little pilgrims, suppose you begin again, not in play, but in earnest, and see how far on you can get before Father comes home.'

'Really, Mother? Where are our bundles?' asked Amy, who was a very literal young lady.

'Each of you told what your burden was just now, except Beth; I rather think she hasn't got any,' said her mother.

'Yes, I have; mine is dishes and dusters, and envying girls with nice pianos, and being afraid of people.'

Beth's bundle was such a funny one that everybody wanted to laugh; but nobody did, for it would have hurt her feelings very much.

'Let us do it,' said Meg, thoughtfully. 'It is only another name for trying to be good, and the story may help us; for though we do want to be good, it's hard work, and we forget, and don't do our best.'

'We were in the Slough of Despond tonight, and Mother came and pulled us out as Help did in the book. We ought to have our roll of directions, like Christian. What shall we do about that?' asked Jo, delighted with the fancy which lent a little romance to the very dull task of doing her duty.

'Look under your pillows, Christmas morning, and you will find your guide-book,' replied Mrs March.

They talked over the new plan while old Hannah cleared the table; then out came the four little work-baskets, and the needles flew as the girls made sheets for Aunt March. It was uninteresting sewing, but tonight no one grumbled. They adopted Jo's plan of dividing the long seams into four parts, and calling the quarters Europe, Asia, Africa and America, and in that way got on capitally, especially when they talked about the different countries, as they stitched their way through them.

At nine they stopped work, and sang, as usual, before they went to bed. No one but Beth could get much music out of the old piano; but she had a way of softly touching the yellow keys, and making a pleasant accompaniment to the simple songs they sang. Meg had a voice like a flute, and she and her mother led the little choir. Amy chirped like a cricket, and Jo wandered through the airs at her own sweet will, always coming out at the wrong place with a croak or a quaver that spoilt the most pensive tune. They had always done this from the time they could lisp

'Crinkle, crinkle, 'ittle 'tar.'

and it had become a household custom, for the mother was a born singer. The first sound in the morning was her voice, as she went about the house singing like a lark; and the last sound at night was the same cheery sound, for the girls never grew too old for that familiar lullaby.

# V
# QUESTIONING

*W Somerset Maugham*
*Edmund Gosse*
*Lord Berners*
*James Joyce*

As a schoolboy at Kings, Canterbury, W Somerset Maugham suffered hell as the result of a severe stammer; in *Of Human Bondage* (1915) which made his name as a novelist after a dazzling career as a playwright, 'Philip Carey' has a more substanial affliction, a club-foot. He prays to God, a child's God, God-as-magician, for deliverance as Maugham must have done. Lack of success simply causes him to suppose that 'one can never have faith enough', not to question the reality of God.

Sir Edmund Gosse (1849–1928) was best known as a critic but was also a poet and playwright and the librarian of the House of Lords. From the once-notorious *Father and Son* comes this desperate attempt to incur the wrath of God through chair-worship. Similarly blasphemous in childhood, the extraordinary Gerald Hugh Tyrwhitt-Wilson, 14th Baron Berners, (1883–1950), became an 'unabashed hedonist' as well as a diplomat, composer, novellist, poet, painter, and bon-viveur, for all of which, he said, he showed 'a certain facile talent'. What is striking about both passages is that the blasphemy is actually a rebellion against temporal not divine authority.

An altogether more weighty figure, James Joyce, provides the final excerpt in this section. Joyce's work has probably been more thoroughly excavated than any other modern writer's. The *Portrait of the Artist as a Young Man* (1916), which although not autobiography show strong leanings that way, is remarkable in that Stephen, the central figure, is treated by the author in a manner which is both detached and ironic. Joyce's brilliant dialogue technique is displayed here in a scene which is both comic and truly tragic, a microcosm of Ireland's social and religious troubles enacted before a child in such a way that Joyce seems to be asking 'What hope has anyone of understanding?'

# W Somerset Maugham

*from:* Of Human Bondage

Then a wave of religiosity passed through the school. Bad language was no longer heard, and the little nastinesses of small boys were looked upon with hostility; the bigger boys, like the lords temporal of the Middle Ages, used the strength of their arms to persuade those weaker than themselves to virtuous course.

Philip, his restless mind avid for new things, became very devout. He heard soon that it was possible to join a Bible League, and wrote to London for particulars. These consisted in a form to be filled up with the applicant's name, age, and school; a solemn declaration to be signed that he would read a set portion of Holy Scripture every night for a year; and a request for half a crown; this, it was explained, was demanded partly to prove the earnestness of the applicant's desire to become a member of the League, and partly to cover clerical expenses. Philip duly sent the papers and the money, and in return received a calendar worth about a penny, on which was set down the appointed passage to be read each day, and a sheet of paper on one side of which was a picture of the Good Shepherd and a lamb, and on the other, decoratively framed in red lines, a short prayer which had to be said before beginning to read.

Every evening he undressed as quickly as possible in order to have time for his task before the gas was put out. He read industriously, as he read always, without criticism, stories of cruelty, deceit, ingratitude, dishonesty, and low cunning. Actions which would have excited his horror in the life about him, in the reading passed through his mind without comment; because they were committed under the direct inspiration of God. The method of the League was to alternate a book of the Old Testament with a book of the New, and one night Philip came across these words of Jesus Christ:

> If ye have faith, and doubt not, ye shall not only do this which is done to the fig-tree, but also if ye shall say unto this mountain, be thou removed, and be thou cast into the sea: it shall be done.

And all this, whatsoever ye shall ask in prayer, believing, ye shall receive.

They made no particular impression on him, but it happened that two or three days later, being Sunday, the Canon in residence chose them for the text of his sermon. Even if Philip had wanted to hear this it would have been impossible, for the boys of King's School sit in the choir, and the pulpit stands at the corner of the transept so that the preacher's back is almost turned to them. The distance also is so great that it needs a man with a fine voice and knowledge of elocution to make himself heard in the choir; and according to long usage the Canons of Tercanbury are chosen for their learning rather than for any qualities which might be of use in a cathedral church. But the words of the text, perhaps because he had read them so short a while before, came clearly enough to Philip's ears, and they seemed on a sudden to have a personal application. He thought about them through most of the sermon, and that night, on getting into bed, he turned over the pages of the gospel and found once more the passage. Though he believed implicitly everything he saw in print, he had learned already that in the Bible things that said one thing quite clearly often mysteriously meant another. There was no one he liked to ask at school, so he kept the question he had in mind till the Christmas holiday, and then one day he made an opportunity. It was after supper and prayers were just finished. Mrs Carey was counting the eggs that Mary Ann had brought in as usual and writing on each one the date. Philip stood at the table and pretended to turn listlessly the pages of the Bible.

'I say, Uncle William, this passage here, does it really mean that?'

He put his finger against it as though he had come across it accidentally.

Mr Carey looked up over his spectacles. He was holding *The Black-stable Times* in front of the fire. It had come in that evening damp from the press, and the Vicar always aired it for ten minutes before he began to read.

'What passage is that?' he asked.

'Why, this about if you have faith you can remove mountains.'

'If it says so in the Bible it is so, Philip,' said Mrs Carey gently, taking up the plate-basket.

Philip looked at his uncle for an answer.

'It's a matter of faith.'

'D'you mean to say that if you really believed you could move mountains you could?'

'By the grace of God,' said the Vicar.

'Now, say good-night to your uncle, Philip,' said Aunt Louisa. 'You're not wanting to move a mountain tonight, are you?'

Philip allowed himself to be kissed on the forehead by his uncle and preceded Mrs Carey upstairs. He had got the information he wanted. His little room was icy, and he shivered when he put on his nightgown. But he always felt that his prayers were more pleasing to God when he said them under conditions of discomfort. The coldness of his hands and feet was an offering to the Almighty. And tonight he sank on his knees, buried his face in his hands, and prayed to God with all his might that He would make his club-foot whole. It was a very small thing beside the moving of mountains. He knew that God could do it if He wished, and his own faith was complete. Next morning, finishing his prayers with the same request, he fixed a date for the miracle.

'Oh, God in Thy living mercy and goodness, if it be Thy will, please make my foot all right on the night before I go back to school.'

He was glad to get his petition into a formula, and he repeated it later in the dining-room during the short pause which the Vicar always made after prayers, before he rose from his knees. He said it again in the evening and again, shivering in his nightshirt, before he got into bed. And he believed. For once he looked forward with eagerness to the end of the holidays. He laughed to himself as he thought of his uncle's astonishment when he ran down the stairs three at a time; and after breakfast he and Aunt Louisa would have to hurry out and buy a new pair of boots. At school they would be astounded.

'Hullo, Carey, what have you done with your foot?'

'Oh, it's all right now,' he would answer casually, as though it were the most natural thing in the world.

He would be able to play football. His heart leaped as he saw himself running, running, faster than any of the other boys. At the end of the Easter term there were the sports, and he would be able to go in for the races; he rather fancied himself over the hurdles. It would be splendid to be like everyone else, not to be stared at curiously by new boys who did not know about his deformity, not at the baths in summer to need incredible precautions, while he was undressing, before he could hide his foot in the water.

He prayed with all the power of his soul. No doubts assailed him. He was confident in the word of God. And the night before he was to go back to school he went up to bed tremulous with excitement. There

101

was snow on the ground, and Aunt Louisa had allowed herself the unaccustomed luxury of a fire in her bedroom; but in Philip's little room it was so cold that his fingers were numb, and he had great difficulty in undoing his collar. His teeth chattered. The idea came to him that he must do something more than usual to attract the attention of God, and he turned back the rug which was in front of his bed so that he could kneel on the bare boards; and then it struck him that his nightshirt was a softness that might displease his Maker, so he took it off and said his prayers naked. When he got into bed he was so cold that for some time he could sleep, but when he did, it was so soundly that Mary Ann had to shake him when she brought in his hot water next morning. She talked to him while she drew the curtains, but he did not answer; he had remembered at once that this was the morning for the miracle. His heart was filled with joy and gratitude. His first instinct was to put down his hand and feel the foot which was whole now, but to do this seemed to doubt the goodness of God. He knew that his foot was well. But at last he made up his mind, and with the toes of his right foot he just touched the ground. Then he passed his hand over it.

He limped downstairs just as Mary Ann was going into the dining-room for prayers, and then he sat down to breakfast.

'You're very quiet this morning, Philip,' said Aunt Louisa presently.

'He's thinking of the good breakfast he'll have at school tomorrow,' said the Vicar.

When Philip answered, it was in a way that always irritated his uncle, with something that had nothing to do with the matter in hand. He called it a bad habit of wool-gathering.

'Supposing you'd asked God to do something,' said Philip, 'and really believed it was going to happen, like moving a mountain, I mean, and you had faith, and it didn't happen, what would it mean?'

'What a funny boy you are!' said Aunt Louisa. 'You asked about moving mountains two or three weeks ago.'

'It would just mean that you hadn't got faith,' answered Uncle William.

Philip accepted the explanation. If God had not cured him, it was because he did not really believe. And yet he did not see how he could believe more than he did. But perhaps he had not given God enough time. He had only asked Him for nineteen days. In a day or two he began his prayer again, and this time he fixed upon Easter. That was the day of His Son's glorious resurrection, and God in His happiness might be mercifully inclined. But now Philip added other means of attaining his desire: he began to wish, when he saw a new moon or a dappled horse, and he looked out for shooting stars; during exeat they had a chicken at the vicarage, and he broke the lucky bone with Aunt Louisa and wished again, each time that his foot might be made whole. He was appealing unconsciously to gods older to his race than the God of Israel. And he bombarded the Almighty with his prayer, at odd times of the day, whenever it occurred to him, in identical words always, for it seemed to him important to make his request in the same terms. But presently the feeling came to him that this time also his faith would not be great enough. He could not resist the doubt that assailed him. He made his own experience into a general rule.

'I suppose no one ever has faith enough,' he said.

It was like the salt which his nurse used to tell him about: you could catch any bird by putting salt on his tail; and once he had taken a little bag of it into Kensington Gardens. But he could never get near enough to put the salt on the bird's tail. Before Easter he had given up the struggle. He felt a dull resentment against his uncle for taking him in. The text which spoke of the moving of mountains was just one of those that said one thing and meant another. He thought his uncle had been playing a practical joke on him.

# Edmund Gosse

*from:* Father and Son

The question of the efficacy of prayer, which has puzzled wiser heads than mine was, began to trouble me. It was insisted on in our household that if anything was desired, you should not, as my Mother said, 'lose any time in seeking for it, but ask God to guide you to it'. In many junctures of life this is precisely what, in sober fact, they did. I will not dwell here on their theories, which my Mother put forth, with unflinching directness, in her published writings. But I found that a difference was made between my privileges in this matter and theirs, and this led to many discussions. My parents said: 'Whatever you need, tell Him and He will grant it, if it is His will.' Very well; I had

103

need of a large painted humming-top which I had seen in a shop-window in the Caledonian Road. Accordingly, I introduced a supplication for this object into my evening prayer, carefully adding the words: 'If it is Thy will.' This, I recollect, placed my Mother in a dilemma, and she consulted my Father. Taken, I suppose, at a disadvantage, my Father told me I must not pray for 'things like that'. To which I answered by another query, 'Why?' And I added that he said we ought to pray for things we needed, and that I needed the humming-top a great deal more than I did the conversion of the heathen or the restitution of Jerusalem to the Jews, two objects of my nightly supplication which left me very cold.

I have reason to believe, looking back upon this scene, conducted by candle-light in the front parlour, that my Mother was much baffled by the logic of my argument. She had gone so far as to say publicly that no 'things or circumstances are too insignificant to bring before the God of the whole earth'. I persisted that this covered the case of the humming-top, which was extremely significant to me. I noticed that she held aloof from the discussion, which was carried on with some show of annoyance by my Father. He had never gone quite so far as she did in regard to this question of praying for material things. I am not sure that she was convinced that I ought to have been checked; but he could not help seeing that it reduced their favourite theory to an absurdity for a small child to exercise the privilege. He ceased to argue, and told me peremptorily that it was not right for me to pray for things like humming-tops, and that I must do it no more. His authority, of course, was paramount, and I yielded; but my faith in the efficacy of prayer was a good deal shaken. The fatal suspicion had crossed my mind that the reason why I was not to pray for the top was because it was too expensive for my parents to buy, that being the usual excuse for not getting things I wished for.

It was about the date of my sixth birthday that I did something very naughty, some act of direct disobedience, for which my Father, after a solemn sermon, chastised me, sacrificially, by giving me several cuts with a cane. This action was justified, as everything he did was justified, by reference to Scripture — 'Spare the rod and spoil the child'. I suppose that there are some children, of a sullen and lymphatic temperament, who are smartened up and made more wide-awake by a whipping. It is largely a matter of convention, the exercise being endured (I am told) with pride by the infants of our aristocracy, but not tolerated by the lower classes. I am afraid that I proved my inherent vulgarity by being made, not contrite or humble, but furiously angry by this caning. I cannot account for the flame of rage which it awakened in my bosom. My dear, excellent Father had beaten me, not very severely, without ill-temper, and with the most genuine desire to improve me. But he was not well-advised especially so far as the 'dedication to the Lord's service' was concerned. This same 'dedication' had ministered to my vanity, and there are some natures which are not improved by being humiliated. I have to confess with shame that I went about the house for some days with a murderous hatred of my Father locked within my bosom. He did not suspect that the chastisement had not been wholly efficacious, and he bore me no malice; so that after a while, I forgot and thus forgave him. But I do not regard physical punishment as a wise element in the education of proud and sensitive children.

My theological misdeeds culminated, however, in an act so puerile and preposterous that I should not venture to record it if it did not throw some glimmering of light on the subject which I have proposed to myself in writing these pages. My mind continued to dwell on the mysterious question of prayer. It puzzled me greatly to know why, if we were God's children, and if he was watching over us by night and day, we might not supplicate for toys and sweets and smart clothes as well as for the conversion of the heathen. Just at this juncture, we had a special service at the Room, at which our attention was particularly called to what we always spoke of as 'the saints' by an excellent Irish The East was represented among 'the saints' by an excellent Irish peer, who had, in his early youth, converted and married a lady of colour; this Asiatic shared in our Sunday morning meetings, and was an object of helpless terror to me; I shrank from her amiable caresses, and vaguely identified her with a personage much spoken of in our family circle, the 'Personal Devil'.

All these matters drew my thoughts to the subject of idolatry, which was severely censured at the missionary meeting. I cross-examined my Father very closely as to the nature of this sin, and pinned him down to the categorical statement that idolatry consisted in praying to any one or anything but God himself. Wood and stone, in the words of the hymn, were peculiarly liable to be bowed down to by the heathen in their blindness. I pressed my Father further on this subject, and he assured me that God would be very angry, and would signify His anger, if anyone in a Christian country bowed down to wood and stone. I cannot recall why I was so pertinacious on this subject, but I remember that my Father became a little restive under my cross-examination. I determined, however, to test the matter for myself, and one morning, when both my parents were safely out of the house, I prepared for the great act of heresy. I was in the morning-room on the ground-floor, where, with much labour, I hoisted a small chair on to the table close to the window. My heart was now beating as if it would leap out of my side, but I pursued my experiment. I knelt down on the carpet in front of the table and looking up I said my daily prayer in a loud voice, only substituting the address 'O Chair!' for the habitual one.

Having carried this act of idolatry safely through, I waited to see what would happen. It was a fine day, and I gazed up at the slip of white sky above the houses opposite, and expected something to appear in it. God would certainly exhibit his anger in some terrible form, and would chastise my impious and wilful action. I was very much alarmed, but still more excited; I breathed the high, sharp air of defiance. But nothing happened; there was not a cloud in the sky, not an unusual sound in the street. Presently I was quite sure that nothing would happen. I had committed idolatry, flagrantly and deliberately, and God did not care.

The result of this ridiculous act was not to make me question the existence and power of God; those were forces which I did not dream of ignoring. But what it did was to lessen still further my confidence in my Father's knowledge of the Divine mind. My Father had said, positively, that if I worshipped a thing made of wood, God would manifest his anger. I had then worshipped a chair, made (or partly made) of wood, and God had made no sign whatever. My Father, therefore, was not really acquainted with the Divine practice in cases of idolatry. And with that, dismissing the subject, I dived again into the unplumbed depths of the *Penny Cyclopaedia*.

# Lord Berners

*from:* First Childhood

## THE BIBLE-THROWING EPISODE

The Bible, during my early years, failed to inspire me with the proper sentiments of reverence and affection. Indeed, I regret to say I even felt an active antipathy for the Holy Book, an attitude which was largely, if not entirely, the fault of my grandmother, Lady Bourchier. The Bible occupied so prominent a position in her scheme of life that I grew to associate it with her own austere personality and the grim little study at Stackwell. I feared that, were I to allow it to become an obsession (as it had become in her case) my own character might end by assuming that same forbidding Calvinistic tinge. I was not sufficiently cultured to be able to appreciate the beauties of biblical language, and the numerous copies of the Bible that my grandmother had thrust into my reluctant hands had been, all of them, cheap, ill-bound editions. The ugly, common bindings, the villainous print and the double columns were not calculated to arouse aesthetic interest, while the rigid numbering of the verses seemed to impart an unpleasantly didactic tone to the contents. Having been told that the book had been written by God himself, I often wondered why One who had shown himself, in most respects, lavish to the point of extravagance should have been so economical in the presentation of his literary efforts to the public.

At Elmley the Bible revenged itself upon me for my lack of consideration by becoming a positive nuisance. There were readings from the Scriptures every morning before early school, and on Sunday mornings we had to learn texts by heart and recite them in turn to the Headmaster. The Bible was thus an essential item of our morning toilet, and just as important as a collar or a tie.

Nearly every morning the wretched volume contrived to get itself lost. It would either burrow down to the bottom of my locker and hide itself under the five-gloves or the cricket bat, or else it would assume protective colouring and look exactly like a Latin grammar or a geography book. At other times it would wedge itself firmly between the back of the locker and the wall so that it could only be retrieved with the greatest difficulty. It seemed to be possessed of a definite animal malevolence and many times it made me late for school so that I got bad marks or an unjustified rebuke for slothfulness.

On Sundays, 'early school' was always taken by Mr Gambril himself. One Sunday morning towards the end of the Summer Term, whilst we were all assembled awaiting his arrival, I entered into a theological discussion with the sanctimonious Creeling, in the course of which he asserted that anyone speaking irreverently of the Bible or maltreating it in any way would inevitably be punished by God.

'What form,' I asked, 'do you suppose the punishment would take?'

107

'Well, you'd probably be struck by lightning, or else lose all your money.'

'What absolute rot!'

'Well, at any rate,' Creeling demurred, 'it would bring frightful bad luck.'

'Supposing,' I suggested, 'I were to get up now and throw my Bible across the room?'

'Just you try it and see!'

He was reckoning on my cowardice, a kind of assumption that arouses the meanest spirit. I at once stood up and hurled my Bible across the room.

At that very moment the door opened and Mr Gambril appeared. The book missed him by a few inches and fell with a thud at his feet. I was paralysed with horror, and he was obliged to ask twice over 'Who threw that book?' before I was able to get my voice into working order.

'Oh, it was you,' he said, in that ominously suave voice which one knew from experience was like the lull preceeding the storm. He bent down and examined the book. Then the storm broke.

'The Bible!' he shouted. 'The Bible, sir! You have thrown the Bible — and on Sunday too! Stand up on the form!'

I climbed up on to the form. My knees were trembling with such violence that I had difficulty in keeping my balance. Somebody laughed.

'Silence!' said Mr Gambril. 'This is no laughing matter!

'Now, sir,' he turned to me, 'may I ask for what reason you threw your Bible?'

I hesitated. I could think of no valid reason.

'What did you throw your Bible for? Answer me at once!'

'I threw it for a bet.'

As the words left my lips I realised their infelicity. I suppose 'bravado' was the word I had meant to use, but panic confused my thought.

'For a bet? Indeed! This makes your offence even worse than I had imagined. You have the effrontery to tell me, sir, that, for a bet, which is in itself reprehensible, you actually threw God's Sacred Book across the room! Are you aware that this constitutes an act of sacrilege, liable in ordinary circumstances to be punished by a long term of imprisonment?'

I was not aware; but it seemed, at that moment, to be quite probable. I was too frightened to recognise it as merely one of those over-statements with which the Head was wont to emphasise his speech.

He turned to the assembled school. 'Never,' he proclaimed, 'in all my long experience of school life have I come across so flagrant a case of wilful blasphemy and godlessness. Boys, I am sure you are all disgusted. You will now express you condemnation of such behaviour by hissing the culprit.'

This was an entirely new form of punishment. To me, as I stood on the form with bowed head, surrounded, as it were, by a roomful of infuriated vipers, it seemed to be the most terrible thing that had ever happened to anyone, and the suggestion of mass-hatred in a peculiarly venomous shape intensified my sense of guilt. I felt as though I were branded for ever with the mark of Cain.

When the hissing had died down the Headmaster said to me in the tones of a judge delivering a death-sentence, 'You will remain standing on the form during the lesson and afterwards you will come to my study.'

This, of course, implied that a birching was in store for me. How I got through the remainder of the lesson would be too painful to relate. There were moments when I would have welcomed annihilation. The horror of seeing what I believed to be a comparatively innocent action transformed in the twinkling of an eye into an appalling crime, followed by public shame, the experience of the pillory and finally the condemned cell. I was also smarting under a sense of injustice, complicated by the horrible doubts as to whether perhaps after all Creeling had not been right in saying that the Bible possessed magic powers of self-protection. In this case, at any rate, the insult offered to it had been followed by swift retribution.

The lesson came to an end at last. I got down from the form and followed the Headmaster out of the room in the midst of a silence that I knew to be fraught with a gloating expectancy.

As I entered the study, Mr Gambril took up one of his birches and laid it on the table. He then proceeded to deliver a forcible homily on sacrilege and wickedness in general, in the course of which he expressed grave misgivings about my future career. But although he fingered the birch and, from time to time, shook it at me menacingly, he finally dismissed me without having used it. The implication was that my offence had been far too serious for mere corporal punishment and that I was lucky to have escaped expulsion. I only thought that I was lucky to have escaped the birch.

It may perhaps seem difficult to believe that so trivial a misdeed as throwing a Bible could have provoked all this fury. But schoolmasters, like many other people in responsible positions, are often overcome by the tedium of their duties, and at such moments, I imagine, they gladly welcome any excuse for working up a violent emotion. It relieves their feelings and acts as a moral pick-me-up. Thus it sometimes happens that small boys, to whom the psychology of their elders is a sealed book, are left with a confusing idea of the relative magnitude of their crimes.

On returning to the schoolroom, I was relieved to find that my act of sacrilege had not really damaged me very seriously in the eyes of my schoolfellows. The hissing was, of course, a perfunctory affair, entered into with zest because the act of hissing was in itself rather enjoyable. Furthermore, it had been a 'command performance' and not in the least a genuine manifestation of public opinion. As a matter of fact, in school life, spectacular disgrace generally produces a reaction of popularity, and I was at once surrounded by an interested crowd. There was, I am bound to say, some slight disappointment when it transpired that I had escaped a birching. However, the sense of being, for the moment, in the public eye helped to dissipate the cloud of guilt that hung over me, and my spirits rose again. Indeed I felt myself almost a hero.

# James Joyce

*from:* Portrait of the Artist as a Young Man

A great fire, banked high and red, flamed in the grate and under the ivytwined branches of the chandelier the Christmas table was spread. They had come home a little late and still dinner was not ready: but it would be ready in a jiffy, his mother had said. They were waiting for the door to open and for the servants to come in, holding the big dishes covered with their heavy metal covers.

All were waiting: uncle Charles, who sat far away in the shadow of the window, Dante and Mr Casey, who sat in the easychairs at either side of the hearth, Stephen, seated on a chair between them, his feet resting on the toasted boss. Mr Dedalus looked at himself in the pierglass above the mantelpiece, waxed out his moustache ends and then, parting his coat tails, stood with his back to the glowing fire: and still from time to time he withdrew a hand from his coat tail to wax out one of his moustache ends. Mr Casey leaned his head to one side and, smiling, tapped the gland of his neck with his fingers. And Stephen smiled too for he knew now that it was not true that Mr Casey had a purse of silver in his throat. He smiled to think how the silvery noise which Mr Casey used to make had deceived him. And when he had tried to open Mr Casey's hand to see if the purse of silver was hidden there he had seen that the fingers could not be straightened out: and Mr Casey had told him that he had got those three cramped fingers making a birthday present for Queen Victoria.

Mr Casey tapped the gland of his neck and smiled at Stephen with sleepy eyes: and Mr Dedalus said to him:

— Yes. Well now, that's all right. O, we had a good walk, hadn't we, John? Yes . . . I wonder if there's any likelihood of dinner this evening. Yes . . . O, well now, we got a good breath of ozone round the Head today. Ay, bedad.

He turned to Dante and said:

— You didn't stir out at all, Mrs Riordan?

Dante frowned and said shortly:

— No.

Mr Dedalus dropped his coat tails and went over to the sideboard. He brought forth a great stone jar of whisky from the locker and filled the decanter slowly, bending now and then to see how much he had poured in. Then replacing the jar in the locker he poured a little of the whisky into two glasses, added a little water and came back with them to the fireplace.

— A thimbleful, John, he said, just to whet your appetite.

Mr Casey took the glass, drank, and placed it near him on the mantelpiece. Then he said:

— Well, I can't help thinking of our friend Christopher manufacturing . . .

He broke into a fit of laughter and coughing and added:

— . . . manufacturing that champagne for those fellows.

Mr Dedalus laughed loudly.

— Is it Christy? he said. There's more cunning in one of those warts on his bald head than in a pack of jack foxes.

He inclined his head, closed his eyes, and, licking his lips profusely, began to speak with the voice of the hotel keeper.

— And he has such a soft mouth when he's speaking to you, don't you know. He's very moist and watery about the dewlaps, God bless him.

Mr Casey was still struggling through his fit of coughing and laughter. Stephen, seeing and hearing the hotel keeper through his father's face and voice, laughed.

Mr Dedalus put up his eyeglass and, staring down at him, said quietly and kindly:

— What are you laughing at, you little puppy, you?

The servants entered and placed the dishes on the table. Mrs Dedalus followed and the places were arranged.

— Sit over, she said.

Mr Dedalus went to the end of the table and said:

— Now, Mrs Riordan, sit over. John, sit you down, my hearty.

He looked round to where uncle Charles sat and said:

— Now then, sir, there's a bird here waiting for you.

When all had taken their seats he laid his hand on the cover and then said quickly, withdrawing it:

— Now, Stephen.

Stephen stood up in his place to say the grace before meals:

*Bless us, O Lord, and these Thy gifts through Thy bounty we are about to receive through Christ our Lord. Amen.*

All blessed themselves and Mr Dedalus with a sigh of pleasure lifted from the dish the heavy cover pearled around the edge with glistening drops.

Stephen looked at the plump turkey which had lain, trussed and skewered, on the kitchen table. He knew that his father had paid a guinea for it in Dunn's of D'Olier Street and that the man had prodded it often at the breastbone to show how good it was: and he remembered the man's voice when he had said:

— Take that one, sir. That's the real Ally Daly.

Why did Mr Barrett in Clongowes call his pandybat a turkey? But Clongowes was far away: and the warm heavy smell of turkey and ham and celery rose from the plates and dishes and the great fire was banked high and red in the grate and the green ivy and red holly made you feel so happy and when dinner was ended the big plum pudding would be carried in, studded with peeled almonds and sprigs of holly, with bluish fire running around it and a little green flag flying from the top.

It was his first Christmas dinner and he thought of his little brothers and sisters who were waiting in the nursery, as he had often waited, till the pudding came. The deep low collar and the Eton jacket made him feel queer and oldish: and that morning when his mother had brought him down to the parlour, dressed for mass, his father had cried. That was because he was thinking of his own father. And uncle Charles had said so too.

Mr Dedalus covered the dish and began to eat hungrily. Then he said:

— Poor old Christy, he's nearly lopsided now with roguery.

— Simon, said Mrs Dedalus, you haven't given Mrs Riordan any sauce.

Mr Dedalus seized the sauceboat.

— Haven't I? he cried. Mrs Riordan, pity the poor blind.

Dante covered her plate with her hands and said:

— No, thanks.

Mr Dedalus turned to uncle Charles.

— How are you off, sir?

— Right as the mail, Simon.

— You, John?

— I'm all right. Go on yourself.

— Mary? Here, Stephen, here's something to make your hair curl.

He poured sauce freely over Stephen's plate and set the boat again on the table. Then he asked uncle Charles was it tender. Uncle Charles could not speak because his mouth was full, but he nodded that it was.

— That was a good answer our friend made to the canon. What? said Mr Dedalus.

— I didn't think he had that much in him, said Mr Casey.

— *I'll pay your dues, father, when you cease turning the house of God into a pollingbooth.*

— A nice answer, said Dante, for any man calling himself a catholic to give to his priest.

— They have only themselves to blame, said Mr Dedalus suavely. If they took a fool's advice they would confine their attention to religion.

— It is religion, Dante said. They are doing their duty in warning the people.

— We go to the house of God, Mr Casey said, in all humility to pray to our Maker and not to hear election addresses.

113

— It is religion, Dante said again. They are right. They must direct their flocks.

— And preach politics from the altar, is it? asked Mr Dedalus.

— Certainly, said Dante. It is a question of public morality. A priest would not be a priest if he did not tell his flock what is right and what is wrong.

Mrs Dedalus laid down her knife and fork, saying:

— For pity sake and for pity sake let us have no political discussion on this day of all days in the year.

— Quite right, ma'am, said uncle Charles. Now Simon, that's quite enough now. Not another word now.

— Yes, yes, said Mr Dedalus quickly.

He uncovered the dish boldly and said:

— Now then, who's for more turkey?

Nobody answered. Dante said:

— Nice language for any catholic to use!

— Mrs Riordan, I appeal to you, said Mrs Dedalus, to let the matter drop now.

Dante turned on her and said:

— And am I to sit here and listen to the pastors of my church being flouted?

— Nobody is saying a word against them, said Mr Dedalus, so long as they don't meddle in politics.

— The bishops and priests of Ireland have spoken, said Dante, and they must be obeyed.

— Let them leave politics alone, said Mr Casey, or the people may leave their church alone.

— You hear? said Dante turning to Mrs Dedalus.

— Mr Casey! Simon! said Mrs Dedalus, let it end now.

— Too bad! Too bad! said uncle Charles.

— What? cried Mr Dedalus. Were we to desert him at the bidding of the English people?

— He was no longer worthy to lead, said Dante. He was a public sinner.

— We are all sinners and black sinners, said Mr Casey coldly.

— *Woe be to the man by whom the scandal cometh!* said Mrs Riordan. *It would be better for him that a millstone were tied about his neck and that he were cast into the depths of the sea rather than that he should scandalize one of these, my least little ones.* That is the language of the Holy Ghost.

— And very bad language if you ask me, said Mr Dedalus coolly.

— Simon! Simon! said uncle Charles. The boy.

— Yes, yes, said Mr Dedalus. I meant about the . . . I was thinking about the bad language of that railway porter. Well now, that's all right. Here, Stephen, show me your plate, old chap. Eat away now. Here.

He heaped up the food on Stephen's plate and served uncle Charles and Mr Casey to large pieces of turkey and splashes of sauce. Mrs Dedalus was eating little and Dante sat with her hands in her lap. She was red in the face. Mr Dedalus rooted with the carvers at the end of the dish and said:

— There's a tasty bit here we call the pope's nose. If any lady or gentleman . . .

He held a piece of fowl up on the prong of the carving-fork. Nobody spoke. He put it on his own plate, saying:

— Well, you can't say but you were asked. I think I had better eat it myself because I'm not well in my health lately.

He winked at Stephen and, replacing the dish cover, began to eat again.

There was a silence while he ate. Then he said:

— Well now, the day kept up fine after all. There were plenty of strangers down, too.

Nobody spoke. He said again:

— I think there were more strangers down than last Christmas.

He looked round at the others whose faces were bent towards their plates and, receiving no reply, waited for a moment and said bitterly:

— Well, my Christmas dinner has been spoiled anyhow.

— There could be neither luck nor grace, Dante said, in a house where there is no respect for the pastors of the church.

Mr Dedalus threw his knife and fork noisily on his plate.

— Respect! he said. Is it for Billy with the lip or for the tub of guts up in Armagh? Respect!

— Princes of the church, said Mr Casey with slow scorn.

— Lord Leitrim's coachman, yes, said Mr Dedalus.

— They are the Lord's anointed, Dante said. They are an honour to their country.

— Tub of guts, said Mr Dedalus coarsely. He has a handsome face, mind you, in repose. You should see that fellow lapping up his bacon and cabbage of a cold winter's day. O Johnny!

He twisted his features into a grimace of heavy bestiality and made a lapping noise with his lips.

— Really, Simon, you should not speak that way before Stephen. It's not right.

— O, he'll remember all this when he grows up, said Dante hotly — the language he heard against God and religion and priests in his own home.

—Let him remember too, cried Mr Casey to her from across the table, the language with which the priests and the priests' pawns broke Parnell's heart and hounded him into his grave. Let him remember that too when he grows up.

— Sons of bitches! cried Mr Dedalus. When he was down they turned on him to betray him and rend him like rats in a sewer. Low-lived dogs! And they look it! By Christ, they look it!

— They behaved rightly, cried Dante. They obeyed their bishops and their priests. Honour to them!

— Well, it is perfectly dreadful to say that not even for one day in the year, said Mrs Dedalus, can we be free from these dreadful disputes!

Uncle Charles raised his hands mildly and said:

— Come now, come now, come now! Can we not have our opinions whatever they are without this bad temper and this bad language? It is too bad surely.

Mrs Dedalus spoke to Dante in a low voice but Dante said loudly:

— I will not say nothing. I will defend my church and my religion when it is insulted and spit on by renegade catholics.

Mr Casey pushed his plate rudely into the middle of the table and, resting his elbows before him, said in a hoarse voice to his host:

— Tell me, did I tell you that story about a very famous spit?

— You did not, John, said Mr Dedalus.

— Why then, said Mr Casey, it is a most instructive story. It happened not long ago in the county Wicklow where we are now.

He broke off and, turning towards Dante, said with quiet indignation:

— And I may tell you, ma'am, that I, if you mean me, am no renegade catholic. I am a catholic as my father was and his father before him and his father before him again when we gave up our lives rather than sell our faith.

— The more shame to you now, Dante said, to speak as you do.

— The story, John, said Mr Dedalus smiling. Let us have the story anyhow.

— Catholic indeed! repeated Dante ironically. The blackest protestant in the land would not speak the language I have heard this

116

evening.

Mr Dedalus began to sway his head to and fro, crooning like a country singer.

— I am no protestant, I tell you again, said Mr Casey flushing.

Mr Dedalus, still crooning and swaying his head, began to sing in a grunting nasal tone:

> O, come all you Roman catholics
> That never went to mass.

He took up his knife and fork again in good humour and set to eating, saying to Mr Casey:

— Let us have the story, John. It will help us to digest.

Stephen looked with affection at Mr Casey's face which stared across the table over his joined hands. He liked to sit near him at the fire, looking up at his dark fierce face. But his dark eyes were never fierce and his slow voice was good to listen to. But why was he then against the priests? Because Dante must be right then. But he had heard his father say that she was a spoiled nun and that she had come out of the convent in the Alleghanies when her brother had got the money from the savages for the trinkets and the chainies. Perhaps that made her severe against Parnell. And she did not like him to play with Eileen because Eileen was a protestant and when she was young she knew children that used to play with protestants and the protestants used to make fun of the litany of the Blessed Virgin. *Tower of Ivory*, they used to say, *House of Gold!* How could a woman be a tower of ivory or a house of gold? Who was right then? And he remembered the evening in the infirmary in Clongowes, the dark waters, the light at the pierhead and the moan′ of sorrow from the people when they had heard.

Eileen had long white hands. One evening when playing tig she had put her hands over his eyes: long and white and thin and cold and soft. That was ivory: a cold white thing. That was the meaning of *Tower of Ivory*.

— The story is very short and sweet, Mr Casey said. It was one day down in Arklow, a cold bitter day, not long before the chief died. May God have mercy on him!

He closed his eyes wearily and paused. Mr Dedalus took a bone from his plate and tore some meat from it with his teeth, saying:

— Before he was killed, you mean.

117

Mr Casey opened his eyes, sighed and went on:

— He was down in Arklow one day. We were down there at a meeting and after the meeting was over we had to make our way to the railway station through the crowd. Such booing and baaing, man, you never heard. They called us all the names in the world. Well there was one old lady, and a drunken old harridan she was surely, that paid all her attention to me. She kept dancing along beside me in the mud bawling and screaming into my face: *Priesthunter! The Paris Funds! Mr Fox! Kitty O'Shea!*

— And what did you do, John? asked Mr Dedalus.

— I let her bawl away, said Mr Casey. It was a cold day and to keep up my heart I had (saving your presence, ma'am) a quid of Tullamore in my mouth and sure I couldn't say a word in any case because my mouth was full of tobacco juice.

— Well, John?

— Well. I let her bawl away, to her heart's content, *Kitty O'Shea* and the rest of it till at last she called that lady a name that I won't sully this Christmas board nor your ears, ma'am, nor my own lips by repeating.

He paused. Mr Dedalus, lifting his head from the bone, asked:

— And what did you do, John?

— Do! said Mr Casey. She stuck her ugly old face up at me when she said it and I had my mouth full of tobacco juice. I bent down to her and *Phth!* says I to her like that.

He turned aside and made the act of spitting.

— Phth! says I to her like that, right into her eye.

He clapped a hand to his eye and gave a hoarse scream of pain.

— *O Jesus, Mary and Joseph!* says she. *I'm blinded! I'm blinded and drownded!*

He stopped in a fit of coughing and laughter, repeating:

— *I'm blinded entirely.*

Mr Dedalus laughed loudly and lay back in his chair while uncle Charles swayed his head to and fro.

Dante looked terrible angry and repeated while they laughed:

— Very nice! Ha! Very nice!

It was not nice about the spit in the woman's eye.

But what was the name the woman had called Kitty O'Shea that Mr Casey would not repeat? He thought of Mr Casey walking through the crowds of people and making speeches from a wagonette. That was what he had been in prison for and he remembered that one night Sergeant O'Neill had come to the house and had stood in the hall, talking in a low voice with his father and chewing nervously at the chinstrap of his cap. And that night Mr Casey had not gone to Dublin by train but a car had come to the door and he had heard his father say something about the Cabinteely road.

He was for Ireland and Parnell and so was his father: and so was Dante too for one night at the band on the esplanade she had hit a gentleman on the head with her umbrella because he had taken off his hat when the band played *God save the Queen* at the end.

Mr Dedalus gave a snort of contempt.

— Ah, John, he said. It is true for them. We are an unfortunate priestridden race and always were and always will be till the end of the chapter.

Uncle Charles shook his head, saying:

— A bad business! A bad business!

Mr Dedalus repeated:

— A priestridden Godforsaken race!

He pointed to the portrait of his grandfather on the wall to his right.

— Do you see that old chap up there, John? he said. He was a good Irishman when there was no money in the job. He was condemned to death as a whiteboy. But he had a saying about our clerical friends, that he would never let one of them put his two feet under his mahogany.

Dante broke in angrily:

— If we are a priestridden race we ought to be proud of it! They are the apple of God's eye. *Touch them not*, says Christ, *for they are the apple of My eye.*

— And can we not love our country then? asked Mr Casey. Are we not to follow the man that was born to lead us?

— A traitor to his country! replied Dante. A traitor, an adulterer! The priests were right to abandon him. The priests were always the true friends of Ireland.

— Were they, faith? said Mr Casey.

He threw his fist on the table and, frowning angrily, protruded one finger after another.

— Didn't the bishops of Ireland betray us in the time of the union when Bishop Lanigan presented an address of loyalty to the Marquess Cornwallis? Didn't the bishops and priests sell the aspirations of their country in 1829 in return for catholic emancipation? Didn't they denounce the fenian movement from the pulpit and in the confession box? And didn't they dishonour the ashes of Terence Bellew

MacManus?

His face was glowing with anger and Stephen felt the glow rise to his own cheek as the spoken words thrilled him. Mr Dedalus uttered a guffaw of coarse scorn.

— O, by God, he cried, I forgot little old Paul Cullen! Another apple of God's eye!

Dante bent across the table and cried to Mr Casey:

— Right! Right! They were always right! God and morality and religion come first.

Mrs Dedalus, seeing her excitement, said to her:

— Mrs Riordan, don't excite yourself answering them.

— God and religion before everything! Dante cried. God and religion before the world!

Mr Casey raised his clenched fist and brought it down on the table with a crash.

— Very well, then, he shouted hoarsely, if it comes to that, no God for Ireland!

— John! John! cried Mr Dedalus, seizing his guest by the coat sleeve.

Dante started across the table, her cheeks shaking. Mr Casey struggled up from his chair and bent across the table towards her, scraping the hair from before his eyes with one hand as though he were tearing aside a cobweb.

— No God for Ireland! he cried. We have had too much God in Ireland. Away with God!

— Blasphemer! Devil! screamed Dante, starting to her feet and almost spitting in his face.

Uncle Charles and Mr Dedalus pulled Mr Casey back into his chair again, talking to him from both sides reasonably. He stared before him out of his dark flaming eyes, repeating:

— Away with God, I say!

Dante shoved her chair violently aside and left the table, upsetting her napkin-ring which rolled slowly along the carpet and came to rest against the foot of an easychair. Mrs Dedalus rose quickly and followed her towards the door. At the door Dante turned round violently and shouted down the room, her cheeks flushed and quivering with rage:

— Devil out of hell! We won! We crushed him to death! Fiend!

The door slammed behind her.

Mr Casey, freeing his arms from his holders, suddenly bowed his head on his hands with a sob of pain.

— Poor Parnell! he cried loudly. My dead king!

He sobbed loudly and bitterly.

Stephen, raising his terrorstricken face, saw that his father's eyes were full of tears.

# VI
# ROLE PLAYING

*Edmund Gosse*
*Flannery O'Connor*
*Mary McCarthy*

It is difficult to decide whether Sir Edmund Gosse's description of his baptism is intended chiefly to amuse or instruct; it combines pathos with sharp observation and mordant wit. Gosse's examination of the relationship of father and son strongly resembles Samuel Butler's in many ways; Butler, the son of the Bishop of Lichfield, was a keen theoretician of the new science, particularly of evolution, which his father regarded as blasphemous. Gosse's father, a zoologist, regarded Darwin in the same light, holding to an austere puritanism which was to wreck his career. Butler's rebellion came later in life than Gosse's, and was perhaps more traumatic; Gosse seems to have developed a sly conformism to his father's authority at a tender age.

Flannery O'Connor (1925–1964), an orthodox Catholic from Georgia, returned again and again in her short writing career to the theme of mankind cut off from God's grace in a tawdry world. Her often grotesque stories are almost all religious in some sense; her characters, drifters, poor white 'trash', criminals and psychotics find salvation perversely through torment or paradox. As, apparently, in this beautifully-written story— through a faith so simple it amounts to a misunderstanding.

In another paradoxical passage, Mary McCarthy's role-playing, pretending a loss of faith, is simple attention-seeking at first and is intended to precede a spectacular 'reconversion'. She finds herself in deep waters, however, and ends up without faith . . . but questioning whether in fact she ever possessed it.

# Edmund Gosse

*from:* Father and Son

The development of my faculties, of which I have spoken, extended to
the religious sphere no less than to the secular. Here, also, as I look
back, I see that I was extremely imitative. I expanded in the warmth of
my Father's fervour, and, on the whole, in a manner that was satisfactory to him. He observed the richer hold that I was now taking on
life; he saw my faculties branching in many directions, and he became
very anxious to secure my maintenance in grace. In earlier years,
certain sides of my character had offered a sort of passive resistance to
his ideas. I had let what I did not care to welcome pass over my mind
in the curious density that children adopt in order to avoid receiving
impressions — blankly, dumbly, achieving by stupidity what they
cannot achieve by argument. I think that I had frequently done this;
that he had been brought up against a dead wall; although on other
sides of my nature I had been responsive and docile. But now, in my
tenth year, the imitative faculty got the upper hand, and nothing
seemed so attractive as to be what I was expected to be. If there was a
doubt now, it lay in the other direction; it seemed hardly normal that
so young a child should appear so receptive and so apt.

My Father believed himself justified, at this juncture, in making a
tremendous effort. He wished to secure me finally, exhaustively, before the age of puberty could dawn, before my soul was fettered with
the love of carnal things. He thought that if I could now be identified
with the 'saints', and could stand on exactly their footing, a habit of
conformity would be secured. I should meet the paganizing tendencies
of advancing years with security if I could be forearmed with all the
weapons of a sanctified life. He wished me, in short, to be received into
the community of the Brethren on the terms of an adult. There were
difficulties in the way of carrying out this scheme, and they were urged
upon him, more or less courageously, by the elders of the church. But
he overbore them. What the difficulties were, and what were the
arguments which he used to sweep those difficulties away, I must now
explain, for in this lay the centre of our future relations as father and
son.

In dealing with the peasants around him, among whom he was engaged in an active propaganda, my Father always insisted on the necessity of conversion. There must be a new birth and being, a fresh creation in God. This crisis he was accustomed to regard as manifesting itself in a sudden and definite upheaval. There might have been prolonged practical piety, deep and true contrition for sin, but these, although the natural and suitable prologue to conversion, were not conversion itself. People hung on at the confines of regeneration, often for a very long time; my Father dealt earnestly with them, the elders ministered to them, with explanation, exhortation and prayer. Such persons were in a gracious state, but they were not in a state of grace. If they should suddenly die, they would pass away in an unconverted condition, and all that could be said in their favour was a vague expression of hope that they would benefit from God's uncovenanted mercies.

But on some day, at some hour and minute, if life was spared to them, the way of salvation would be revealed to these persons in such an aspect that they would be enabled instantaneously to accept it. They would take it consciously, as one takes a gift from the hand that offers it. This act of taking was the process of conversion, and the person who so accepted was a child of God now, although a single minute ago he had been a child of wrath. The very root of human nature had to be changed, and, in the majority of cases, this change was sudden, patent, palpable.

I have just said, 'in the majority of cases', because my Father admitted the possibility of exceptions. The formula was, 'If any man hath not the Spirit of Christ, he is none of his.' As a rule, no one could possess the Spirit of Christ, without a conscious and full abandonment of the soul, and this, however carefully led up to, and prepared for with tears and renunciations, was not, could not, be made, except at a set moment of time. Faith, in an esoteric and almost symbolic sense, was necessary, and could not be a result of argument, but was a state of heart. In these opinions my Father departed in no wise from the strict evangelical doctrine of the Protestant churches, but he held it in a mode and with a severity peculiar to himself. Now, it is plain that this state of heart, this voluntary deed of acceptance, presupposed a full and rational consciousness of the relations of things. It might be clearly achieved by a person of humble cultivation, but only by one who was fully capable of independent thought, in other words by a more or less adult person. The man or woman claiming the privileges of conversion must be able to understand and to grasp what his religious education was aiming at.

It is extraordinary what trouble it often gave my Father to know whether he was justified in admitting to the communion people of very limited powers of expression. A harmless, humble labouring man would come with a request to be allowed to 'break bread'. It was only by the use of strong leading questions that he could be induced to mention Christ as the ground of his trust at all. I recollect an elderly agricultural labourer being closeted for a long time with my Father, who came out at last, in a sort of dazed condition, and replied to our inquiries, — with a shrug of his shoulders as he said it, — 'I was obliged to put the Name and Blood and Work of Jesus into his very mouth. It is true that he assented cordially at last, but I confess I was grievously daunted by the poor intelligence!'

But there was, or there might be, another class of persons, whom early training, separation from the world, and the care of godly parents had so early familiarized with the acceptable calling of Christ that their conversion had occurred, unperceived and therefore un-recorded, at an extraordinarily early age. It would be in vain to look for a repetition of the phenomenon in those cases. The heavenly fire must not be expected to descend a second time; the lips are touched with the burning coal once, and once only. If, accordingly, these precociously selected spirits are to be excluded because no new birth is observed in them at a mature age, they must continue outside in the cold, since the phenomenon cannot be repeated. When, therefore, there is not possible any further doubt of their being in possession of salvation, longer delay is useless, and worse than useless. The fact of conversion, though not recorded nor even recollected, must be accepted on the evidence of confession of faith, and as soon as the intelligence is evidently developed, the person not merely may, but should be accepted into communion, although still immature in body, although in years still even a child. This my Father believed to be my case, and in this rare class did he fondly persuade himself to station me.

As I have said, the congregation, — although docile and timid, and little able, as units, to hold their own against their minister, — behind his back were faintly hostile to this plan. None of their own children had even been so much as suggested for membership, and each of themselves, in ripe years, had been subjected to severe cross-examination. I think it was rather a bitter pill for some of them to swallow that a pert little boy of ten should be admitted, as a grown-up person, to all the hard-won privileges of their order. Mary Grace Burmington came back from her visits to the cottagers, reporting disaffection here and there, grumblings in the rank and file. But quite as many, especially of the women, enthusiastically supported my Father's wish, gloried aloud in the manifestations of my early piety, and professed to see in it something of miraculous promise. The expression 'another Infant Samuel' was widely used. I became quite a subject of contention. A war of the sexes threatened to break out over me; I was a disturbing element at cottage breakfasts. I was mentioned at public prayer-meetings, not indeed by name but, in the extra-ordinary allusive way customary in our devotions, as 'one amongst us of tender years' or as 'a sapling in the Lord's vineyard'.

To all this my Father put a stop in his own high-handed fashion. After the morning meeting, one Sunday in the autumn of 1859, he desired the attention of the Saints to a personal matter which was, perhaps, not unfamiliar to them by rumour. That was, he explained, the question of the admission of his beloved little son to the communion of saints in the breaking of bread. He allowed — and I sat there in evidence, palely smiling at the audience, my feet scarcely touching the ground — that I was not what is styled adult; I was not, he frankly admitted, a grown-up person. But I was adult in a knowledge of the Lord; I possessed an insight into the plan of salvation which many a hoary head might envy for its fullness, its clearness, its conformity with Scripture doctrine. This was a palpable hit at more than one stumbler and fumbler after the truth, and several hoary heads were bowed.

My Father then went on to explain very fully the position which I have already attempted to define. He admitted the absence in my case of a sudden, apparent act of conversion resulting upon conviction of sin. But he stated the grounds of his belief that I had, in still earlier infancy, been converted, and he declared that if so, I ought no longer to be excluded from the privileges of communion. He said, moreover, that he was willing on this occasion to waive his own privilege as a minister, and that he would rather call on Brother Fawkes and Brother Bere, the leading elders, to examine the candidate in his stead. This was a master-stroke, for Brothers Fawkes and Bere had been suspected of leading the disaffection, and this threw all the burden of responsi-bility on them. The meeting broke up in great amiability, and my Father and I went home together in the very highest of spirits. I, indeed, in my pride, crossed the verge of indiscretion by saying: 'When I have been admitted to fellowship, Papa, shall I be allowed to call you "beloved Brother"?' My Father was too well pleased with the morning's work to be critical. He laughed, and answered: 'That, my Love, though strictly correct, would hardly, I fear, be thought judicious!'

It was suggested that my tenth birthday, which followed this public announcement by a few days, would be a capital occasion for me to go through the ordeal. Accordingly, after dark (for our new lamp was lighted for the first time in honour of the event), I withdrew alone into our drawing-room, which had just, at length, been furnished, and which looked, I thought, very smart. Hither came to me, first Brother Fawkes, by himself; then Brother Bere, by himself; and then both together, so that you may say, if you are pedanticaly inclined, that I underwent three successive interviews. My Father, out of sight somewhere, was, of course, playing the part of stage manager.

I felt not at all shy, but so highly strung that my whole nature seemed to throb with excitement. My first examiner, on the other hand, was extremely confused. Fawkes, who was a builder in a small business of his own, was short and fat; his complexion, which wore a deeper and more uniform rose-colour than usual, I observed to be starred with dew-drops of nervous emotion, which he wiped away at intervals with a large bandana handkerchief. He was so long in coming to the point, that I was obliged to lead him to it himself, and I sat up on the sofa in the full lamplight, and testified my faith in the atonement with a fluency that surprised myself. Before I had done, Fawkes, a middle-aged man with the reputation of being a very stiff employer of labour, was weeping like a child.

Bere, the carpenter, a long, thin and dry man, with a curiously immobile eye, did not fall so easily a prey to my fascinations. He put me through my paces véry sharply, for he had something of the temper of an attorney mingled with his religiousness. However, I was equal to him, and he, too, though he held his own head higher, was not less impressed than Fawkes had been, by the surroundings of the occasion. Neither of them had ever been in our drawing-room since it was furnished, and I thought that each of them noticed how smart the wallpaper was. Indeed, I believe I drew their attention to it. After the two solitary examinations were over, the elders came in again, as I have said, and they prayed for a long time. We all three knelt at the sofa, I between them. But by this time, to my great exaltation of spirits there had succeeded an equally dismal depression. It was my turn now to weep, and I dimly remember my Father coming into the room, and my being carried up to bed, in a state of collapse and fatigue, by the silent and kindly Miss Marks.

On the following Sunday morning, I was the principal subject which occupied an unusually crowded meeting. My Father, looking whiter and yet darker than usual, called upon Brother Fawkes and Brother Bere to state to the assembled saints what their experiences had been in connection with their visits to 'one' who desired to be admitted to the breaking of bread. It was tremendously exciting for me to hear myself spoken of with this impersonal publicity, and I had no fear of the result.

Events showed that I had no need of fear. Fawkes and Bere were sometimes accused of a rivalry, which indeed broke out a few years later, and gave my Father much anxiety and pain. But on this occasion their unanimity was wonderful. Each strove to exceed the other in the tributes which they paid to my piety. My answers had been so full and clear, my humility (save the mark!) had been so sweet, my acquaintance with Scripture so amazing, my testimony to all the leading principles of salvation so distinct and exhaustive, that they could only say that they had felt confounded, and yet deeply cheered and led far along their own heavenly path, by hearing such accents fall from the lips of a babe and a suckling. I did not like being described as a suckling, but every lot has its crumpled rose-leaf, and in all other respects the report of the elders was a triumph. My Father then clenched the whole matter by rising and announcing that I had expressed an independent desire to confess the Lord by the act of public baptism, immediately after which I should be admitted to communion 'as an adult'. Emotion ran so high at this, that a large portion of the congregation insisted on walking with us back to our garden-gate, to the stupefaction of the rest of the villagers.

My public baptism was the central event of my whole childhood. Everything, since the earliest dawn of consciousness, seemed to have been leading up to it. Everything, afterwards, seemed to be leading down and away from it. The practice of immersing communicants on the sea-beach at Oddicombe had now been completely abandoned, but we possessed as yet no tank for a baptismal purpose in our own Room. The Room in the adjoining town, however, was really quite a large chapel and it was amply provided with the needful conveniences. It was our practice, therefore, at this time, to claim the hospitality of our neighbours. Baptisms were made an occasion for friendly relations between the two congregations, and led to pleasant social intercourse. I believe that the ministers and elders of the two meetings arranged to combine their forces at these times, and to baptize communicants from both congregations.

The minister of the town meeting was Mr S., a very handsome old gentleman, of venerable and powerful appearance. He had snowy hair and a long white beard, but from under shaggy eyebrows there blazed out great black eyes which warned the beholder that the snow was an ornament and not a sign of decrepitude. The eve of my baptism at length drew near; it was fixed for October 12, almost exactly three weeks after my tenth birthday. I was dressed in old clothes, and a suit of smarter things was packed up in a carpet-bag. After a nightfall, this carpet-bag, accompanied by my Father, myself, Miss Marks and Mary Grace, was put in a four-wheeled cab, and driven, a long way in the dark, to the chapel of our friends. There we were received, in a blaze of lights, with a pressure of hands, with a murmur of voices, with ejaculations and even with tears, and were conducted, amid unspeakable emotion, to places of honour in the front row of the congregation.

The scene was one which would have been impressive, not merely to such hermits as we were, but even to worldly persons accustomed to life and to its curious and variegated experiences. To me it was dazzling beyond words, inexpressibly exciting, an initiation to every kind of publicity and glory. There were many candidates, but the rest of them, — mere grown-up men and women, — gave thanks aloud that it was their privilege to follow where I led. I was the acknowledged hero of the hour. Those were days when newspaper enterprise was scarcely in its infancy, and the event owed nothing to journalistic effort. In spite of that, the news of this remarkable ceremony, the immersion of a little boy of ten years old 'as an adult', had spread far and wide through the county in the course of three weeks. The chapel of our hosts was, as I have said, very large; it was commonly too large for their needs, but on this night it was crowded to the ceiling, and the crowd had come — as every soft murmur assured me — to see *me*.

There were people there who had travelled from Exeter, from Dartmouth, from Totnes, to witness so extraordinary a ceremony. There was one old woman of eighty-five who had come, my neighbours whispered to me, all the way from Moreton-Hampstead, on purpose to see me baptized. I looked at her crumpled countenance with amazement, for there was no curiosity, no interest visible in it. She sat there perfectly listless, looking at nothing, but chewing between her toothless gums what appeared to be a jujube.

In the centre of the chapel-floor a number of planks had been taken up, and revealed a pool which might have been supposed to be a small swimming-bath. We gazed down into this dark square of mysterious waters, from the tepid surface of which faint swirls of vapour rose. The whole congregation was arranged, tier above tier, about the four straight sides of this pool; every person was able to see what happened in it without any unseemly struggling or standing on forms. Mr S. now rose, an impressive hieratic figure, commanding attention and imploring perfect silence. He held a small book in his hand, and he was preparing to give out the number of a hymn, when an astounding incident took place.

There was a great splash, and a tall young woman was perceived to be in the baptismal pool, her arms waving above her head, and her figure held upright in the water by the inflation of the air underneath her crinoline which was blown out like a bladder, as in some extravagant old fashion-plate. Whether her feet touched the bottom of the font I cannot say, but I suppose they did so. An indescribable turmoil of shrieks and cries followed on this extraordinary apparition. A great many people excitedly called upon other people to be calm, and an instance was given of the remark of James Smith that

> He who, in quest of quiet, 'Silence!' hoots
> Is apt to make the hubbub he imputes.

The young woman, in a more or less fainting condition, was presently removed from the water, and taken into the sort of tent which was prepared for candidates. It was found that she herself had wished to be a candidate and had earnestly desired to be baptized, but that this had been forbidden by her parents. On the supposition that she fell in by accident, a pious coincidence was detected in this affair; the Lord had pre-ordained that she should be baptized in spite of all opposition. But my Father, in his shrewd way, doubted. He pointed out to us, next morning, that, in the first place, she had not, in any sense, been baptized, as her head had not been immersed; and that, in the second place, she must have deliberately jumped in, since, had she stumbled and fallen forward, her hands and face would have struck the water, whereas they remained quite dry. She belonged, however, to the neighbour congregation, and we had no responsibility to pursue the inquiry any further.

Decorum being again secured, Mr S., with unimpaired dignity, proposed to the congregation a hymn, which was long enough to occupy them during the preparations for the actual baptism. He then retired to the vestry, and I (for I was to be the first to testify) was led by Miss Marks and Mary Grace into the species of tent of which I have just spoken. Its pale sides seemed to shake with the jubilant singing of the saints outside, while part of my clothing was removed and I was prepared for immersion. A sudden cessation of the hymn warned us that the Minister was now ready, and we emerged into the glare of lights and faces to find Mr S. already standing in the water up to his knees. Feeling as small as one of our microscopical specimens, almost infinitesimally tiny as I descended into his Titanic arms, I was handed down the steps to him. He was dressed in a kind of long surplice, underneath which — as I could not, even in that moment, help observing — the air gathered in long bubbles which he strove to flatten out. The end of his noble beard he had tucked away; his shirt-sleeves were turned up at the wrist.

The entire congregation was now silent, so silent that the uncertain splashing of my feet as I descended seemed to deafen me. Mr S., a little embarrassed by my short stature, succeeded at length in securing me with one palm on my chest and the other between my shoulders. He said, slowly, in a loud, sonorous voice that seemed to enter my brain and empty it, 'I baptize thee, my Brother, in the name of the Father and of the Son and of the Holy Ghost!' Having intoned this formula, he then gently flung me backwards until I was wholly under the water, and then — as he brought me up again, and tenderly steadied my feet on the steps of the font, and delivered me, dripping and spluttering, into the anxious hands of the women, who hurried me to the tent — the whole assembly broke forth in a thunder of song, a paean of praise to God for this manifestation of his marvellous goodness and mercy. So great was the enthusiasm, that it could hardly be restrained so as to allow the other candidates, the humdrum adults who followed in my wet and glorious footsteps, to undergo a ritual about which, in their case, no one in the congregation pretended to be able to take even the most languid interest.

My Father's happiness during the next few weeks it is now pathetic to me to look back upon. His sternness melted into a universal complaisance. He laughed and smiled, he paid to my opinions the tribute of the gravest considerations, he indulged — utterly unlike his wont — in shy and furtive caresses. I could express no wish that he did not attempt to fulfil, and the only warning which he cared to give me was one, very gently expressed, against spiritual pride.

This was certainly required, for I was puffed out with a sense of my own holiness. I was religiously confidential with my Father, condescending with Miss Marks (who I think had given up trying to make it all out), haughty with the servants, and insufferably patronizing with those young companions of my own age with whom I was now beginning to associate.

I would fain close this remarkable episode on a key of solemnity, but alas! if I am to be loyal to the truth, I must record that some of the other little boys presently complained to Mary Grace that I put out my tongue at them in mockery, during the service in the Room, to remind them that I now broke bread as one of the Saints and that they did not.

# *Flannery O'Connor*

*from:* A Good Man is Hard to Find

## THE RIVER

The child stood glum and limp in the middle of the dark living room while his father pulled him into a plaid coat. His right arm was hung in the sleeve but the father buttoned the coat anyway and pushed him forward toward a pale spotted hand that stuck through the half-open door.

"He ain't fixed right," a loud voice said from the hall.

"Well then for Christ's sake fix him," the father muttered. "It's six o'clock in the morning." He was in his bathrobe and barefooted. When he got the child to the door and tried to shut it, he found her looming in it, a speckled skeleton in a long pea-green coat and felt helmet.

"And his and my carfare," she said, "It'll be twice we have to ride the car."

He went in the bedroom again to get the money and when he came back, she and the boy were both standing in the middle of the room. She was taking stock. "I couldn't smell those dead cigarette butts long if I was ever to come sit with you," she said, shaking him down in his coat.

"Here's the change," the father said. He went to the door and opened it wide and waited.

After she had counted the money she slipped it somewhere inside her coat and walked over to a watercolor hanging near the phonograph. "I know what time it is," she said, peering closely at the black lines crossing into broken planes of violent color. "I ought to. My shift goes on at 10 p.m. and don't get off till 5 and it takes me one hour to ride the Vine Street car."

"Oh, I see," he said; "well, we'll expect him back tonight, about eight or nine?"

"Maybe later," she said. "We're going to the river to a healing. This particular preacher don't get around this way often. I wouldn't have paid for that," she said, nodding at the painting, "I would have drew it myself."

"All right, Mrs. Connin, we'll see you then," he said, drumming on the door.

A toneless voice called from the bedroom, "Bring me an icepack."

"Too bad his mamma's sick," Mrs. Connin said. "What's her trouble?"

"We don't know," he muttered.

"We'll ask the preacher to pray for her. He's healed a lot of folks. The Reverend Bevel Summers. Maybe she ought to see him sometime."

"Maybe so," he said. "We'll see you tonight," and he disappeared into the bedroom and left them to go.

The little boy stared at her silently, his nose and eyes running. He was four or five. He had a long face and bulging chin and half-shut eyes set far apart. He seemed mute and patient, like an old sheep waiting to be let out.

"You'll like this preacher," she said. "The Reverend Bevel Summers. You ought to hear him sing."

The bedroom door opened suddenly and the father stuck his head out and said, "Good-by, old man. Have a good time."

"Good-by," the little boy said and jumped as if he had been shot.

Mrs. Connin gave the watercolor another look. Then they went out into the hall and rang for the elevator. 'I wouldn't have drew it," she said.

Outside the gray morning was blocked off on either side by the unlit empty buildings. "It's going to fair up later," she said, "but this is the last time we'll be able to have any preaching at the river this year. Wipe your nose, Sugar Boy."

He began rubbing his sleeve across it but she stopped him. "That ain't nice," she said. "Where's your handkerchief?"

He put his hands in his pockets and pretended to look for it while she waited. "Some people don't care how they send one off," she murmured to her reflection in the coffee shop window. "You pervide." She took a red and blue flowered handkerchief out of her pocket and stooped down and began to work on his nose. "Now blow," she said and he blew. "You can borry it. Put it in your pocket."

He folded it up and put it in his pocket carefully and they walked on to the corner and leaned against the side of a closed drugstore to wait for the car. Mrs. Connin turned up her coat collar so that it met her hat in the back. Her eyelids began to droop and she looked as if she might go to sleep against the wall. The little boy put a slight pressure on her hand.

"What's your name?" she asked in a drowsy voice. "I don't know but only your last name. I should have found out your first name."

His name was Harry Ashfield and he had never thought at any time before of changing it. "Bevel," he said.

Mrs. Connin raised herself from the wall. "Why ain't that a coincident!" she said. "I told you that's the name of this preacher!"

"Bevel," he repeated.

She stood looking down at him as if he had become a marvel to her. "I'll have to see you meet him today," she said. "He's no ordinary preacher. He's a healer. He couldn't do nothing for Mr. Connin though. Mr. Connin didn't have the faith but he said he would try anything once. He had this griping in his gut."

The trolley appeared as a yellow spot at the end of the deserted street.

"He's gone to the government hospital now," she said, "and they taken one-third of his stomach. I tell him he better thank Jesus for what he's got left but he says he ain't thanking nobody. Well I declare," she murmured, "Bevel!"

They walked out to the tracks to wait. "Will he heal me?" Bevel asked.

"What you got?"

"I'm hungry," he decided finally.

"Didn't you have your breafast?"

"I didn't have time to be hungry yet then," he said.

"Well when we get home we'll both have us something," she said. "I'm ready myself."

They got on the car and sat down a few seats behind the driver and Mrs. Connin took Bevel on her knees. "Now you be a good boy," she said, "and let me get some sleep. Just don't get off my lap." She lay her head back and as he watched, gradually her eyes closed and her mouth fell open to show a few long scattered teeth, some gold and some darker than her face; she began to whistle and blow like a musical skeleton. There was no one in the car but themselves and the driver and when he saw she was asleep, he took out the flowered handkerchief and unfolded it and examined it carefully. Then he folded it up again and unzipped a place in the innerlining of his coat and hid it in there and shortly he went to sleep himself.

Her house was a half-mile from the end of the car line, set back a little from the road. It was tan paper brick with a porch across the front of it and a tin top. On the porch there were three little boys of different sizes with identical speckled faces and one tall girl who had her hair up in so many aluminium curlers that it glared like the roof. The three boys followed them inside and closed in on Bevel. They looked at him silently, not smiling.

"That's Bevel," Mrs. Connin said, taking off her coat. "It's a coincident he's named the same as the preacher. These boys are J.C., Spivey, and Sinclair, and that's Sarah Mildred on the porch. Take off that coat and hang it on the bed post, Bevel."

The three boys watched him while he unbuttoned the coat and took it off. Then they watched him hang it on the bed post and then they stood, watching the coat. They turned abruptly and went out the door and had a conference on the porch.

Bevel stood looking around him at the room. It was part kitchen and part bedroom. The entire house was two rooms and two porches. Close to his foot the tail of a light-colored dog moved up and down between two floor boards as he scratched his back on the underside of the house. Bevel jumped on it but the hound was experienced and had already withdrawn when his feet hit the spot.

The walls were filled with pictures and calendars. There were two round photographs of an old man and woman with collapsed mouths and another picture of a man whose eyebrows dashed out of two bushes of hair and clashed in a heap on the bridge of his nose; the rest of his face stuck out like a bare cliff to fall from. "That's Mr. Connin," Mrs. Connin said, standing back from the stove for a second to admire the face with him, "but it don't favor him any more." Bevel turned from Mr. Connin to a colored picture over the bed of a man wearing a

137

white sheet. He had long hair and a gold circle around his head and he was sawing on a board while some children stood watching him. He was going to ask who that was when the three boys came in again and motioned for him to follow them. He thought of crawling under the bed and hanging onto one of the legs but the three boys only stood there, speckled and silent, waiting, and after a second he followed them at a little distance out on the porch and around the corner of the house. They started off through a field of rough yellow weeds to the hog pen, a five-foot boarded square full of shoats, which they intended to ease him over into. When they reached it, they turned and waited silently, leaning against the side.

He was coming very slowly, deliberately bumping his feet together as he had trouble walking. Once he had been beaten up in the park by some strange boys when his sitter forgot him, but he hadn't known anything was going to happen that time until it was over. He began to smell a strong odor of garbage and to hear the noises of a wild animal. He stopped a few feet from the pen and waited, pale but dogged.

The three boys didn't move. Something seemed to have happened to them. They stared over his head as if they saw something coming behind him but he was afraid to turn his own head and look. Their speckles were pale and their eyes were still and gray as glass. Only their ears twitched slightly. Nothing happened. Finally, the one in the middle said, "She'd kill us," and turned, dejected and hacked, and climbed up on the pen and hung over, staring in.

Bevel sat down on the ground, dazed with relief, and grinned up at them.

The one sitting on the pen glanced at him severely. "Hey you," he said after a second, "if you can't climb up and see these pigs you can lift that bottom board off and look in thataway." He appeared to offer this as a kindness.

Bevel had never seen a real pig but he had seen a pig in a book and knew they were small fat pink animals with curly tails and round grinning faces and bow ties. He leaned forward and pulled eagerly at the board.

"Pull harder," the littlest boy said. "It's nice and rotten. Just lift out thet nail."

He eased a long reddish nail out of the soft wood.

"Now you can lift up the board and put your face to the . . ." a quiet voice began.

He had already done it and another face, gray, wet and sour, was

138

pushing into his, knocking him down and back as it scraped out under the plank. Something snorted over him and charged back again, rolling him over and pushing him up from behind and then sending him forward, screaming through the yellow field, while it bounded behind.

The three Connins watched from where they were. The one sitting on the pen held the loose board back with his dangling foot. Their stern faces didn't brighten any but they seemed to become less taut, as if some great need had been partly satisfied. "Maw ain't going to like him lettin out thet hawg," the smallest one said.

Mrs. Connin was on the back porch and caught Bevel up as he reached the steps. The hog ran under the house and subsided, panting, but the child screamed for five minutes. When she had finally calmed him down, she gave him his breakfast and let him sit on her lap while he ate it. The shoat climbed the two steps onto the back porch and stood outside the screen door, looking in with his head lowered sullenly. He was long-legged and hump-backed and part of one of his ears had been bitten off.

"Git away!" Mrs. Connin shouted. "That one yonder favors Mr. Paradise that has the gas station," she said. "You'll see him today at the healing. He's got the cancer over his ear. He always comes to show he ain't been healed."

The shoat stood squinting a few seconds longer and then moved off slowly. "I don't want to see him," Bevel said.

They walked to the river, Mrs. Connin in front with him and the three boys strung out behind and Sarah Mildred, the tall girl, at the end to holler if one of them ran out on the road. They looked like the skeleton of an old boat with two pointed ends, sailing slowly on the edge of the highway. The white Sunday sun followed at a little distance, climbing fast through a scum of gray cloud as if it meant to overtake them. Bevel walked on the outside edge, holding Mrs. Connin's hand and looking down into the orange and purple gulley that dropped off from the concrete.

It occurred to him that he was lucky this time that they had found Mrs. Connin who would take you away for the day instead of an ordinary sitter who only sat where you lived or went to the park. You found out more when you left where you lived. He had found out already this morning that he had been made by a carpenter named Jesus Christ. Before he had thought it had been a doctor named

Sladewall, a fat man with a yellow mustache who gave him shots and thought his name was Herbert, but this must have been a joke. They joked a lot where he lived. If he had thought about it before, he would have thought Jesus Christ was a word like "oh" or "damn" or "God," or maybe somebody who had cheated them out of something sometime. When he had asked Mrs. Connin who the man in the sheet in the picture over her bed was, she had looked at him a while with her mouth open. Then she had said, "That's Jesus," and she had kept on looking at him.

In a few minutes she had got up and got a book out of the other room. "See here," she said, turning over the cover, "this belonged to my great grandmamma. I wouldn't part with it for nothing on earth." She ran her finger under some brown writing on a spotted page. "Emma Stevens Oakley, 1832," she said. "Ain't that something to have? And every word of it the gospel truth." She turned the next page and read him the name: "The Life of Jesus Christ for Readers Under Twelve." Then she read him the book.

It was a small book, pale brown on the outside with gold edges and a smell like old putty. It was full of pictures, one of the carpenter driving a crowd of pigs out of a man. They were real pigs, gray and sour-looking, and Mrs. Connin said Jesus had driven them all out of this one man. When she finished reading, she let him sit on the floor and look at the pictures again.

Just before they left for the healing, he had managed to get the book inside his innerlining without her seeing him. Now it made his coat hang down a little farther on one side than the other. His mind was dreamy and serene as they walked along and when they turned off the highway onto a long red clay road winding between banks of honeysuckle, he began to make wild leaps and pull forward on her hand as if he wanted to dash off and snatch the sun which was rolling away ahead of them now.

They walked on the dirt road for a while and then they crossed a field stippled with purple weeds and entered the shadows of a wood where the ground was covered with thick pine needles. He had never been in woods before and he walked carefully, looking from side to side as if he were entering a strange country. They moved along a bridle-path that twisted downhill through crackling red leaves, and once, catching at a branch to keep himself from slipping, he looked into two frozen green-gold eyes enclosed in the darkness of a tree hole. At the bottom of the hill, the woods opened suddenly onto a pasture dotted here and there with black and white cows and sloping down, tier after tier, to a broad orange stream where the reflection of the sun was set like a diamond.

There were people standing on the near bank in a group, singing. Long tables were set up behind them and a few cars and trucks were parked in a road that came up by the river. They crossed the pasture, hurrying, because Mrs. Connin, using her hand for a shed over her eyes, saw the preacher already standing out in the water. She dropped her basket on one of the tables and pushed the three boys in front of her into the knot of people so that they wouldn't linger by the food. She kept Bevel by the hand and eased her way up to the front.

The preacher was standing about ten feet out in the stream where the water came up to his knees. He was a tall youth in khaki trousers that he had rolled up higher than the water. He had on a blue shirt and a red scarf around his neck but no hat and his light-colored hair was cut in sideburns that curved into the hollows of his cheeks. His face was all bone and red light reflected from the river. He looked as if he might have been nineteen years old. He was singing in a high twangy voice, above the singing on the bank, and he kept his hands behind him and his head tilted back.

He ended the hymn on a high note and stood silent, looking down at the water and shifting his feet in it. Then he looked up at the people on the bank. They stood close together, waiting; their faces were solemn but expectant and every eye was on him. He shifted his feet again.

"Maybe I know why you come," he said in the twangy voice, "maybe I don't."

"If you ain't come for Jesus, you ain't come for me. If you just come to see can you leave your pain in the river, you ain't come for Jesus. You can't leave your pain in the river," he said. "I never told nobody that." He stopped and looked down at his knees.

"I seen you cure a woman once!" a sudden high voice shouted from the hump of people. "Seen that woman git up and walk out straight where she had limped in!"

The preacher lifted one foot and then the other. He seemed almost but not quite to smile. "You might as well go home if that's what you come for," he said.

Then he lifted his head and arms and shouted, "Listen to what I got to say, you people! There ain't but one river and that's the River of Life, made out of Jesus' Blood. That's the river you have to lay your pain in, in the River of Faith, in the River of Life, in the River of Love,

141

in the rich red river of Jesus' Blood, you people!"

His voice grew soft and musical. "All the rivers come from that one River and go back to it like it was the ocean sea and if you believe, you can lay your pain in that River and get rid of it because that's the River that was made to carry sin. It's a River full of pain itself, pain itself, moving toward the Kingdom of Christ, to be washed away, slow, you people, slow at this here old red water river round my feet.

"Listen," he sang, "I read in Mark about an unclean man, I read in Luke about a blind man, I read in John about a dead man! Oh you people hear! The same blood that makes this River red, made that leper clean, made that blind man stare, made that dead man leap! You people with trouble," he cried, "lay it in that River of Blood, lay it in that River of Pain, and watch it move away toward the Kingdom of Christ."

While he preached, Bevel's eyes followed drowsily the slow circles of two silent birds revolving high in the air. Across the river there was a low red and gold grove of sassafras with hills of dark blue trees behind it and an occasional pine jutting over the skyline. Behind, in the distance, the city rose like a cluster of warts on the side of the mountain. The birds revolved downward and dropped lightly in the top of the highest pine and sat hunch-shouldered as if they were supporting the sky.

"If it's this River of Life you want to lay your pain in, then come up," the preacher said, "and lay your sorrow here. But don't be thinking this is the last of it because this old red river don't end here. This old red suffering stream goes on, you people, slow to the Kingdom of Christ. This old red river is good to Baptize in, good to lay your faith in, good to lay your pain in, but it ain't this muddy water here that saves you. I been all up and down this river this week," he said. "Tuesday I was in Fortune Lake, next day in Ideal, Friday me and my wife drove to Lulawillow to see a sick man there. Them people didn't see no healing," he said and his face burned redder for a second. "I never said they would."

While he was talking a fluttering figure had begun to move forward with a kind of butterfly movement — an old woman with flapping arms whose head wobbled as if it might fall off any second. She managed to lower herself at the edge of the bank and let her arms churn in the water. Then she bent farther and pushed her face down in it and raised herself up finally, streaming wet; and still flapping, she turned a time or two in a blind circle until someone reached out and

142

pulled her back into the group.

"She's been that way for thirteen years," a rough voice shouted. "Pass the hat and give this kid his money. That's what he's here for." The shout, directed out to the boy in the river, came from a huge old man who sat like a humped stone on the bumper of a long ancient gray automobile. He had on a gray hat that was turned down over one ear and up over the other to expose a purple bulge on his left temple. He sat bent forward with his hands hanging between his knees and his small eyes half closed.

Bevel stared at him once and then moved into the folds of Mrs. Connin's coat and hid himself.

The boy in the river glanced at the man quickly and raised his fist. "Believe Jesus or the devil!" he cried. "Testify to one or the other!"

"I know from my own self-experience," a woman's mysterious voice called from the knot of people, "I know from it that this preacher can heal. My eyes have been opened! I testify to Jesus!"

The preacher lifted his arms quickly and began to repeat all that he had said before about the River and the Kingdom of Christ and the old man sat on the bumper, fixing him with a narrow squint. From time to time Bevel stared at him again from around Mrs. Connin.

A man in overalls and a brown coat leaned forward and dipped his hand in the water quickly and shook it and leaned back, and a woman held a baby over the edge of the bank and splashed its feet with water. One man moved a little distance away and sat down on the bank and took off his shoes and waded out into the stream; he stood there for a few minutes with his face tilted as far back as it would go, then he waded back and put on his shoes. All this time, the preacher sang and did not appear to watch what went on.

As soon as he stopped singing, Mrs. Connin lifted Bevel up and said, "Listen here, preacher, I got a boy from town today that I'm keeping. His mamma's sick and he wants you to pray for her. And this is a coincident — his name is Bevel! Bevel," she said, turning to look at the people behind her, "same as his. Ain't that a coincident, though?"

There were some murmurs and Bevel turned and grinned over her shoulder at the faces looking at him. "Bevel," he said in a loud jaunty voice.

"Listen," Mrs. Connin said, "have you ever been Baptized, Bevel?"

He only grinned.

"I suspect he ain't ever been Baptized," Mrs. Connin said, raising her eyebrows at the preacher.

"Swang him over here," the preacher said and took a stride forward and caught him.

He held him in the crook of his arm and looked at the grinning face. Bevel rolled his eyes in a comical way and thrust his face forward, close to the preacher's. "My name is Bevvvuuuuul," he said in a loud deep voice and let the tip of his tongue slide across his mouth.

The preacher didn't smile. His bony face was rigid and his narrow gray eyes reflected the almost colorless sky. There was a loud laugh from the old man sitting on the car bumper and Bevel grasped the back of the preacher's collar and held it tightly. The grin had already disappeared from his face. He had the sudden feeling that this was not a joke. Where he lived everything was a joke. From the preacher's face, he knew immediately that nothing the preacher said or did was a joke. "My mother named me that," he said quickly.

"Have you even been Baptized?" the preacher asked.

"What's that?" he murmured.

"If I Baptize you," the preacher said, "you'll be able to go to the Kingdom of Christ. You'll be washed in the river of suffering, son, and you'll go by the deep river of life. Do you want that?"

"Yes," the child said, and thought, I won't go back to the apartment then, I'll go under the river.

"You won't be the same again," the preacher said. "You'll count." Then he turned his face to the people and began to preach and Bevel looked over his shoulder at the pieces of the white sun scattered in the river. Suddenly the preacher said, "All right, I'm going to Baptize you now," and without more warning, he tightened his hold and swung him upside down and plunged his head into the water. He held him under while he said the words of Baptism and then he jerked him up again and looked sternly at the gasping child. Bevel's eyes were dark and dilated. "You count now," the preacher said. "You didn't even count before."

The little boy was too shocked to cry. He spit out the muddy water and rubbed his wet sleeve into his eyes and over his face.

"Don't forget his mamma," Mrs. Connin called. "He wants you to pray for his mamma. She's sick."

"Lord," the preacher said, "we pray for somebody in affliction who isn't here to testify. Is your mother sick in the hospital?" he asked. "Is she in pain?"

The child stared at him. "She hasn't got up yet," he said in a high dazed voice. "She has a hangover." The air was so quiet he could hear the broken pieces of the sun knocking in the water.

The preacher looked angry and startled. The red drained out of his face and the sky appeared to darken in his eyes. There was a loud guffaw from the bank and Mr Paradise shouted, "Haw! Cure the afflicted woman with the hangover!" and began to beat his knee with his fist.

"He's had a long day," Mrs. Connin said, standing with him in the door of the apartment and looking sharply into the room where the party was going on. "I reckon it's past his regular bedtime." One of Bevel's eyes was closed and the other half closed; his nose was running and he kept his mouth open and breathed through it. The damp plaid coat dragged down on one side.

That would be her, Mrs. Connin decided, in the black britches — long black satin britches and barefoot sandals and red toenails. She was lying on half the sofa, with her knees crossed in the air and her head propped on the arm. She didn't get up.

"Hello Harry," she said. "Did you have a big day?" She had a long pale face, smooth and blank, and straight sweet-potato-coloured hair, pulled back.

The father went off to get the money. There were two other couples. One of the men, blond with little violet-blue eyes, leaned out of his chair and said, "Well Harry, old man, have a big day?"

"His name ain't Harry. It's Bevel," Mrs. Connin said.

"His name is Harry," *she* said from the sofa. "Whoever heard of anybody named Bevel?"

The little boy had seemed to be going to sleep on his feet, his head drooping farther and farther forward; he pulled it back suddenly and opened one eye; the other was stuck.

"He told me this morning his name was Bevel," Mrs. Connin said in a shocked voice. "The same as our preacher. We been all day at a preaching and healing at the river. He said his name was Bevel, the same as the preacher's. That's what he told me."

"Bevel!" his mother said. "My God! what a name."

"This preacher is name Bevel and there's no better preacher around," Mrs. Connin said. "And furthermore," she added in a defiant tone, "he Baptized this child this morning!"

His mother sat straight up. "Well the nerve!" she muttered.

"Furthermore," Mrs. Connin said, "he's a healer and he prayed for you to be healed."

"Healed!" she almost shouted. "Healed of what for Christ's sake?" "Of your affliction," Mrs. Connin said icily.

The father had returned with the money and was standing near Mrs. Connin waiting to give it to her. His eyes were lined with red threads. "Go on, go on," he said, "I want to hear more about her affliction. The exact nature of it has escaped . . ." He waved the bill and his voice trailed off. "Healing by prayer is mighty inexpensive," he murmured.

Mrs. Connin stood a second, staring into the room, with a skeleton's appearance of seeing everything. Then, without taking the money, she turned and shut the door behind her. The father swung around, smiling vaguely, and shrugged. The rest of them were looking at Harry. The little boy began to shamble toward the bedroom.

"Come here, Harry," his mother said. He automatically shifted his direction toward her without opening his eye any farther. "Tell me what happened today," she said when he reached her. She began to pull off his coat.

"I don't know," he muttered.

"Yes you do know," she said, feeling the coat heavier on one side. She unzipped the innerlining and caught the book and a dirty handkerchief as they fell out. "Where did you get these?"

"I don't know," he said and grabbed for them. "They're mine. She gave them to me."

She threw the handkerchief down and held the book too high for him to reach and began to read it, her face after a second assuming an exaggerated comical expression. The others moved around and looked at it over her shoulder. "My God," somebody said.

One of the men peered at it sharply from behind a thick pair of glasses. "That's valuable," he said. "That's a collector's item," and he took it away from the rest of them and retired to another chair.

"Don't let George go off with that," his girl said.

"I tell you it's valuable," George said. "1832."

Bevel shifted his direction again toward the room where he slept. He shut the door behind him and moved slowly in the darkness to the bed and sat down and took off his shoes and got under the cover. After a minute a shaft of light let in the tall silhouette of his mother. She tiptoed lightly across the room and sat down on the edge of his bed. "What did that dolt of a preacher say about me?" she whispered. "What lies have you been telling today, honey?"

He shut his eye and heard her voice from a long way away, as he were under the river and she on top of it. She shook his shoulder. "Harry," she said, leaning down and putting her mouth to his ear, "tell me what he said." She pulled him into a sitting position and he felt as if he had been drawn up from under the river. "Tell me," she whispered and her bitter breath covered his face.

He saw the pale oval close to him in the dark. "He said I'm not the same now," he muttered. "I count."

After a second, she lowered him by his shirt front onto the pillow. She hung over him an instant and brushed her lips against his forehead. Then she got up and moved away, swaying her hips lightly through the shaft of light.

He didn't wake up early but the apartment was still dark and close when he did. For a while he lay there, picking his nose and eyes. Then he sat up in bed and looked out of the window. The sun came in palely, stained gray by the glass. Across the street at the Empire Hotel, a colored cleaning woman was looking down from an upper window, resting her face on her folded arms. He got up and put on his shoes and went to the bathroom and then into the front room. He ate two crackers spread with anchovy paste, that he found on the coffee table, and drank some ginger ale left in a bottle and looked around for his book but it was not there.

The apartment was silent except for the faint humming of the refrigerator. He went into the kitchen and found some raisin bread heels and spread a half jar of peanut butter between them and climbed up on the tall kitchen stool and sat chewing the sandwich slowly, wiping his nose every now and then on his shoulder. When he finished he found some chocolate milk and drank that. He would rather have had the ginger ale he saw but they left the bottle openers where he couldn't reach them. He studied what was left in the refrigerator for a while — some shriveled vegetables that she had forgot were there and a lot of brown oranges that she bought and didn't squeeze; there were three or four kinds of cheese and something fishy in a paper bag; the rest was a pork bone. He left the refrigerator door open and wandered back into the dark living room and sat down on the sofa.

He decided they would be out cold until one o'clock and that they would all have to go to a restaurant for lunch. He wasn't high enough for the table yet and the waiter would bring a highchair and he was too big for a highchair. He sat in the middle of the sofa, kicking it with his heels. Then he got up and wandered around the room, looking into the ashtrays at the butts as if this might be a habit. In his own room he had picture books and blocks but they were for the most part torn up; he found the way to get new ones was to tear up the ones he had. There was very little to do at any time but eat; however, he was not a fat boy.

He decided he would empty a few of the ashtrays on the floor. If he only emptied a few, she would think they had fallen. He emptied two, rubbing the ashes carefully into the rug with his finger. Then he lay on the floor for a while, studying his feet which he held up in the air. His shoes were still damp and he began to think about the river.

Very slowly, his expression changed as if he were gradually seeing appear what he didn't know he'd been looking for. Then all of a sudden he knew what he wanted to do.

He got up and tiptoed into their bedroom and stood in the dim light there, looking for her pocketbook. His glance passed her long pale arm hanging off the edge of the bed down to the floor, and across the white mound his father made, and past the crowded bureau, until it rested on the pocketbook hung on the back of a chair. He took a car-token out of it and half a package of Life Savers. Then he left the apartment and caught the car at the corner. He hadn't taken a suitcase because there was nothing from there he wanted to keep.

He got off the car at the end of the line and started down the road he and Mrs. Connin had taken the day before. He knew there wouldn't be anybody at her house because the three boys and the girl went to school and Mrs. Connin had told him she went out to clean. He passed her yard and walked on the way they had gone to the river. The paper brick houses were far apart and after a while the dirt place to walk on ended and he had to walk on the edge of the highway. The sun was pale yellow and high and hot.

He passed a shack with an orange gas pump in front of it but he didn't see the old man looking out at nothing in particular from the doorway. Mr. Paradise was having an orange drink. He finished it slowly, squinting over the bottle at the small plaid-coated figure disappearing down the road. Then he set the empty bottle on a bench and, still squinting, wiped his sleeve over his mouth. He went in the shack and picked out a peppermint stick, a foot long and two inches thick, from the candy shelf, and stuck it in his hip pocket. Then he got in his car and drove slowly down the highway after the boy.

By the time Bevel came to the field speckled with purple weeds, he was dusty and sweating and he crossed it at a trot to get into the woods as fast as he could. Once inside, he wandered from tree to tree, trying to find the path they had taken yesterday. Finally he found a line worn in the pine needles and followed it until he saw the steep trail twisting down under the trees.

Mr. Paradise had left his automobile back some way on the road and had walked to the place where he was accustomed to sit almost every day, holding an unbaited fishline in the water while he stared at the river passing in front of him. Anyone looking at him from a distance would have seen an old boulder half hidden in the bushes.

Bevel didn't see him at all. He only saw the river, shimmering reddish yellow, and bounded into it with his shoes and his coat on and took a gulp. He swallowed some and spit the rest out and then stood there in water up to his chest and looked around him. The sky was a clear pale blue, all in one piece — except for the hole the sun made — and fringed around the bottom with treetops. His coat floated to the surface and surrounded him like a strange gay lily pad and he stood grinning in the sun. He intended not to fool with preachers any more but to Baptize himself and to keep on going this time until he found the Kingdom of Christ in the river. He didn't mean to waste any more time. He put his head under the water at once and pushed forward.

In a second he began to gasp and sputter and his head reappeared on the surface; he started under again and the same thing happened. The river wouldn't have him. He tried again and came up, choking. This was the way it had been when the preacher held him under — he had had to fight with something that pushed him back in the face. He stopped and thought suddenly: it's another joke, it's just another joke! He thought how far he had come for nothing and he began to hit and splash and kick the filthy river. His feet were already treading on nothing. He gave one low cry of pain and indignation. Then he heard a shout and turned his head and saw something like a giant pig bounding after him shaking a red and white club and shouting. He plunged under once and this time, the waiting current caught him like a long gentle hand and pulled him swiftly forward and down. For an instant he was overcome with surprise; then since he was moving quickly and knew that he was getting somewhere, all his fury and his fear left him.

Mr. Paradise's head appeared from time to time on the surface of the water. Finally, far downstream, the old man rose like some ancient water monster and stood empty-handed, staring with his dull eyes as far down the river line as he could see.

# Mary McCarthy

*from:* Memories of a Catholic Girlhood

## C'EST LE PREMIER PAS QUI COÛTE

I came back in the autumn, as a full-time boarder, with a certain set to my jaw, determined to go it alone. A summer passed in thoughtful isolation, rowing on a mountain lake, diving from a pier, had made me perfectly reckless. I was going to get myself recognized at whatever price. It was in this cold, empty gambler's mood, common to politicians and adolescents, that I surveyed the convent set-up. If I could not win fame by goodness, I was ready to do it by badness, and I looked to the past for precedents. Anything that had happened once in a Sacred Heart convent became, so to speak, fossilized in the institutions of the order. Once, long ago, perhaps here or in Bruges or Chicago or nineteenth-century France, a girl had eloped with the music master, so now our piano lessons were chaperoned by a fat sister, one of the domestics, who reclined, snoring gently, in a chair just behind the Baron's. For a few weeks during the autumn, the prospect of an elopement held first claim on my thoughts. My twelve-year-old hands trembled with hope whenever, in the stretch of an octave, they grazed the white hands of the professor; he had a few little blond glinting hairs on his plump fingers, which seemed to hint of virility dormant but vibrato, like the sleeping nun. I grew faint when my laced shoe encountered his spatted Oxford on the loud pedal. Examples of child marriages among the feudal nobility crowded through my head, as if to encourage the Baron, but at length I had to bow to the force of American custom and face it: he probably thought I was too young.

The decision to lose my faith followed swiftly on this disappointment. People are always asking me how I came to lose my faith, imagining a period of deep inward struggle. The truth is the whole momentous project simply jumped at me, ready-made, out of one of Madame MacIllvra's discourses. I had decided to do it before I knew what it was, when it was merely an interweaving of words, lose-your-faith, like the ladder made of sheets on which the daring girl had descended into the arms of her Romeo. 'Say you've lost your faith,' the devil prompted, assuring me that there was no risk if I chose my moment carefully. Starting Monday morning, we were going to have a retreat, to be preached by a stirring Jesuit. If I lost my faith on, say, Sunday, I could regain it during the three days of retreat, in time for Wednesday confessions. Thus there would be only four days in which my soul would be in danger if I should happen to die suddenly. The only real sacrifice would be foregoing Communion on Sunday. He who hesitates is lost; *qui ne risque rien n'a rien*, observed the devil, lapsing into French, as is his wont. If I did not do it, someone else might — that awful Beryl, for instance. It was a miracle that someone had not thought of it already, the idea seemed so obvious, like a store waiting to be robbed.

Surprised looks were bent on me Sunday morning in the chapel when the line formed for Communion and I knelt unmoving in my pew. I was always an ostentatious communicant. Now girls clambered over me, somebody gave me a poke, but I shook my head sorrowfully, signifying by my expression that I was in a state of mortal sin and dared not approach the table. At lunch, eating little, I was already a centre of attention at my table; I maintained a mournful silence, rehearsing what I would say to Madame MacIllvra in her office as soon as the meal was over. Having put in my request for an appointment, I was beginning to be slightly frightened. After lunch, as I stood waiting outside her door, I kept licking my lips. Yet this fear, I argued, was a token of sincerity; naturally you would be frightened if you had just lost your faith.

'*Ma Mère,* I have lost my faith.' At her roll-top desk, Madame MacIllvra started; one plump white hand fluttered to her heart. She gave me a single searching look. Evidently, my high standing in my studies had prepared her for this catastrophe, for she did not ransack me further as I stood there quaking and bowing and trying to repress a foolish giveaway grin. I had been expecting a long questioning, but she reached, sighing, for the telephone, as though I had appendicitis or the measles.

'Pray, my child,' she murmured as she summoned Father Dennis, our chaplain, from the neighbouring Jesuit college. 'I can't pray,' I promptly responded. A classical symptom of unbelief was the inability to pray, as I knew from her own lectures. Madame MacIllvra nodded, turning a shade paler; she glanced at the watch in her bosom. 'Go to your room,' she said perturbedly. 'You are not to speak to anyone. You will be sent for when Father Dennis comes. I will pray for you myself.'

Some of her alarm had communicated itself to me. I had not realized that what I had said was so serious. I felt quite frightened now by what I had done and by the prospect of a talk with Father Dennis, who was an old, dry, forbidding man, very different from the handsome missionary father who was going to preach our retreat. The idea of backing down presented itself with more and more attraction, but I did not see how I could do this without being convicted of shallowness. Moreover, I doubted very much that Madame MacIllvra would believe me if I said now that I had got my faith back all at once. She would make me talk to Father Dennis anyway. Once the convent machinery had got into motion, there was no way of stopping it, as I knew from horrendous experience. It was like the mills of the gods.

By the time I reached my cubicle I was thoroughly scared. I saw that I was going to have to go through with this or be exposed before them all as a liar, and for the first time it occurred to me that I would have to have arguments to make my doubts sound real. At the same shaken moment I realized that I knew nothing whatever of atheism. If I were out in the world, I could consult the books that had been written on the subject, but here in the convent, obviously, there could be no access to atheistic literature. From the playground outside floated the voices of the girls, laughing. I went to the window and looked down at them, feeling utterly cut off and imprisoned within my own emptiness. There was no one to turn to but God, yet this was one occasion when prayer would be unavailing. A prayer for atheistic arguments (surely?) would only bring out the stern side of God. What was I going to do?

I sat down on my bed and tried to count my resources. After all, I said to myself suddenly, I did know something about scepticism, thanks to Madame MacIllvra herself. The sceptics' arguments were based on science — false science, said Madame MacIllvra — which reasoned that there was no God because you could not see Him. This was a silly materialistc 'proof' to which, unfortunately, I knew the answer. Could you see the wind? And yet its touch was everywhere, like God's invisible grace blowing on our souls. Sceptics denied the life after death and said there was no Heaven, only the blue of space in the celestial vault. Science proved that, they said, and science proved, too, that there was no Hell burning under the earth. We had had the answer to that one, only last week in Christian Doctrine, in Saint Paul's steely words, which we had had to memorize: 'That eye hath not seen, nor ear heard, neither hath it entered into the heart of man, what things God hath prepared for them that love Him.' I sank into a dull despair. Was I going to have to offer 'proofs' that any fool could see through? Any fool knew that man's scientific calipers could not grasp God directly. Hell and Heaven were not contradictory to science but something different altogether, beyond science. But what about miracles?

I sat up suddenly. Miracles were not invisible. They were supposed to happen right here on earth, today. They were attested in the photographs of Lourdes by all the crutches hanging up in token of thankfulness for cures. Nevertheless, I said to myself delightedly, *I* had never seen a miracle, and perhaps all these people were lying or deluded. Christian Science claimed cures, too, and we knew that that was just imagination. Voltaire was an intelligent man and he had laughed at miracles. Why not I?

As I sat there searching my memory, doubts that I had hurriedly stowed away, like contraband in a bureau drawer, came back to me, reassuringly. I found that I had always been a little suspicious of the life after death. Perhaps it was really true that the dead just rotted and I would never rejoin my parents in Heaven? I scratched a spot on my uniform watching it turn white under my thumb-nail. Another memory was tapping at my consciousness: the question of the Resurrection of the Body. At the last trump, all the bodies of men, from Adam onward, were supposed to leap from their graves and rejoin the souls that had left them; this was why the Church forbade cremation. But somewhere, not so long ago, I had heard a priest quote scornfully a materialistic argument against this. The materialist said (yes, that was it!) that people rotted and turned into fertilizer, which went into vegetables, and then other people ate the vegetables, so that when the Resurrection came there would not be enough bodies to go around. The priest answered that for God, anything was possible; if God made man from clay, He could certainly make some extra bodies. But in that case, I thought, pouncing, why did He object to cremation? And in any case they would not be the *same* bodies, which was the whole point. And I could think of an even stronger instance: What about cannibals? If God divided the cannibal into the component bodies he had digested, what would become of the cannibal? God could start with whatever flesh the cannibal had had when he was a baby, before he began eating missionaries, but if his father and mother had been cannibals too, what flesh would he really have that he could call his own?

At that time, I did not know that this problem had been treated by Aquinas, and with a child's pertinacity, I mined away at the foundations of the Fortress Rock. Elation had replaced fear. I could hardly wait now to meet Father Dennis and confront him with these doubts, so remarkable in one of my years. Parallels with the young Jesus, discoursing with the scribes and doctors, bounded through my head: 'And all that heard Him were astonished at His Wisdom and His answers.' No one now, I felt certain, would dare accuse me of faking. I strolled along proudly with the messenger who had come to fetch me; just as her knock sounded, I had reached the stage of doubting the divinity of Christ. I could see in the wondering looks this Iris was shedding on me that already I was a credit to the milieu.

In the dark parlour, the priest was waiting, still in his cassock — a wrinkled, elderly man with a hairless face and brown, dead curly hair that looked like a wig. He had a weary, abstracted air as he turned away from the window, as though he had spent his life in the confessional box. His voice was hollow; everything about him was colourless and dry. As chaplain to Madame MacIllvra, he must have become a sort of spiritual factotum, like an upper servant in an apron, and there was despondency in his manner, as though his *Nunc Dimittis* would never be pronounced. It was clear that he did not have the resilience of our clever nuns.

'You have doubts, Mother says,' he began in a low, listless voice, pointing me to a straight chair opposite him and then seating himself in an arm-chair, with half-averted face, as priests do in the confessional. I nodded self-importantly. 'Yes, Father,' I recited. 'I doubt the divinity of Christ and the Resurrection of the Body and the real existence of Heaven and Hell.' The priest raised his scanty eyebrows, like two little wigs, and sighed. 'You have been reading atheistic literature?' I shook my head. 'No, Father. The doubts came all by themselves.' The priest cupped his chin in his hand. 'So,' he murmured. 'Let us have them then.'

I was hurt when he interrupted me right in the middle of the cannibals. 'These are scholastic questions,' he said curtly. 'Beyond the reach of your years. Believe me, the Church has an answer for them.' A feeling of disappointment came over me; it seemed to me that I had a right to know the answer to the cannibal question, since I had thought it up all by myself, but my 'Why can't I know nows' were brushed aside, just as though I had been asking about how babies were born. 'No,' said Father Dennis, with finality. My first excitement was punctured and I began to be suspicious of him, in the manner of adolescents. What, I asked myself shrewdly, was the Church trying to hide from me?

'Let us come to more important matters.' He leaned forward in his chair, with the first sign of interest he had given. 'You doubt the divinity of Our Lord?' I felt a peculiar avidity in his question that made we wish to hold back. A touch of fear returned to me. 'I *think* so,' I said dubiously, half ready to abandon my ground. '*Think!* Don't you know?' he demanded, raising his voice like a frail thunderbolt. Quailing, I produced my doubt — I was one of those cowards who are afraid not to be brave. Nevertheless, I spoke hurriedly, in gulps, as if swallowing medicine. 'We are supposed to know that He was God because He rose from the dead — that was His sign to us that He was more than man. But you can't prove that He rose from the dead. That's only what the Apostles said. How do we know they were telling the truth? They were very ignorant, superstitious men — just fishermen, weren't they? People like that nowadays believe in fairies and spirits.' I looked appealingly up at him, half begging recognition for my doubt and half waiting for him to settle it.

The priest passed a hand across his forehead. 'You consider Our Lord a liar, then?' he said in a sepulchral tone. 'You think He deceived the poor, ignorant Apostles by pretending to be the Son of God. That is what you are saying, my child, though you do not know it yourself. You are calling Our Blessed Saviour a liar and a cheat.' 'He might have been mistaken,' I objected, feeling rather cross. 'He might have *thought* He was God.' Father Dennis closed his eyes. 'You must have faith, my child,' he said abruptly, rising from his chair and taking a few quick steps, his cassock bobbing.

I gazed at him in humble perplexity. For the first time, he seemed to me rather holy, as if the word 'faith' had elicited something sweet and sanctified from his soul, but by the same token he seemed very remote from me, as if he were feeling something that I was unable to feel. Yet he was not answering my arguments; in fact, he was looking down at me with a grave, troubled expression, as if he, too, were suddenly conscious of a gulf between us, a gulf that could not be bridged by words. The awesome thought struck me that perhaps I *had* lost my faith. Could it have slipped away without my knowing it? 'Help me, Father,' I implored meekly, aware that this was the right thing to say but meaning it nevertheless.

I seemed to have divided into two people, one slyly watching as the priest sank back into the arm-chair, the other anxious and aghast at the turn the interview was taking. 'The wisdom and goodness of Jesus,' Father Dennis said slowly, 'as we find it in His life and teachings — do you think mere man was capable of *this*?' I pondered. 'Why not?' I queried, soberly. But the priest glanced at me with reproach, as if I were being fresh. 'You don't know your history, I see. Among the prophets and the pagans, among the kings and philosophers, among the saints and scholars, was there ever such a One?' A little smile glinted in the corners of his mouth. 'No,' I admitted. The priest nodded. 'There, you see, my child. Such a departure from our ordinary human nature signifies the Divine intervention. If we had only Christ's teaching, we could know that He was God. But in addition we have His miracles, the firm assurance of tradition, and the Living Church, the Rock on which He built and which survived the buffets of the ages, where the false religions foundered and were lost to the mind of man.'

He took out his watch and peered at it in the dusk. My pride, again, was offended. 'It's not only good things that survive,' I said boldly. 'There's sin, for instance.' 'The devil is eternal,' said Father Dennis, sighing, with a quick glance at me.

'But then the Church could be the instrument of the devil, couldn't it?' Father Dennis swooped. 'Then the teaching of Jesus, which it guards, are of diabolical origin?' I flushed. 'Other religions have lasted,' I said, retreating. 'The Jewish religion and Mohammedanism. Is that because they are diabolic?' I spoke with an air of ingenuousness, but I knew I had him in a corner; there were Jewish girls in the convent. 'They had a partial truth,' Father Dennis murmured. 'Hence they have been preserved.' I became impatient with this sparring, which was taking me away from a real point I had glimpsed. 'Yes, Father,' I said. 'But still I don't see that the fact that Christ was an exception proves that He was God.' 'There are no exceptions in nature,' retorted Father Dennis. 'Oh, Father!' I cried. 'I can think of lots.'

I was burning to pursue this subject, for it had come to me, slowly, that Christ really *could* have been a man. The idea of Christ as simply man had something extraordinary and joyous about it that was different, I perceived, from the condescension of God to the flesh. I was glad I had started this discussion, for I was learning something new every second. All fear had left me and all sense of mere wilful antagonism. I was intent on showing Father Dennis the new possibilities that opened; my feeling for him was comradely.

But once more he shut me off. 'You must accept what I tell you,' he said, almost sharply. 'You are too young to understand these things. You must have faith.' 'But you're supposed to give me faith, Father,' I protested. 'Only God can do that,' he answered. 'Pray, and He will grant it.' 'I can't pray,' I said automatically. 'You know your prayers,' he said. 'Say them.' He rose, and I made my curtsy. 'Father!' I cried out suddenly, in desperation at the way he was leaving me. 'There's something else!'

He turned back, fatiguedly, but the wild look on my face must have alarmed him. 'What is it, my child?' he came a little nearer, peering at me with a concerned, kindly expression. 'My child,' he said gravely, 'do you doubt the existence of God?' 'Yes,' I breathed, in exultant agony, knowing that it was true.

He sat down with me again and took my hand. Very gently, seeing that this was what I seemed to want from him, he recited for me the five *a posteriori* proofs of God's existence: the argument of the unmoved Mover, the argument of efficient causes, the argument of the Necessary Being implied by contingent beings, the argument of graduated perfections, the argument of the wonderful order and design in the universe. Most of what he said I did not understand, but the gist was clear to me. It was that every effect must have a cause and the cause was, of course, God. The universe could not exist unless some self-sufficient Being had created it and put it in motion. I listened earnestly, trying to test what he said, almost convinced and yet not quite. It was as though the spirit of doubt had wormed its way into the very tissue of my thinking, so that axioms that had seemed simple and clear only an hour or so before now became perplexing and murky. 'Why, Father,' I asked finally, 'does everything *have* to have a cause? Why couldn't the universe just be there, causing itself?'

Father Dennis lit the lamp on the table beside him; the bell rang for *goûter;* a girl poked her head in and hurriedly withdrew. 'Because,' he said patiently, 'I have just explained to you, every effect must have a proportionate cause.' I turned this over in my head, reminding myself that I was a child and that he probably thought I did not comprehend him. 'Except God,' I repeated helpfully. The priest nodded. 'But, Father,' I cried, with a sudden start of discovery, 'why can't the universe be self-sufficient if God can? Why can't something in matter be the uncaused cause? Like electricity?'

The priest shook his head sorrowfully. 'I cannot tell you, my child.' He dropped into a different tone, caustic and reproachful. 'I cannot

157

open eyes that blindly refuse to see. Can inert matter give birth to spirit? Did inert matter give you your conscience? Who deny causal necessity make the world a chaos where vice and anarchy reign!' His hollow voice reverberated as if he were addressing a whole dockful of secular philosophers, arraigned in a corner of the room. 'Oh, my child,' he concluded, rising, 'give up reading that atheistic filth. Pray to God for faith and make a good confession.' He left the room swiftly, his cassock swelling behind him.

Father Dennis's failure made a great impression on the convent. Wherever I went, eyes regarded me respectfully: there went the girl a Jesuit had failed to convince. The day girls and five-day boarders, returning on Monday, quickly heard the news. Little queens who had never noticed my existence gathered round me at recess and put me whispered questions, for we were not supposed to talk during the retreat. The co-incidence of the holy fervour of the retreat with my unsanctified state heightened the sense of the prodigious. It was thought that Father Heeney, the curly-haired, bronzed missionary who had got such results among the Eskimos, was pitting his oratory against me. In her office, at a second interview, Madame MacIllvra wiped the corners of her eyes with her plain cambric handkerchief. She felt that she had betrayed a trust reposed in her, from Heaven, by my dead mother. Tears came readily to her, as to most pretty lady principals, especially when she felt that the *convent* might be open to criticism. By Wednesday, the third time she saw me, we had come to a serious pass. My deskmate, Louise, had bet me that I would not get my faith back by Wednesday; as one fiery sermon followed another and I remained unswayed, a sort of uneasiness settled down over the convent. It was clear to everyone, including me, that I would *have* to get my faith back to put an end to this terrible uncertainty.

I was as much concerned now as Madame MacIllvra herself. I was trying, with all my power, to feel faith, if only as a public duty, but the more I tapped and tested myself, the more I was forced to recognize that there was no belief inside me. My very soul had fled, as far as I could make out. Curiously enough, for the first time, seeing what I had wrought, I had a sense of obligation to others and not to my own soul or to God, which was a proof in itself that I had lost God, for our chief obligation in life was supposed to be to please Him. God (if there was a God) would certainly not be pleased if I *pretended* to regain my faith to satisfy Madame MacIllvra and Madame Barclay and my new friend and double, Louise, who was mischievous but a good Catholic. Yet this was the decision I came to after a second unfruitful session in the parlour, this time with Father Heeney, who could convert me, I felt leadenly, if anybody could. He had said all the same things that Father Dennis had said, though calling me by my first name and laughing when I told him that my father and grandfather were lawyers, as though my serious doubts were part of what he called the gift of the gab. He, too, seemed convinced that I had been reading atheistic literature and warned me, jestingly, of the confessional when I denied it. These priests, I thought bitterly, seemed to imagine that you could do nothing for yourself, that everything was from inheritance and reading, just as they imagined that Christ could not have been a 'mere man', and just, for that matter, as they kept saying that you must have 'faith', a word that had become more and more irritating to me during the past few days. 'Natural reason, Mary,' expatiated Father Heeney, 'will not take you the whole way today. There's a little gap that we have to fill with faith.' I looked up at him measuringly. So there *was* a gap, then. How was it that they had never mentioned this interesting fact to us before?

As I left the parlour, I decided to hold Father Heeney personally responsible for the deception he was forcing me into. 'I'll see you in the confessional,' he called after me in his full, warm voice, but it was not me, I promised myself, that he was going to see but a mere pious effigy of myself. By failing to convert me and treating my case so lightly — calling me Thomasina, for instance, in a would-be funny reference to doubting Thomas — he was driving me straight into fraud. Thanks to his incompetence, the only thing left for me to do was to enact a simulated conversion. But I had no intention of giving him the credit. I was going to pretend to be converted in the night, by a dream.

And I did not feel a bit sorry, even on Thursday morning, kneeling in my white veil at the altar railing to receive the Host. Behind me, the nuns, I knew, were rejoicing, as good nuns should, over the reclamation of a soul. Madame MacIllvra's blue eyes were probably misting. Beside me, Pork Barrel was bursting her seams with envy. Louise (I had just informed her in the veiling room) had invited me to spend the night with her during Christmas vacation. My own chief sensation was one of detached surprise at how far I had come from my old mainstays, as once, when learning to swim, I had been doing the dead-man's float and looked back, raising my doused head, to see my water wings drifting, far behind me, on the lake's surface.

# VII
# ENCOUNTERING GOODNESS

*Susan Hill*
*Christopher Milne*
*Maxim Gorki*
*Charlotte Brontë*
*Frank O'Connor*

In a piece written for this collection, Susan Hill (b. 1942), well-known children's writer, sets out the incidents and ideas which have guided her own decisions concerning the education of her daughter. Herself a protestant educated at Catholic schools, she selects what she sees as positive in such an education but concludes that whilst no school, no family can provide a complete preparation for life, if "you can tell of love", and show it, then "everything else follows".

Christopher Milne, better known as Christopher Robin, has the courage to refute A A Milne's sentimental (and 'cynical') portrait of him as a boy, and to argue that a child of five is not too young to be taught about God, but too old.

The passage from *Jane Eyre* is familiar; the other two pieces less so. Maxim Gorki is one of the heroes of Soviet Socialist Realism but was never an orthodox Bolshevik, quarrelled with Lenin and died under mysterious circumstances at the height of Stalin's purges having been welcomed back from a long exile as a hero in 1928. An orphan, he spent much of his youth wandering sourthern Russia and the Ukraine; the heroes of his books are always nonconformists, often gypsies and beggars. The Old Testament ethos of his grandfather and the New Testament idealism of his grandmother were of lasting influence; his work, which was the first to deal realistically with the life of the industrial proletariat, is characterised by a split between the old, harsh and authoritarian and the new, kindly and hopeful.

Frank O'Connor (Michael O'Donovan) was imprisoned after fighting as a republican in the Civil War, became a librarian and then at the urging of W B Yeats a director of the Abbey Theatre. His first love was poetry; he wrote in both Gaelic and English and translated much Irish verse. The story of his *First Confession* is hilarious and heart-warming.

# Susan Hill

Recently, an old friend with whom I had renewed contact brought me a pile of school magazines, dating from more than thirty years ago, when she and I were contemporaries in the kindergarten department of a Roman Catholic convent.

My own family was not, in fact, Catholic, but this had been the only good school in the area willing to take children very young; my mother ran a business full-time, I was an only child in need of companionship and stimulus, and she was, for some obscure reason — for I doubt if she had ever had much to do with them — a great 'believer in nuns'.

So off I went, to be taught, to play, and to attend chapel and be indoctrinated along with the little R.C.s.

As a matter of fact, in many essential respects, my mother was quite right about the nuns. Particularly when we were small (things got harsher as we grew older) they loved us, cared for and about us, and they were mostly also good fun. And because they themselves live in the Convent, which also took some boarders, it had an atmosphere rather like a home as well as like a school.

I was as happy and as unhappy as many another child similarly placed. This is not a piece of embittered reminiscence of the horrors of a Catholic convent education, nor a self-pitying reflection on the ways in which it blighted my life.

I imbibed a great deal of gobbledegook, of course, some of it of little importance, and some which mattered more and from which it took me years to free myself. I attended enough masses, said enough decades of the Rosary, learned enough catechism by rote, to qualify me for remission of a good many years in the purgatory to which, of course, I was doomed, as a Protestant.

And it all came back to me, right down to the choking, sickly-sweet smell of the incense, as I leafed through those magazines. For the most part, it seems to have been quite irrelevant to life — my life, real life, contemporary life, non-Catholic life, *anybody's* life. Occasionally I shuddered, recalling Lenten retreats, and bread without margarine, sermons on hell-fire, the mumbo-jumbo of Latin. But it was when I came to one of the form diaries that I actually began to smile, and then to laugh, and then to see it all in perspective once again, as well as to feel gloriously liberated. It read, "Next month is Reverend Mother's Feast Day. We are planning to present her with a clock for the assembly hall and a spiritual bouquet, and all of us are practising as many Acts of Virtue as we can. Form Four is concentrating on Obedience and Purity of Thought."

It has always struck me as surprising that nine year old girls could have been considered capable of very much in the way of *impure* thought. It did so at the time. Indeed, I used to ask searching questions as to what exactly constituted those impure thoughts, and received no very satisfactory replies, but only a decade of the Rosary as a penance for raising the matter!

And as I sat, mulling it all over, I began to compare how things were with me, and so many others then, with how a Christian upbringing and education are for my own daughter, now aged seven and to see how very different it all is, and how altogether better.

I do not think that there are, or should be, any easy formulae to follow, any set blueprints to make the Christian education of young children work successfully. I don't think there are any pat, slick, closed-ended formulae in Christianity, or human life, at all. It is all infinitely more complex, subtle, individual, and spontaneous than that. I have never accepted anybody's version of 'do this, believe that, say the other, sign here, hand yourself over to us and you will be saved,' and one thing I am very sure of is that I don't want my daughter to fall for any of that, either. Mistrust *anyone* who tells you they have the right answer, the one simple, foolproof system — anyone except God; but then, he never does it. If nothing else, I may save her from the clutches of the Moonies.

Yet, paradoxically, in another sense the whole thing *is* simple and straightforward. Well — isn't it? Love. That's all. Love.

When we went to look round the school to which we were hoping to send Jessica, I suppose we had several vague requirements in mind, though we were not rigid, didn't quite know what we were looking for. We just knew, at once, that we had found it. It was all there around us, in the attitude, the approach, the atmosphere, the very air we were breathing — caring happiness, concern. Love. Oh, yes, and busyness, purposefulness and bright little faces. We didn't bother to look at any other schools, and we were right, this one is everything I ask of a Christian school. It is non-denominational and not in any sense sectarian, but neither Anglican, non-conformist, nor perhaps even latterday Catholic would feel anything but happy and familiar with the teaching and the worship.

What the children learn and what they are shown, rather than merely told and taught, is that they should love one another, care for and about one another, as they are objects of loving concern to the staff. They are taught to show interest, respect, sensitivity, sympathy, for one another. My daughter came home one day when she was six with a story about the naughtiest, toughest boy in the school who had gone round the playground at break-time 'looking for someone who'd fallen over, so he could help them!'

They rejoice at each other's glad tidings and they are also encouraged to weep with one another, to bear each other's burdens. Last year, we had a second child, who was born prematurely, and who died at the age of five weeks. Jessica was able to share her confusion, unhappiness, anxiety, anger, grief, at school with teachers and other children. It helped her. It helped us. Last year, too, they all learned about the cruel reality of human suffering, sickness, hunger, death. They learned about the famine in Africa. And talked about what they themselves could do. And did it. I remember that we used to collect halfpennies for the 'Catholic black-babies' but it all seemed very remote, very alien and I'm not sure exactly what the pennies were for.

There is discipline in the school, there are rewards and punishments. But, what my daughter and her friends seemed so blessedly free from is what has scarred and maimed more human souls in the name of Christianity than anything else — 'a sense of sin.' To know right from wrong, and why; to do, want to do, understand why it is better to do, the former and refrain from the latter — well of course, of course. To recognise evil in all its cunning manifestations, to muster under the banner of righteousness, to learn about it both in life and in art, to read *A Pilgrim's Progress* — all of this I would have her do. But not to be dogged by any sense of sin, and guilt, to be made to feel 'bad' without exactly knowing why, to be obliged to search the young soul and confess aloud to man, to feel fear of punishment in both this, but principally, in the next world, to be riddled through like a maggotty fruit, with self-blame and its henchman, self-loathing — I would walk through fire to keep her from all of this.

I remember thinking when I was quite young that there seemed to be two particularly important messages in the teachings of Jesus which a lot of people either ignored or distorted. I still think so. They form the basis of what I try to teach my daughter. The first is that you should love your neighbour *as yourself*. Love, not denigration and hatred, of self, gratitude for one's self and its uniqueness, joy in one's self-ness — that is how much we should love others. But all we seemed to hear about was self-denial, putting self last, the insignificance and wickedness of selfish desires. It has caused untold human misery and lack of fulfilment, and even, it seems clear, physical and mental ill-health.

And the other truth is that 'God *so loved the world,* that he gave his only begotten son . . .' Yet what did we hear about but the wicked ways of the world, and how it was a dreadful place in which to have the misfortune to be, how worldly desires were to be shunned, how those who renouced the world took the finer and better way. But, I still read, God loved the world, God made the world, He looked upon it and saw that it was good.

Yes. That is what she must grow up knowing, believing, feeling, being certain of in her bones. She is being taught to celebrate the world, its joys, its glories, its teeming life, its excitements and possibilities and challenges, its gifts; to praise for it, thank for it, respect it, love it, share it, revel in it. And somehow, bound up with all of that, to accept if only in order to fight, everything else that is inextricably bound up in it — pain, loneliness, injustice, cruelty, deprivation, sickness, death. The 'shirt of flame, which human hands cannot remove.'

That is indeed hard to teach, impossible to explain. All of it can only be learned by living. But my daughter has seen something of it already, and been helped to bear and to fight it, though she cannot understand, for who does? She is loved, cared for, helped, but she cannot be shielded or spared, by them, by me, by anyone in this world. All she can be given is 'the whole armour of God', to wear on her pilgrimage.

And as I look back and remember, it dawns upon me that in spite of everything, in spite of the nonsenses and falsitites, which are blown away like so many cobwebs on the wind, that is what happened to me. I was brought up hearing, knowing, believing, a child of light, not left to walk in darkness.

For no one's Christian upbringing is exactly right. How can it be, there are too many imponderables, too much depends upon human frailty, human ignorance and confusion. What matters is the attempt, the strength of the conviction that these things are worth knowing, this man's teaching, this way of living, is a good way and better than good.

Children do best when we leave it to them to show us what kind of people they are, and where their particular strengths and talents lie, when we encourage each one's uniqueness, rather than when we impose our own ideas, plans, desires, vision, upon them. They do best when given freedom and a wide open space, yet when there is a framework beyond that space. They do best of all when they are shown, not merely told. You can tell of love, but it will mean nothing, unless and until you also show it.

After that, everything else follows.

# *Christopher Milne*

*from:* Enchanted Places

Before I come to the second poem that I must disown—and the reader may start guessing which one it will be—I must quote from something my father wrote in a 'Preface to Parents' for a special edition of the verses and which he later reprinted in his autobiography.

> In real life very young children have an artless beauty, an innocent grace, an unstudied abandon of movement, which, taken together, make an appeal to our emotions similar in kind to that made by any other young and artless creatures: kittens, puppies, lambs: but greater in degree, for the reason that the beauty of childhood seems in some way to transcend the body. Heaven, that is, does really appear to lie about the child in its infancy, as it does not lie about even the most attractive kitten. But with this outstanding physical quality there is a natural lack of moral quality, which expresses itself, as Nature always insists on expressing herself, in an egotism entirely ruthless . . . The mother of a little boy of three has disappeared, and is never seen again. The child's reaction to the total loss of his mother is given in these lines:
>
> James James
> Morrison Morrison

> (Commonly known as Jim)
> Told his
> Other relations
> Not to go blaming *him*.

And that is all. It is the truth about a child: children are, indeed,
as heartless as that. . .

Is it? Are they? Was I? I cannot pretend to know for sure how I felt
about anything at the age of three. I can only guess that though I
might not have missed my mother had she disappeared, and would
certainly not have missed my father, I would have missed Nanny—
most desolately. A young child's world is a small one and within it
things may have odd values. A teddy bear may be worth more than a
father. But the egotism with which (I will admit) a child is born, surely
very quickly disappears as attachments are made and relationships
established. When a child plays with his bear the bear comes alive and
there is at once a child-bear relationship which tries to cope with the
Nanny-child relationship. Then the child gets inside his bear and
looks at it the other way round: that's how *bear* feels about it. And at
once sympathy is born and egotism has died. A poem in which my
father really does express what I feel is the truth about a child is
'Market Square', which ends up:

> So I'm sorry for the people who sell fine saucepans,
> I'm sorry for the people who sell fresh mackerel,
> I'm sorry for the people who sell sweet lavender,
> 'Cos they haven't got a rabbit, not anywhere there!

How well I remember this feeling of sympathy—totally misplaced, of
course—yet agonizingly sincere!

Undoubtedly children can be selfish, but so, too, can adults. By
accusing the young of heartless egotism are we perhaps subconsciously
reassuring ourselves that, selfish though we still may be, there was
once a time when we were worse. . .

This brings me to the second poem I must disown—'Vespers'. It is
one of my father's best known and one that has brought me over the
years more toe-curling, fist-clenching, lip-biting embarrassment than
any other. So let me, for the first time in my life, look it clearly in the
eyes and see how things stand between us.

The general impression left by 'Vespers'—especially with anyone who has heard Vera Lynn singing it—is of a rather soppy poem about a good little boy who is saying his prayers. But if one reads it rather more carefully, one will see that it is nothing of the sort. It is a poem about a rather naughty little boy who is *not* saying his prayers. He is merely pretending; and to his and the author's surprise he had managed to fool a great many people. 'Vespers', then, is not a sentimental poem at all: it is a mildly cynical one. But even so, nothing to get worked up about. After all, everyone is naughty sometimes.

So you might think. But it is not quite what my father thought. Let us see what he had to say in that 'Preface to Parents'.

Finally, let me refer to the poem which has been more sentimentalized over than any other in the book: 'Vespers'. Well, if mothers and aunts and hard-headed reviewers have been sentimental over it, I am glad; for the spectacle in real life of a child of three at its prayers is one over which thousands have been sentimental. It is indeed calculated to bring a lump to the throat. But even so one must tell the truth about the matter. Not 'God bless Mummy, because I love her so', but 'God bless Mummy, I know that's right'; not 'God bless Daddy, because he buys me food and clothes' but 'God bless Daddy, I quite forgot'; not even the egotism of 'God bless Me, because I'm the most important person in the house', but the super-egotism of feeling so impregnable that the blessing of this mysterious God for Oneself is the very last thing for which it would seem necessary to ask. And since this is the Truth about a Child, let us get all these things into the poem, and the further truth that prayer means nothing to a child of three, whose thoughts are engaged with other, more exciting matters. . .

'Vespers', it seems, is not just about what a certain little boy did on a certain occasion. It is the Truth (with a capital T) about a Child (with a capital C). And although I knew that this was my father's general feeling, I had entirely forgotten how uncompromisingly he had expressed himself.

It was at this point, while I was collecting my thoughts together, wondering how to go on, that I noticed the quotation from Wordsworth. It comes in the first of the two passages I have quoted:

Heaven lies about us in our infancy

This is a line from Wordsworth's 'Intimations of Immortality'. At first glance it seemed at home in its context. But on looking closer I saw that this was far from the case. For the line had been given a new and altogether different meaning. Wordsworth had been saying that Heaven appeared *to the child* to lie around him. My father was saying that this was how it seemed to the *onlooker*. So then I read the whole poem. It is, of course, the Truth about a Child as Wordsworth sees it, and it is the complete reverse of my father's view. And at once it awakened an echo in my heart—as it must have awakened many another echo in many another heart.

> Those first affections,
> Those shadowy recollections,
> Which, be they what they may,
> Are yet the fountain light of all our day.

In those days of splendour and glory I certainly felt myself nearer to God—both the God that Nanny was telling me about who lived up in the sky and the God who painted the buttercups—than I do today. And so, asked to choose between these two views of childhood, I am bound to say that I'm for Wordsworth. Maybe he is just being sentimental. Maybe the infant William has fooled the middle-aged poet in the same way that the kneeling Christopher Robin fooled so many of his readers. Maybe my cynical father is right. But this is not how I feel about it.

Today it is fashionable to maintain that at the age of five a child is too young to be taught about God. The Divine is beyond his comprehension. One should wait until he is older. Dare I suggest that the reverse might be true: that the child of five is not too young; he is really too old.

I don't really want to get too involved either with Poetry or with Religious Instruction, nor do I want to spend too long on my infant knees. Furthermore, in a world heavily over-populated with sociologists, psychologists and research workers generally, I am reluctant to set up theories backed by nothing more than memory against the statistics and case histories of the opposition. However, this I must say. The Christopher Robin of that wretched poem is indeed me at the age of three. I retain the most vivid memories of saying my prayers as a child. They go back a long way, but I cannot date them. I well recall how I knelt, how Nanny sat, her hands round mine, and what we said aloud together. Did my thoughts wander? Were they engaged on other, more exciting things? The answer—and let me say it loudly and clearly—is NO. Would I agree that prayer meant nothing to a child of three? If the stress is on the last word, I must be careful: I may be thinking of a child of four. All I can accurately say is that I can recall no occasion when this was so.

At this point a picture floats uninvited into my mind. Nothing that ever happened, nothing to do with my parents, purely imaginary. Papa and Mama in church. Both kneeling. Mama's mind, disconnected from her ears, hovering around the Sunday lunch. Papa, squinting through his fingers, studying the hats in the pew in front. No, it's not only the three year old whose thoughts wander.

I said earlier than I was going to have things out with 'Vespers'. Partly, I must confess, I wanted to get my own back. But there was another reason.

# Maxim Gorki

*from:* My Childhood

I was not long in grasping the fact that there was one God for grandfather and another for grandmother. The frequency with which this difference was brought to my notice made it impossible to ignore it.

Sometimes grandmother woke up in the morning and sat a long while on the bed combing her wonderful hair. Holding her head firmly, she would draw the comb with its jagged teeth through every thread on that black, silky mane, whispering the while, not to wake me:

"Bother you! The devil take you for sticking together like this!"

When she had thus taken all the tangles out, she quickly wove it into a thick plait, washed in a hurry, with many angry tossings of her head, and without washing away the signs of irritation from her large face, which was creased by sleep, she placed herself before the ikon and began her real morning ablutions, by which her whole being was instantly refreshed.

She straightened her crooked back, and raising her head, gazed upon the round face of Our Lady of Kazan, and after crossing herself reverently, said in a loud, fierce whisper:

"Most Glorious Virgin! Take me under thy protection this day, dear Mother."

Having made a deep obeisance, she straightened her back with difficulty, and then went on whispering ardently, and with deep feeling:

"Source of our Joy! Stainless Beauty! Apple tree in bloom!"

Every morning she seemed to find fresh words of praise; and for that reason I used to listen to her prayers with strained attention.

"Dear Heart, so pure, so heavenly! My Defence and my Refuge! Golden Sun! Mother of God! Guard me from temptation; grant that I may do no one harm, and may not be offended by what others do to me thoughtlessly."

With her dark eyes smiling, and a general air of rejuvenation about her, she crossed herself again, with that slow and ponderous movement of her hand.

"Jesus Christ, Son of God, have mercy on me, a sinner, for Thy Mother's sake!"

Her prayers were always non-liturgical, full of sincere praise, and very simple.

She did not pray long in the mornings because she had to get the samovar ready, for grandfather kept no servants, and if the tea was not made to the moment, he used to give her a long and furious scolding.

Sometimes he was up before her, and would come up to the attic. Finding her at prayer, he would stand for some minutes listening to her, contemptuously curling his thin, dark lips, and when he was drinking his tea, he would growl:

"How often have I taught you how to say your prayers, blockhead. But you are always mumbling some nonsense, you heretic! I can't think why God puts up with you."

"He understands," grandmother would reply confidently, "what we don't say to Him. He looks into everything."

"You cursed dullard! U—u—ugh, *you!*" was all he said to this.

Her God was with her all day; she even spoke to the animals about Him. Evidently this God, with willing submission, made Himself subject to all creatures — to men, dogs, bees, and even the grass of the field; and He was impartially kind and accessible to everyone on earth.

Once the petted cat belonging to the innkeeper's wife — an artful,

pretty, coaxing creature, smoke-coloured with golden eyes—caught a
starling in the garden. Grandmother took away the nearly exhausted
bird and punished the cat, crying:

"Have you no fear of God, you spiteful wretch?"

The wife of the innkeeper and the porter laughed at these words, but
she said to them angrily:

"Do you think that animals don't understand about God? All
creatures understand about Him better than you do, you heartless
things!"

When she harnessed Sharapa, who was growing fat and melancholy, she used to hold a conversation with him.

"Why do you look so miserable, toiler of God? Why? You are getting
old, my dear, that's what it is." And the horse would sigh and toss his
head.

And yet she did not utter the name of God as frequently as grandfather did. Her God was quite comprehensible to me, and I knew that
I must not tell lies in His presence; I should be ashamed to do so. The
thought of Him produced such an invincible feeling of shame, that I
never lied to grandmother. It would be simply impossible to hide
anything from this good God; in fact, I had not even a wish to do so.

One day the innkeeper's wife quarrelled with grandfather and
abused him, and also grandmother who had taken no part in the
quarrel; nevertheless she abused her bitterly, and even threw a carrot
at her.

"You are a fool, my good woman," said grandmother very quietly;
but I felt the insult keenly, and resolved to be revenged on the spiteful
creature.

For a long time I could not make up my mind as to the best way to
punish this sandy-haired, fat woman, with two chins and no eyes to
speak of. From my own experience of feuds between people living
together, I knew that they avenged themselves on one another by
cutting off the tails of their enemy's cats, by chasing his dogs, by killing
his cocks and hens, by creeping into his cellar in the night and
pouring kerosene over the cabbages and cucumbers in the tubs, and
letting the kvass run out of the barrels; but nothing of this kind
appealed to me. I wanted something less crude, and more terrifying.

At last I had an idea. I lay in wait for the innkeeper's wife, and as
soon as she went down to the cellar, I shut the trap door on her,
fastened it, danced a jig on it, threw the key on to the roof, and rushed
into the kitchen where grandmother was busy cooking. At first she

173

could not understand why I was in such an ecstasy of joy, but when she had grasped the cause, she slapped me — on that part of my anatomy provided for the purpose, dragged me out to the yard, and sent me up to the roof to find the key. I gave it to her with reluctance, astonished at her asking for it, and ran away to a corner of the yard, whence I could see how she set the captive free, and how they laughed together in a friendly way as they crossed the yard.

"I'll pay you for this!" threatened the innkeeper's wife, shaking her plump fist at me; but there was a good-natured smile on her eyeless face.

Grandmother dragged me back to the kitchen by the collar. "Why did you do that?" she asked.

"Because she threw a carrot at you."

"That means that you did it for me? Very well! This is what I will do for you — I will horsewhip you and put you amongst the mice under the oven. A nice sort of protector you are! 'Look at a bubble and it will burst directly.' If I were to tell grandfather he would skin you. Go up to the attic and learn your lesson."

She would not speak to me for the rest of the day, but before she said her prayers that night she sat on the bed and uttered these memorable words in a very impressive tone:

"Now, Lenka, my darling, you must keep yourself from meddling with the doings of grown-up persons. Grown-up people are given responsibilities and they have to answer for them to God; but it is not so with you yet, you live by a child's conscience. Wait till God takes possession of your heart, and shows you the work you are to do, and the way you are to take. Do you understand? It is no business of yours to decide who is to blame in any matter. God judges, and punishes; that is for Him, not for us."

She was silent for a moment while she took a pinch of snuff; then, half-closing her right eye, she added:

"Why, God Himself does not always know where the fault lies."

"Doesn't God know everything?" I asked in astonishment.

"If He knew everything, a lot of things that are done would not be done. It is as if He, the Father, looks and looks from Heaven at the earth, and sees how often we weep, how often we sob, and says: 'My people, my dear people, how sorry I am for you!' "

She was crying herself as she spoke; and drying her wet cheeks, she went into the corner to pray.

From that time her God became still closer and still more comprehensible to me.

Grandfather, in teaching me, also said that God was a Being — Omnipresent, Omniscient, All-seeing, the kind Helper of people in all their affairs; but he did not pray like grandmother. In the morning, before going to stand before the ikon, he took a long time washing himself; then, when he was fully dressed, he carefully combed his sandy hair, brushed his beard, and looking at himself in the mirror, saw that his shirt sat well, and tucked his black cravat into his waistcoat — after which he advanced cautiously, almost stealthily, to the ikon. He always stood on one particular board of the parquet floor, and with an expression in his eyes which made them look like the eyes of a horse, he stood in silence for a minute, with bowed head, and arms held straight down by his sides in soldier fashion; then, upright, and slender as a nail, he began impressively:

"In the name of the Father, and of the Son, and of the Holy Ghost."

After these words it always seemed to me that the room became extraordinarily quiet; the very flies seemed to buzz cautiously.

There he stood, with his head thrown back, his eyebrows raised and bristling, his golden beard sticking out horizontally, and recited the prayers, in a firm tone, as if he were repeating a lesson, and with a voice which was very distinct and very imperious.

"It will be useless when the Judge comes, and every action is laid bare —"

Striking himself lightly on the breast, he prayed fervently:

"To Thee alone can sinners come. Oh turn Thy face away from my misdeeds."

He recited the "I believe," using the prescribed words only; and all the while his right leg quivered, as if it were noiselessly keeping time with his prayers, and his whole form, straining towards the ikon, seemed to become taller, leaner, and drier — so clean he was, so neat, and so persistent in his demands.

"Heavenly Physician, heal my soul of its long-lived passions. To thee, Holy Virgin, I cry from my heart; to thee I offer myself with fervour."

And with his green eyes full of tears he wailed loudly:

"Impute to me, my God, faith instead of works, and be not mindful of deeds which can by no means justify me!"

Here he crossed himself frequently at intervals, tossing his head as if he were about to butt at something, and his voice became squeaky and cracked. Later, when I happened to enter a synagogue, I realised that grandfather prayed like a Jew.

By this time the samovar would have been snorting on the table for some minutes, and a hot smell of rye-cakes would be floating through the room. Grandmother, frowning, strolled about, with her eyes on the floor, the sun looked cheerfully in at the window from the garden, the dew glistened like pearls on the trees, the morning air was deliciously perfumed by the smell of dill, and currant-bushes, and ripening apples, but grandfather went on with his prayers — quavering and squeaking.

"Extinguish in me the flame of passion, for I am in misery and accursed."

I knew all the morning prayers by heart, and even in my dreams I could say what was to come next, and I followed with intense interest to hear if he made a mistake or missed out a word — which very seldom happened; but when it did, it aroused a feeling of malicious glee in me.

When he had finished his prayers, grandfather used to say "Good morning!" to grandmother and me, and we returned his greeting and sat down to table. Then I used to say to him:

"You left out a word this morning."

"Not really?" grandfather would say with an uneasy air of incredulity.

"Yes. You should have said, 'This, my Faith, reigns supreme,' but you did not say 'reigns.'"

"There now!" he would exclaim, much perturbed, and blinking guiltily.

Afterwards he would take a cruel revenge on me for pointing out his mistake to him; but for the moment, seeing how disturbed he was, I was able to enjoy my triumph.

One day grandmother said to him jokingly:

"God must get tired of listening to your prayers, Father. You do nothing but insist on the same things over and over again."

"What's that?" he drawled in an ominous voice. "What are you nagging about now?"

"I say that you do not offer God so much as one little word from your own heart, so far as I can hear."

He turned livid, and quivering with rage, jumped up on his chair and threw a dish at her head, yelping with a sound like that made by a saw on a piece of wood:

"Take that, you old hag!"

When he spoke of the omnipotence of God, he always emphasised its cruelty above every other attribute. "Man sinned, and the Flood was sent; sinned again, and his towns were destroyed by fire; then God punished people by famine and plague, and even now He is always holding a sword over the earth — a scourge for sinners. All who have wilfully broken the commandments of God will be punished by sorrow and ruin." And he emphasised this by rapping his fingers on the table.

It was hard for me to believe in the cruelty of God, and I suspected grandfather of having made it all up on purpose to inspire me with fear not of God but of himself; so I asked him frankly:

"Are you saying all this to make me obey you?"

And he replied with equal frankness:

"Well, perhaps I am. Do you mean to disobey me again?"

"And how about what grandmother says?"

"Don't you believe the old fool!" he admonished me sternly. "From her youth she has always been stupid, illiterate, and unreasonable. I shall tell her she must not dare to talk to you again on such an important matter. Tell me, now — how many companies of angels are there?"

I gave the required answer, and then I asked:

"Are they limited companies?"

"Oh, you scatter-brain!" he laughed, covering his eyes and biting his lips. "What have companies to do with God . . . they belong to life on earth . . . they are founded to set the laws at naught."

"What are laws?"

"Laws! Well, they are really derived from custom," the old man explained, with pleased alacrity; and his intelligent, piercing eyes sparkled. "People living together agree amongst themselves — 'Such and such is our best course of action; we will make a custom of it — a rule'; finally it becomes a law. For example, before they begin a game, children will settle amongst themselves how it is to be played, and what rules are to be observed. Laws are made in the same way."

"And what have companies to do with laws?"

"Why, they are like an impudent fellow, they come along and make the laws of no account."

"But why?"

"Ah! that you would not understand," he replied, knitting his brows heavily; but afterwards, as if in explanation, he said:

"All the actions of men help to work out God's plans. Men desire one thing, but He wills something quite different. Human institutions are never lasting. The Lord blows on them, and they fall into dust and ashes."

I had reason for being interested in "companies," so I went on inquisitively:

"But what does Uncle Jaakov mean when he sings:

> 'The Angels bright
> For God will fight,
> But Satan's slaves
> Are Companies'?

Grandfather raised his hand to his beard, thus hiding his mouth, and closed his eyes. His cheeks quivered, and I guessed that he was laughing inwardly.

"Jaakov ought to have his feet tied together and be thrown into the water," he said. "There was no necessity for him to sing or for you to listen to that song. It is nothing but a silly joke which is current in Kalonga — a piece of schismatical, heretical nonsense." And looking, as it were, through and beyond me, he murmured thoughtfully: "U—u—ugh, *you!*"

But though he had set God over mankind, as a Being to be very greatly feared, none the less did he, like grandmother, invoke Him in all his doings.

The only saints grandmother knew were Nikolai, Youry, Frola, and Lava, who were full of kindness and sympathy with human-nature, and went about in the villages and towns sharing the life of the people, and regulating all their concerns; but grandfather's saints were nearly all males, who cast down idols, or defied the Roman emperors, and were tortured, burned or flayed alive in consequence.

Sometimes grandfather would say musingly:

"If only God would help me to sell that little house, even at a small profit, I would make a public thanksgiving to St Nicholas."

But grandmother would say to me, laughingly:

"That's just like the old fool! Does he think St Nicholas will trouble himself about selling a house? Hasn't our little Father Nicholas something better to do?"

I kept by me for many years a church calendar which had belonged to grandfather, containing several inscriptions in his handwriting. Amongst others, opposite the day of Joachim and Anne, was written in red ink, and very upright characters:

"My benefactors, who averted a calamity."

I remember that "calamity."

In his anxiety about the maintenance of his very unprofitable children, grandfather set up as a moneylender, and used to receive articles in pledge secretly. Someone laid an information against him, and one night the police came to search the premises. There was a great fuss, but it ended well, and grandfather prayed till sunrise the next morning, and before breakfast, and in my presence, wrote those words in the calendar.

Before supper he used to read with me the Psalms, the breviary, or the heavy book of Ephraim Sirine; but as soon as he had supped he began to pray again, and his melancholy words of contrition resounded in the stillness of evening:

"What can I offer to Thee, or how can I atone to Thee, O generous God, O King of Kings! . . . Preserve us from all evil imaginations . . . O Lord, protect me from certain persons! . . . My tears fall like rain, and the memory of my sins . . ."

But very often grandmother said:

"Oie, I am dog-tired! I shall go to bed without saying my prayers."

Grandfather used to take me to church — to vespers on Saturday, and to High Mass on Sundays and festivals — but even in church I made a distinction as to which God was being addressed; whatever the priest or the deacon recited — that was to grandfather's God; but the choir always sang to grandmother's God. Of course I can only crudely express this childish distinction which I made between these two Gods, but I remember how it seemed to tear my heart with terrific violence, and how grandfather's God aroused in my mind a feeling of terror and unpleasantness. A Being Who loved no one, He followed all of us about with His severe eyes, seeking and finding all that was ugly, evil, and sinful in us. Evidently He put no trust in man, He was always insisting on penance, and He loved to chastise.

In those days my thoughts and feelings about God were the chief nourishment of my soul and were the most beautiful ones of my existence. All other impressions which I received did nothing but disgust me by their cruelty and squalor, and awaken in me a sense of repugnance and ferocity. God was the best and brightest of all the beings who lived about me — grandmother's God, that Dear Friend of all creation; and naturally I could not help being disturbed by the question — "How is it that grandfather cannot see the Good God?"

# *Charlotte Brontë*

*from:* Jane Eyre

Close by Miss Temple's bed, and half covered with its white curtains, there stood a little crib. I saw the outline of a form under the clothes, but the face was hid by the hangings; the nurse I had spoken to in the garden sat in an easy-chair, asleep; an unsnuffed candle burnt dimly on the table. Miss Temple was not to be seen: I knew afterwards that she had been called to a delirious patient in the fever-room. I advanced: then paused by the crib side: my hand was on the curtain, but I preferred speaking before I withdrew it. I still recoiled at the dread of seeing a corpse.

'Helen!' I whispered softly; 'are you awake?'

She stirred herself, put back the curtain, and I saw her face, pale, wasted, but quite composed; she looked so little changed, that my fear was instantly dissipated.

'Can it be you Jane?' she asked, in her own gentle voice.

'Oh!' I thought, 'she is not going to die; they are mistaken; she could not speak and look so calmly if she were.'

I got on to her crib and kissed her: her forehead was cold, and her cheek both cold and thin, and so were her hand and wrist: but she smiled as of old.

'Why are you come here, Jane? It is past eleven o'clock: I heard it strike some minutes since.'

'I came to see you, Helen: I heard you were very ill, and I could not sleep till I had spoken to you.'

'You came to bid me good-bye, then: you are just in time probably.'

'Are you going somewhere, Helen? Are you going home?'

'Yes; to my long home — my last home.'

'No, no, Helen!' I stopped distressed. While I tried to devour my tears, a fit of coughing seized Helen; it did not, however, wake the nurse. When it was over, she lay some minutes exhausted; then she whispered —

'Jane, your little feet are bare; lie down and cover yourself with my quilt.'

I did so: she put her arm over me, and I nestled close to her. After a long silence, she resumed, still whispering —

'I am very happy, Jane; and when you hear that I am dead, you must be sure and not grieve: there is nothing to grieve about. We all must die one day, and the illness which is removing me is not painful; it is gentle and gradual; my mind is at rest. I leave no one to regret me much: I have only a father, and he is lately married, and will not miss me. By dying young, I shall escape great sufferings. I had not qualities or talents to make my way very well in the world: I should have been continually at fault.'

'But where are going to, Helen? Can you see? Do you know?'

'I believe; I have faith: I am going to God.'

'Where is God? What is God?'

'My Maker and yours, who will never destroy what He created. I rely implicitly on His power, and confide wholly in His goodness: I count the hours till that eventful one arrives which shall restore me to Him, reveal Him to me.'

'You are sure, then, Helen, that there is such a place as heaven; and that our souls can get to it when we die?'

'I am sure there is a future state; I believe God is good; I can resign my immortal part to Him without any misgiving. God is my father; God is my friend; I love Him; I believe He loves me.'

'And shall I see you again, Helen, when I die?'

'You will come to the same region of happiness: be received by the same mighty universal Parent, no doubt, dear Jane.'

Again I questioned; but this time only in thought. 'Where is that region? Does it exist?' And I clasped my arms closer round Helen; she seemed dearer to me than ever; I felt as if I could not let her go; I lay with my face hidden on her neck. Presently she said in the sweetest tone —

'How comfortable I am! The last fit of coughing has tired me a little; I feel as if I could sleep; but don't leave me, Jane; I like to have you near me.'

'I'll stay with you, *dear* Helen: no one shall take me away.'

'Are you warm, darling?'

'Yes.'

'Good-night, Jane.'

'Good-night, Helen.'

She kissed me, and I her, and we both soon slumbered.

When I awoke it was day: an unusual movement roused me; I looked up; I was in somebody's arms; the nurse held me; she was carrying me through the passage back to the dormitory. I was not reprimanded for leaving my bed; people had something else to think about; no explanation was afforded then to my many questions; but a day or two afterwards I learned that Miss Temple, on returning to her own room at dawn, had found me laid in a little crib; my face against Helen Burns's shoulder, my arms round her neck. I was asleep, and Helen was — dead.

Her grave is in Brocklebridge Churchyard: for fifteen years after her death it was only covered by a grassy mound; but now a gray marble tablet marks the spot, inscribed with her name, and the word '*Resurgam*'.


# Frank O'Connor

## *from:* First Confession


All the trouble began when my grandfather died and my grandmother — my father's mother — came to live with us. Relations in the one house are a strain at the best of times, but, to make matters worse, my grandmother was a real old countrywoman and quite unsuited to the life in town. She had a fat, wrinkled old face, and, to Mother's great indignation, went round the house in bare feet — the boots had her crippled, she said. For dinner she had a jug of porter and a pot of potatoes with — sometimes — a bit of salt fish, and she poured out the potatoes on the table and ate them slowly, with great relish, using her fingers by way of a fork.

Now, girls are supposed to be fastidious, but I was the one who suffered most from this. Nora, my sister, just sucked up to the old woman for the penny she got every Friday out of the old-age pension, a thing I could not do. I was too honest, that was my trouble; and when I was playing with Bill Connell, the sergeant-major's son, and saw my grandmother steering up the path with the jug of porter sticking out from beneath her shawl, I was mortified. I made excuses not to let him come into the house, because I could never be sure what she would be up to when we went in.

When Mother was at work and my grandmother made the dinner I wouldn't touch it. Nora once tried to make me, but I hid under the table from her and took the bread-knife with me for protection. Nora let on to be very indignant (she wasn't, of course, but she knew Mother saw through her, so she sided with Gran) and came after me. I lashed out at her with the bread-knife, and after that she left me alone. I stayed there till Mother came in from work and made my dinner, but when Father came in later Nora said in a shocked voice: 'Oh, Dadda, do you know what Jackie did at dinner-time?' Then, of course, it all came out; Father gave me a flaking; Mother interfered, and for days after that he didn't speak to me and Mother barely spoke to Nora. And all because of that old woman! God knows, I was heart-scalded.

Then, to crown my misfortunes, I had to make my first confession and communion. It was an old woman called Ryan who prepared us for these. She was about the one age with Gran; she was well-to-do, lived in a big house on Montenotte, wore a black cloak and bonnet, and came every day to school at three o'clock when we should have been going home, and talked to us of hell. She may have mentioned the other place as well, but that could only have been by accident, for hell had the first place in her heart.

She lit a candle, took out a new half-crown, and offered it to the first boy who would hold one finger — only one finger! — in the flame for five minutes by the school clock. Being always very ambitious I was tempted to volunteer, but I thought it might look greedy. Then she asked were we afraid of holding one finger — only one finger! — in a little candle flame for five minutes and not afraid of burning all over in roasting hot furnaces for all eternity. 'All eternity! Just think of that! A whole lifetime goes by and it's nothing, not even a drop in the ocean of your sufferings.' The woman was really interesting about hell, but my attention was all fixed on the half-crown. At the end of the lesson she put it back in her purse. It was a great disappointment; a religious woman like that, you wouldn't think she'd bother about a thing like a half-crown.

Another day she said she knew a priest who woke one night to find a fellow he didn't recognize leaning over the end of his bed. The priest was a bit frightened — naturally enough — but he asked the fellow what he wanted, and the fellow said in a deep, husky voice that he wanted to go to confession. The priest said it was an awkward time and wouldn't it do in the morning, but the fellow said that last time he went to confession, there was one sin he kept back, being ashamed to mention it, and now it was always on his mind. Then the priest knew it was a bad case, because the fellow was after making a bad confession and committing a mortal sin. He got up to dress, and just then the cock crew in the yard outside, and — lo and behold! — when the priest looked round there was no sign of the fellow, only a smell of burning timber, and when the priest looked at his bed didn't he see the print of two hands burned in it? That was because the fellow had made a bad confession. This story made a shocking impression on me.

But the worst of all was when she showed us how to examine our conscience. Did we take the name of the Lord, our God, in vain? Did we honour our father and our mother? (I asked her did this include grandmothers and she said it did.) Did we love our neighbours as ourselves? Did we covet our neighbour's goods? (I thought of the way I felt about the penny that Nora got every Friday.) I decided that, between one thing and another, I must have broken the whole ten commandments, all on account of that old woman, and so far as I could see, so long as she remained in the house I had no hope of ever doing anything else.

I was scared to death of confession. The day the whole class went I let on to have a toothache, hoping my absence wouldn't be noticed; but at three o'clock, just as I was feeling safe, along comes a chap with a message from Mrs Ryan that I was to go to confession myself on Saturday and be at the chapel for communion with the rest. To make it worse, Mother couldn't come with me and sent Nora instead.

Now, that girl had ways of tormenting me that Mother never knew of. She held my hand as we went down the hill, smiling sadly and saying how sorry she was for me, as if she were bringing me to the hospital for an operation.

'Oh, God help us!' she moaned. 'Isn't it a terrible pity you weren't a good boy? Oh, Jackie, my heart bleeds for you! How will you ever think of all your sins? Don't forget you have to tell him about the time you kicked Gran on the shin.'

'Lemme go!' I said, trying to drag myself free of her. 'I don't want to go to confession at all.'

'But sure, you'll have to go to confession, Jackie,' she replied in the same regretful tone. 'Sure, if you didn't, the parish priest would be up to the house, looking for you. 'Tisn't, God knows, that I'm sorry for you. Do you remember the time you tried to kill me with the bread-knife under the table? And the language you used to me? I don't know what he'll do with you at all, Jackie. He might have to send you up to the bishop.'

I remember thinking bitterly that she didn't know the half of what I had to tell — if I told it. I knew I couldn't tell it and understood perfectly why the fellow in Mrs Ryan's story made a bad confession; it seemed to me a great shame that people wouldn't stop criticising him. I remember that steep hill down to the church, and the sunlit hillsides beyond the valley of the river, which I saw in the gaps between the houses like Adam's last glimpse of Paradise.

Then, when she had manoeuvred me down the long flight of steps to the chapel yard, Nora suddenly changed her tone. She became the raging malicious devil she really was.

'There you are!' she said with a yelp of triumph, hurling me through the church door. 'And I hope he'll give you the penitential psalms, you dirty little caffler.'

I knew then I was lost, given up to eternal justice. The door with the coloured-glass panels swung shut behind me, the sunlight went out and gave place to deep shadow, and the wind whistled outside so that the silence within seemed to crackle like ice under my feet. Nora sat in front of me by the confession box. There were a couple of old women ahead of her, and then a miserable-looking poor devil came and wedged me in at the other side, so that I couldn't escape even if I had the courage. He joined his hands and rolled his eyes in the direction of the roof, muttering aspirations in an anguished tone, and I wondered had he a grandmother too. Only a grandmother could account for a fellow behaving in that heart-broken way, but he was better off than I, for he at least could go and confess his sins while I would make a bad confession and then die in the night and be continually coming back and burning people's furniture.

Nora's turn came, and I heard the sound of something slamming, and then her voice as if butter wouldn't melt in her mouth, and then another slam, and out she came. God, the hypocrisy of women! Her eyes were lowered, her head was bowed, and her hands were joined very low down on her stomach, and she walked up the aisle to the side altar looking like a saint. You never saw such an exhibition of devotion; and I remembered the devilish malice with which she had tormented me all the way from our door, and wondered were all religious people like that, really. It was my turn now. With the fear of damnation in my soul I went in, and the confessional door closed of itself behind me.

It was pitch-dark and I couldn't see priest or anything else. Then I really began to be frightened. In the darkness it was a matter between

God and men, and He had all the odds. He knew what my intentions were before I even started; I had no chance. All I had ever been told about confession got mixed up in my mind, and I knelt to one wall and said: 'Bless me, father, for I have sinned; this is my first confession.' I waited for a few minutes, but nothing happened, so I tried it on the other wall. Nothing happened there either. He had me spotted all right.

It must have been then that I noticed the shelf at about one height with my head. It was really a place for grown-up people to rest their elbows, but in my distracted state I thought it was probably the place you were supposed to kneel. Of course, it was on the high side and not very deep, but I was always good at climbing and managed to get up all right. Staying up was the trouble. There was room only for my knees, and nothing you could get a grip on but a sort of wooden moulding a bit above it. I held on to the moulding and repeated the words a little louder, and this time something happened all right. A slide was slammed back; a little light entered the box, and a man's voice said: 'Who's there?'

"'Tis me, father,' I said for fear he mightn't see me and go away again. I couldn't see him at all. The place the voice came from was under the moulding, about the level with my knees, so I took a good grip of the moulding and swung myself down till I saw the astonished face of a young priest looking up at me. He had to put his head on one side to see me, and I had to put mine on one side to see him, so we were more or less talking to one another upside-down. It struck me as a queer way of hearing confessions, but I didn't feel it my place to criticise.

'Bless me, father, for I have sinned; this is my first confession,' I rattled off all in one breath, and swung myself down the least shade more to make it easier for him.

'What are you doing up there?' he shouted in an angry voice, and the strain the politeness was putting on my hold of the moulding, and the shock of being addressed in such an uncivil tone, were too much for me. I lost my grip, tumbled, and hit the door an unmerciful wallop before I found myself flat on my back in the middle of the aisle. The people who had been waiting stood up with their mouths open. The priest opened the door of the middle box and came out, pushing his biretta back from his forehead; he looked something terrible. Then Nora came scampering down the aisle.

'Oh, you dirty little caffler!' she said. 'I might have known you'd do it. I might have known you'd disgrace me. I can't leave you out of my sight for one minute.'

Before I could even get to my feet to defend myself she bent down and gave me a clip across the ear. This reminded me that I was so stunned I had even forgotten to cry, so that people might think I wasn't hurt at all, when in fact I was probably maimed for life. I gave a roar out of me.

'What's all this about?' the priest hissed, getting angrier than ever and pushing Nora off me. 'How dare you hit the child like that, you little vixen?'

'But I can't do my penance with him, father,' Nora cried, cocking an outraged eye up at him.

'Well, go and do it, or I'll give you some more to do,' he said, giving me a hand up. 'Was it coming to confession you were, my poor man?' he asked me.

''Twas, father,' said I with a sob.

'Oh,' he said respectfully, 'a big hefty fellow like you must have terrible sins. Is this your first?'

''Tis, father,' said I.

'Worse and worse,' he said gloomily. 'The crimes of a lifetime. I don't know will I get rid of you at all today. You'd better wait now till I'm finished with these old ones. You can see by the looks of them they haven't much to tell.'

'I will, father,' I said with something approaching joy.

The relief of it was really enormous. Nora stuck out her tongue at me from behind his back, but I couldn't even be bothered retorting. I knew from the very moment that man opened his mouth that he was intelligent above the ordinary. When I had time to think, I saw how right I was. It only stood to reason that a fellow confessing after seven years would have more to tell than people that went every week. The crimes of a lifetime, exactly as he said. It was only what he expected, and the rest was the cackle of old women and girls with their talk of hell, the bishop, and the penitential psalms. That was all they knew. I started to make my examination of conscience, and barring the one bad business of my grandmother it didn't seem so bad.

The next time, the priest steered me into the confession box himself and left the shutter back the way I could see him get in and sit down at the further side of the grille from me.

'Well, now,' he said, 'what do they call you?'

'Jackie, father,' said I.

'And what's a-trouble to you, Jackie?'

'Father,' I said, feeling I might as well get it over while I had him in good humour, 'I had it all arranged to kill my grandmother.'

He seemed a bit shaken by that, all right, because he said nothing for quite a while.

'My goodness,' he said at last, 'that'd be a shocking thing to do. What put that into your head?'

'Father,' I said, feeling very sorry for myself, 'she's an awful woman.'

'Is she?' he asked. 'What way is she awful?'

'She takes porter, father,' I said, knowing well from the way Mother talked of it that this was a mortal sin, and hoping it would make the priest take a more favourable view of my case.

'Oh, my!' he said, and I could see he was impressed.

'And snuff, father,' said I.

'That's a bad case, sure enough, Jackie,' he said.

'And she goes round in her bare feet, father,' I went on in rush of self-pity, 'and she know I don't like her, and she gives pennies to Nora and none to me, and my da sides with her and flakes me, and one night I was so heart-scalded I made up my mind I'd have to kill her.'

'And what would you do with the body?' he asked with great interest.

'I was thinking I could chop that up and carry it away in a barrow I have,' I said.

'Begor, Jackie,' he said, 'do you know you're a terrible child?'

'I know, father,' I said, for I was just thinking the same thing myself. 'I tried to kill Nora too with a bread-knife under the table, only I missed her.'

'Is that the little girl that was beating you just know?' he asked.

''Tis, father.'

'Someone will go for her with a bread-knife one day, and he won't miss her,' he said rather cryptically. 'You must have great courage. Between ourselves, there's a lot of people I'd like to do the same to but I'd never have the nerve. Hanging is an awful death.'

'Is it, father?' I asked with the deepest interest — I was always very keen on hanging. 'Did you ever see a fellow hanged?'

'Dozens of them,' he said solemnly. 'And they all died roaring.'

'Jay!' I said.

'Oh, a horrible death!' he said with great satisfaction. 'Lots of the fellows I saw killed their grandmothers too, but they all said, 'twas never worth it.'

He had me there for a full ten minutes talking, and then walked out the chapel yard with me. I was genuinely sorry to part with him, because he was the most entertaining character I'd ever met in the religious line. Outside, after the shadow of the church, the sunlight was like the roaring of waves on a beach; it dazzled me; and when the frozen silence melted and I heard the screech of trams on the road my heart soared. I knew now I wouldn't die in the night and come back leaving marks on my mother's furniture. It would be a great worry to her, and the poor soul had enough.

Nora was sitting on the railing, waiting for me, and she put on a very sour puss when she saw the priest with me. She was mad jealous because a priest had never come out of the church with her.

'Well,' she asked coldly, after he left me, 'what did he give you?'

'Three Hail Marys,' I said.

'Three Hail Marys,' she repeated incredulously. 'You mustn't have told him anything.'

'I told him everything,' I said confidently.

'About Gran and all?'

'About Gran and all.'

(All she wanted was to be able to go home and say I'd made a bad confession.)

'Did you tell him you went for me with the bread-knife?' she asked with a frown.

'I did to be sure.'

'And he only gave you three Hail Marys?'

'That's all.'

She slowly got down from the railing with a baffled air. Clearly, this was beyond her. As we mounted the steps back to the main road she looked at me suspiciously.

'What are you sucking?' she asked.

'Bullseyes.'

'Was it the priest gave them to you?'

''Twas.'

'Lord God,' she wailed bitterly, 'some people have all the luck! 'Tis no advantage to anybody trying to be good. I might just as well be a sinner like you.'

# VIII
# THE AWAKENING CONSCIENCE

*Juliana Horatia Ewing*

*Charles Lamb*

*Frances Hodgson Burnett*

Juliana Horatia Ewing (1841–1885) the daughter of a famous writer for children, was, like Louisa M Alcott, the editor of a children's magazine, *Aunt Judy's*, which numbered Lewis Caroll, F Anstey and Mrs Molesworth among its contributors. *Flat Iron for a Farthing* (1870) one of her many now largely-forgotten works, shows a disinclination to moralising which is refreshing for the period, and doubly so when dealing with a subject like this one.

The story of 'Barbara S——', too, is narrated by Charles Lamb in a pleasantly dry and unsentimental, at times almost conversational manner which belies its skilful construction as narrative. *The Last Essays of Elia* (1833) were collected from his contributions to the *London Magazine*.

A similar episode, but intended for a young audience, forms the last extract of this book, by Frances Hodgson Burnett (c. 1849–1924). Born in England, but having grown up in Knoxville, Tennessee, Burnett's first novels were unremarkable. *Little Lord Fauntleroy* (1886) brought her lasting fame, but her reputation today rests largely on the children's books of 1900–1910, in particular *The Secret Garden* and *The Little Princess*. Although the story of Sara and the beggar-girl must have hundreds of close counterparts in Victorian fiction, it is handled with a simplicity which is disarming, and the girl's fantasy-world, which she uses to forget her surroundings, is convincing; "Sometimes I can," she admits, "and sometimes I can't."

# Juliana Horatia Ewing

*from:* A Flat Iron for a Farthing

I must not forget to speak of an incident which had a considerable influence on my character at this time. The church which my uncle and his family "attended," as it was called, was one of those most dreary places of worship too common at that time, in London and elsewhere. It was ugly outside, but the outside ugliness was as nothing compared with the ugliness within. The windows were long and bluntly rounded at the top, and the sunlight was modified by scanty calico blinds, which, being yellow with age and smoke, *toned* the light in rather an agreeable manner. Mouldings of a pattern one sees about common fireplaces ran everywhere with praiseworthy impartiality. But the great principle of the ornamental work throughout was a principle only too prevalent at the date when this particular church was last "done up." It was imitations of things not really there, and which would have been quite out of place if they had been there. For instance, pillars and looped-up curtains painted on flat walls, with pretentious shadows, having no reference to the real direction of the light. At the east end some Hebrew letters, executed as journeymen painters usually do execute them, had a less cheerful look than the highly-coloured lion and unicorn on the gallery in front. The clerk's box, the reading-desk, and the pulpit, piled one above another, had a symmetrical effect, to which the umbrella-shaped sounding-board above gave a distant resemblance to a Chinese pagoda. The only things which gave warmth or colour to the interior as a whole were the cushions and pew curtains. There were plenty of them, and they were mostly red. These same curtains added to the sense of isolation, which was already sufficiently attained by the height of the pew walls and their doors and bolts. I think it was this — and the fact that, as the congregation took no outward part in the prayers except that of listening to them, Polly and I had nothing to do — and we could not even hear the old gentleman who usually "read prayers" — which led us into the very reprehensible habit of "playing at houses" in Uncle Ascott's gorgeously furnished pew. Not that we left our too tightly stuffed seats for one moment, but as we sat or stood, unable to see

193

anything beyond the bombazine curtains (which, intervening between us and the distant parson, made our hearing what he said next
to impossible), we amused ourselves by mentally "pretending" a good
deal of domestic drama, in which the pew represented a house; and we
related our respective "plays" to each other afterwards when we went
home.

Wrong as it was, we did not intend to be irreverent, though I had the
grace to feel slightly shocked when after a cheerfully lighted evening
service, at which the claims of a missionary society had been enforced,
Polly confided to me, with some triumph in her tone, "I pretended a
theatre, and when the man was going round with the box upstairs, I
pretended it was oranges in the gallery."

I had more than once felt uneasy at our proceedings, and I now told
Polly that I thought it was not right, and that we ought to "try to
attend." I rather expected her to resent my advice, but she said that
she had "sometimes thought it was wrong" herself; and we resolved to
behave better for the future, and indeed really did give up our un-
seasonable game.

Few religious experiences fill one with more shame and self-reproach
than the large results from very small efforts in the right direction.
Polly and I prospered in our efforts to "attend." I may say for myself
that, child as I was, I began to find a satisfaction and pleasure in going
to church, though the place was hideous, the ritual dreary, and the
minister mumbling. When by chance there was a nice hymn, such as,
"Glory to Thee," or "O God, our help in ages past," we were quite
happy. We also tried manfully to "attend" to the sermons, which,
considering the length and abstruseness of them, was, I think, credit-
able to us. I fear we felt it to be so, and that about this time we began to
be proud of the texts we knew, and of our punctilious propriety in the
family pew, and of the resolve which we had taken in accordance with
my proposal to Polly —

"Let us be very religious."

One Saturday Miss Blomfield was a good deal excited about a
certain clergyman who was to preach in our church next Sunday, and
as the services were now a matter of interest to us, Polly and I were
excited too. I had been troubled with toothache all the week, but this
was now better, and I was quite able to go to church with the rest of the
family.

The general drift of the sermon, even its text, have long since faded
from my mind; but I do remember that it contained so highly coloured

a peroration on the Day of Judgement and the terrors of Hell, that my horror and distress knew no bounds; and when the sermon was ended, and we began to sing, "From lowest depths of woe," I burst into a passion of weeping. The remarkable part of the incident was that the rest of the party, having sat with their noses in the air quite undistressed by the terrible eloquence of the preacher, Aunt Maria never for a moment guessed at the real cause of my tears. But as soon as we were all in the carriage (it was a rainy evening, and we had driven to church), she said —

"That poor child will never have a minute's peace while that tooth's in his head. Thomas! Drive to Dr. Pepjohn's."

Polly did say, "Is it very bad, Regie?" But Aunt Maria answered for me — "Can't you see it's bad, child? Leave him alone."

I was ashamed to confess the real cause of my outburst, and suffered for my disingenuousness in Dr. Pepjohn's consulting-room.

"Show Dr. Pepjohn which it is, Regie," said my aunt; and, with tears that had now become simply hysterical, I pointed to the tooth that had ached.

"Just allow me to touch it," said Dr. Pepjohn, inserting his fat finger and thumb into my mouth. "I won't hurt you, my little man," he added, with the affable mendaciousness of his craft. Fortunately for me it was rather loose, and a couple of hard wrenches from the doctor's expert fingers brought it out.

"You think me very cruel, now, don't you, my little man?" said the jocose gentleman, as we were taking leave.

"I don't think you're cruel," I answered, candidly; "but I think you tell fibs, for it *did* hurt."

The doctor laughed long and loudly, and said I was quite an original, which puzzled me extremely. Then he gave me sixpence, with which I was much pleased, and we parted good friends.

My father was with us on the following Sunday, and he did not go to the church Aunt Maria went to. I went to the one to which he went. This church was very well built and appropriately decorated. The music was good, and the responses of the congregation hearty, and the service altogether was much better adapted to awaken and sustain the interest of a child than those I had hitherto been to in London.

"You know we *couldn't* play houses in the church where Papa goes," I told Polly on my return, and I was very anxious that she should go with us to the evening service. She did go, but I am bound to confess that she decided on a loyal preference for the service to which she had been accustomed, and, like sensible people, we agreed to differ in our tastes.

"There's no clerk at your church, you know," said Polly, to whom a gap in the threefold ministry of clerk, reader and preacher, symbolized by the "threedecker" pulpit, was ill atoned for by the chanting of the choir.

In quite a different way, I was as much impressed by the sermons at the new church as I had been by that which cost me a tooth.

One sermon especially, upon the duties of visiting the sick and imprisoned, feeding the hungry, and clothing the naked, made an impression on me that years did not efface. I made the most earnest resolutions to be active in deeds of kindness "when I was a man," and, not being troubled by considerations of political economy, I began my charitable career by dividing what pocket money I had in hand amongst the street-sweepers and mendicants nearest to our square.

I soon converted Polly to my way of thinking; and we put up a money-box in the nursery, in imitation of the alms-box in church. I am ashamed to confess that I was guilty of the meanness of changing a sixpence which I had dedicated to our "charity-box" into twelve half-pence, that I might have the satisfaction of making a dozen distinct contributions to the fund.

But, despite all its follies, vanities, and imperfections (and what human efforts for good are not stained with folly, vanity, and imperfection?), our benevolence was not without sincerity or self-denial, and brought its own invariable reward of increased willingness to do more; according to the deep wisdom of the poet —

> "In doing is this knowledge won:
> To see what yet remains undone."

We really did forego many a toy and treat to add to our charitable store; and I began then a habit of taxing what money I possessed, by taking off a fixed proportion for "charity," which I have never discontinued, and to the advantages of which I can most heartily testify. When a self-indulgent civilization goads all classes to live beyond their incomes, and tempts them not to include the duty of almsgiving in the expenditure of those incomes, it is well to remove a due proportion of what one has beyond the reach of the evergrowing monster of extravagance; and, being decided upon in an unbiassed and calm moment, it is the less likely to be too much for one's domestic claims, or too little for one's religious duty. It frees one for ever from that grudging and often comical spasm of meanness which attacks so many even wealthy people when they are asked to give, because among all the large "expenses" to which their goods are willingly made liable the expense of giving alms of those goods has never been fairly counted as an item not less needful, not less imperative, not less to be felt as a deduction from the remainder, not less lifelong and daily, than the expenses of rent, and dress, and dinner-parties.

We had, as I say, no knowledge of political economy, and it must be confessed that the objects of our charity were on more than one occasion most unworthy.

"Oh, Regie, dear," Polly cried one day, rushing up to me as she returned from a walk (I had a cold, and was in the nursery), "there is such a poor, poor man at the corner of ——— Street. I do think we ought to give him all that's left in the box. He's quite blind, and he reads out of a book with such queer letters. It's one of the Gospels, he says; so he must be very good, for he reads it all day long. And he can't have any home, for he sits in the street. And he's got a ticket on his back to say 'Blind,' and 'Taught at the Blind School.' And as I passed he was reading quite loud. And I heard him say, 'Now Barabbas was a robber.' Oh, he *is* such a poor man! And you know, Regie, he *must* be good, for *we* don't sit reading our Bibles all day long."

I at once gave my consent to the box being emptied in favour of this very poor and very pious man; and at the first opportunity Polly took the money to her *protégé*.

"He was so much pleased!" she reported on her return. "He seemed quite surprised to get so much. And he said, 'God bless you, miss!' I wish you'd been there, Regie. I said, 'It's not all from me.' He *was* so much pleased!"

"How did he know you were a *miss*, I wonder?" said I.

"I suppose it was my voice," said Polly, after a pause.

As soon as I could go out, I went to see the blind man. As I drew near, he was—as Polly told me—reading aloud. The regularity and rapidity with which his fingers ran over line after line, as if he were rubbing out something on a slate, were most striking; and as I stood beside him I distinctly heard him read the verse, "Now Barabbas was a robber." It was a startling coincidence to find him still reading the words which Polly overheard, especially as they were not in any way remarkably adapted for the subject of a prolonged meditation.

Much living alone with grown-up people had, I think, helped

towards my acquiring a habit I had of "brown studying," turning things over, brewing them, so to speak, in my mind. I stood pondering the peculiarities of the object of our charity for some moments, during which he was elaborately occupied in turning over a leaf of his book. Presently I said—

"What makes you say it out aloud when you read?"

He turned his head towards me, blinking and rolling his eyes, and replied in impressive tones—

"It's the pleasure I takes in it, sir."

Now as he blinked I watched his eyes with mingled terror, pity, and curiosity. At this moment a stout and charitable-looking old gentleman was passing, between whom and my blind friend I was standing. And as he passed he threw the blind man some coppers. But in the moment before he did so, and when there seemed a possibility of his passing without what I suspect was a customary dole, such a sharp expression came into the scarcely visible pupils of the blind man's half-shut eyes that (never suspecting that his blindness was feigned, but for the moment convinced that he had seen the old gentleman) I exclaimed, without thinking of the absurdity of my inquiry—

"Was it at the Blind School you learnt to see so well with your blind eyes?"

The "very poor man" gave me a most unpleasant glance out of his "sightless orbs," and taking up his stool, and muttering something about its being time to go home, he departed.

Some time afterwards I learnt what led me to believe that he had the best possible reason for being able to "see so well with his blind eyes." He was not blind at all.

# *Charles Lamb*

*from:* The Last Essays of Elia

## BARBARA S———

On the noon of the 14th of November, 1743 or 4, I forget which it was, just as the clock had struck one, Barbara S———, with her accustomed punctuality, ascended the long rambling staircase, with awkward interposed landing-places, which led to the office, or rather a sort of box with a desk in it, whereat sat the then Treasurer of (what few of our readers may remember) the Old Bath Theatre. All over the island it was the custom, and remains so I believe to this day, for the players to receive their weekly stipend on the Saturday. It was not much that Barbara had to claim.

This little maid had just entered her eleventh year; but her important station at the theatre, as it seemed to her, with the benefits which she felt to accrue from her pious application of her small earnings, had given an air of womanhood to her steps and to her behaviour. You would have taken her to have been at least five years older.

Till latterly she had merely been employed in choruses, or where children were wanted to fill up the scene. But the manager, observing a diligence and adroitness in her above her age, had for some few months past intrusted to her the performance of whole parts. You may guess the self-consequence of the promoted Barbara. She had already drawn tears in young Arthur; had rallied Richard with infantine petulance in the Duke of York; and in her turn had rebuked that petulance when she was Prince of Wales. She would have done the elder child in Morton's pathetic afterpiece to the life; but as yet the *Children in the Wood* was not.

Long after this little girl was grown an aged woman, I have seen some of these small parts, each making two or three pages at most, copied out in the rudest hand of the then prompter, who doubtless transcribed a little more carefully and fairly for the grown-up tragedy ladies of the establishment. But such as they were, blotted and scrawled, as for a child's use, she kept them all; and in the zenith of her after reputation it was a delightful sight to behold them bound up in costliest morocco, each single—each small part making a *book*—with fine clasps, gilt-splashed, etc.

She had conscientiously kept them as they had been delivered to her; not a blot had been effaced or tampered with. They were precious to her for their affecting remembrancings. They were her principia, her rudiments; the elementary atoms; the little steps by which she pressed forward to perfection. "What," she would say, "could India-rubber, or a pumice-stone, have done for these darlings?"

I am in no hurry to begin my story—indeed I have little or none to tell—so I will just mention an observation of her connected with that interesting time.

Not long before she died I had been discoursing with her on the quantity of real present emotion which a great tragic performer experiences during acting. I ventured to think, that though in the first instance such players must have possessed the feelings which they so powerfully called up in others, yet by frequent repetition those feelings must become deadened in great measure, and the performer trust to the memory of past emotion, rather than express a present one.

She indignantly repelled the notion, that with a truly great tragedian the operation, by which such effects were produced upon an audience, could ever degrade itself into what was purely mechanical. With much delicacy, avoiding to instance in her *self*-experience, she told me, that so long ago as when she used to play the part of the Little Son to Mrs. Porter's Isabella (I think it was), when that impressive actress has been bending over her in some heart-rending colloquy, she has felt real hot tears come trickling from her, which (to use her powerful expression) have perfectly scalded her back.

I am not quite so sure that it was Mrs. Porter; but it was some great actress of that day. The name is indifferent; but the fact of the scalding tears I most distinctly remember.

I was always fond of the society of players, and am not sure that an impediment in my speech (which certainly kept me out of the pulpit) even more than certain personal disqualifications, which are often got over in that profession, did not prevent me at one time of life from adopting it. I have had the honour (I must ever call it) once to have been admitted to the tea-table of Miss Kelly. I have played at serious whist with Mr. Liston. I have chattered with ever good-humoured Mrs. Charles Kemble. I have conversed as friend to friend with her accomplished husband. I have been indulged with a classical conference with Macready; and with a sight of the Player-picture gallery, at Mr. Mathews's, when the kind owner, to remunerate me for my love of the old actors (whom he loves so much), went over it with me, supplying to his capital collection, what alone the artist could not give them—voice; and their living motion. Old tones, half-faded, of Dodd, and Parsons, and Baddeley, have lived again for me at his bidding. Only Edwin he could not restore to me. I have supped with ——; but I am growing a coxcomb.

As I was about to say—at the desk of the then treasurer of the Old Bath Theatre—not Diamond's—presented herself the little Barbara S——.

The parents of Barbara had been in reputable circumstances. The father had practised, I believe, as an apothecary in the town. But his practice, from causes which I feel my own infirmity too sensibly that way to arraign—or perhaps from that pure infelicity which accompanies some people in their walk through life, and which it is impossible to lay at the door of imprudence—was now reduced to nothing. They were in fact in the very teeth of starvation, when the manager, who knew and respected them in better days, took the little Barbara into his company.

At the period I commenced with, her slender earnings were the sole support of the family, including two younger sisters. I must throw a veil over some mortifying circumstances. Enough to say, that her Saturday's pittance was the only chance of a Sunday's (generally their only) meal of meat.

One thing I will only mention, that in some child's part, where in her theatrical character she was to sup off a roast fowl (O joy to Barbara) some comic actor, who was for the night caterer of this dainty—in the misguided humour of his part, threw over the dish such a quantity of salt (O grief and pain of heart to Barbara) that when she crammed a portion of it into her mouth, she was obliged sputteringly to reject it; and what with shame of her ill-acted part, and pain of real appetite at missing such a dainty, her little heart sobbed almost to breaking, till a flood of tears, which the well-fed spectators were totally unable to comprehend, mercifully relieved her.

This was the little starved, meritorious maid, who stood before old Ravenscroft, the treasurer, for her Saturday's payment.

Ravenscroft was a man, I have heard many old theatrical people besides herself say, of all men least calculated for a treasurer. He had no head for accounts, paid away at random, kept scarce any books, and summing up at the week's end, if he found himself a pound or so deficient, blest himself that it was no worse.

Now Barbara's weekly stipend was a bare half guinea. By mistake he popped into her hand— a whole one.

Barbara tripped away.

She was entirely unconscious at first of the mistake: God knows, Ravenscroft would never have discovered it.

But when she had got down to the first of those uncouth landing-places, she became sensible of an unusual weight of metal pressing her little hand.

Now mark the dilemma.

She was by nature a good child. From her parents and those about her she had imbibed no contrary influence. But then they had taught her nothing. Poor men's smoky cabins are not always porticoes of moral philosophy. This little maid had no instinct to evil, but then she might be said to have no fixed principle. She had heard honesty commended, but never dreamed of its application to herself. She thought of it as something which concerned grown-up people, men and women. She had never known temptation, or thought of preparing resistance against it.

Her first impulse was to go back to the old treasurer, and explain to him his blunder. He was already so confused with age, besides a natural want of punctuality, that she would have had some difficulty in making him understand it. She saw *that* in an instant. And then it was such a bit of money! and then the image of a larger allowance of butcher's-meat on their table next day came across her, till her little eyes glistened, and her mouth moistened. But then Mr. Ravenscroft had always been so good-natured, had stood her friend behind the scenes, and even recommended her promotion to some of her little parts.

But again the old man was reputed to be worth a world of money. He was supposed to have fifty pounds a year clear of the theatre. And then came staring upon her the figures of her little stockingless and shoeless sisters. And when she looked at her own neat white cotton stockings, which her situation at the theatre had made it indispensable for her mother to provide for her, with hard straining and pinching from the family stock, and thought how glad she should be to cover their poor feet with the same—and how then they could accompany her to rehearsals, which they had hitherto been precluded from doing, by reason of their unfashionable attire—in these thoughts she reached the second landing-place—the second, I mean, from the top—for there was still another left to traverse.

Now virtue support Barbara!

And that never-failing friend *did* step in—for at that moment a strength not her own, I have heard her say, was revealed to her—a reason above reasoning—and without her own agency, as it seemed (for she never felt her feet to move), she found herself transported back to the individual desk she had just quitted, and her hand in the old hand of Ravenscroft, who in silence took back the refunded treasure, and who had been sitting (good man) insensible to the lapse of minutes, which to her were anxious ages, and from that moment a deep peace fell upon her heart, and she knew the quality of honesty.

A year or two's unrepining application to her profession brightened up the feet and the prospects of her little sisters, set the whole family upon their legs again, and released her from the difficulty of discussing moral dogmas upon a landing-place.

I have heard her say that it was a surprise, not much short of mortification to her, to see the coolness with which the old man pocketed the difference, which had caused her such mortal throes.

This anecdote of herself I had in the year 1800, from the mouth of the late Mrs. Crawford, then sixty-seven years of age (she died soon after); and to her struggles upon this childish occasion I have sometimes ventured to think her indebted for that power of rending the heart in the representation of conflicting emotions, for which in after years she was considered as little inferior (if at all so in the part of Lady Randolph) even to Mrs. Siddons.

# Frances Hodgson Burnett

*from:* A Little Princess

The winter was a wretched one. There were days on which Sara tramped through snow when she went on her errands; there were worse days when the snow melted and combined itself with mud to form slush; there were others when the fog was so thick that the lamps in the streets were lighted all day and London looked as it had looked the afternoon several years ago, when the cab had driven through the thoroughfares with Sara tucked up on its seat, leaning against her father's shoulder. On such days the windows of the house of the Large Family always looked delightfully cosy and alluring, and the study in which the Indian gentleman sat glowed with warmth and rich colour. But the attic was dismal beyond words. There were no longer sunsets or sunrises to look at, and scarcely ever any stars, it seemed to Sara. The clouds hung low over the skylight, and were either grey or mud-colour, or dropping heavy rain. At four o'clock in the afternoon, even when there was no special fog, the daylight was at an end. If it was necessary to go to her attic for anything, Sara was obliged to light a candle. The women in the kitchen were depressed, and that made them more ill-tempered than ever. Becky was driven like a little slave.

"Twarn't for you, miss,' she said hoarsely to Sara one night when she had crept into the attic—"twarn't for you, an' the Bastille, an' bein' the prisoner in the next cell, I should die. That there does seem real now, doesn't it? The missus is more like the head jailer every day she lives. I can jest see them big keys you say she carries. The cook, she's like one of the under-jailers. Tell me some more, please, miss— tell me about the subt'ranean passage we've dug under the walls.'

'I'll tell you something warmer,' shivered Sara. 'Get your coverlet and wrap it round you, and I'll get mine, and we will huddle it close together on the bed, and I'll tell you about the tropical forest where the Indian gentleman's monkey used to live. When I see him sitting on the table near the window and looking out into the street with that mournful expression, I always feel sure he is thinking about the tropical forest where he used to swing by his tail from coconut-trees. I wonder who caught him, and if he left a family behind who had depended on him for coconuts.'

'That is warmer, miss,' said Becky gratefully, 'but, someways, even the Bastille is sort of heatin' when you gets to tellin' about it.'

'That is because it makes you think of something else,' said Sara, wrapping the coverlet round her until only her small dark face was to be seen looking out of it. 'I've noticed this. What you have to do with your mind, when your body is miserable, is to make it think of something else.'

'Can you do it, miss?' faltered Becky, regarding her with admiring eyes.

Sara knitted her brows a moment.

'Sometimes I can and sometimes I can't,' she said stoutly. 'But when I *can* I'm all right. And what I believe is that we always could—if we practised enough. I've been practising a good deal lately, and it's beginning to be easier than it used to be. When things are horrible— just horrible—I think as hard as ever I can of being a princess. I say to myself: "I am a princess, and I am a fairy one, and because I am a fairy nothing can hurt me or make me uncomfortable." You don't know how it makes you forget'—with a laugh.

She had many opportunities of making her mind think of something else, and many opportunities of proving to herself whether or not she was a princess. But one of the strongest tests she was ever put to came on a certain dreadful day which, she often thought afterward, would never quite fade out of her memory even in the years to come.

For several days it had rained continuously; the streets were chilly and sloppy and full of dreary, cold mist; there was mud everywhere—

sticky London mud—and over everything the pall of drizzle and fog. Of course there were several long and tiresome errands to be done— there always were on days like this—and Sara was sent out again and again, until her shabby clothes were damp through. The absurd old feathers on her forlorn hat were more draggled and absurd than ever, and her down-trodden shoes were so wet that they could not hold any more water. Added to this, she had been deprived of her dinner, because Miss Minchin had chosen to punish her. She was so cold and hungry and tired that her face began to have a pinched look, and now and then some kind-hearted person passing her in the street glanced at her with sudden sympathy. But she did not know that. She hurried on, trying to make her mind think of something else. It was really very necessary. Her way of doing it was to 'pretend' and 'suppose' with all the strength that was left in her. But really this time it was harder than she had ever found it, and once or twice she thought it almost made her more cold and hungry instead of less so. But she persevered obstinate- ly and as the muddy water squelched through her broken shoes and the wind seemed trying to drag her thin jacket from her, she talked to herself as she walked, though she did not speak aloud or even move her lips.

'Suppose I had dry clothes on,' she thought. 'Suppose I had good shoes and a long, thick coat and merino stockings and a whole umbrella. And suppose—suppose—just when I was near a baker's where they sold hot buns, I should find sixpence—which belonged to nobody. *Suppose*, if I did, I should go into the shop and buy six of the hottest buns and eat them all without stopping.'

Some very odd things happen in this world sometimes.

It certainly was an odd thing that happened to Sara. She had to cross the street just when she was saying this to herself. The mud was dreadful—she almost had to wade. She picked her way as carefully as she could, but she could not save herself much; only, in picking her way, she had to look down at her feet and the mud, and in looking down—just as she reached the pavement—she saw something shining in the gutter. It was actually a piece of silver—a tiny piece trodden upon by many feet, but still with spirit enough left to shine a little. Not quite a sixpence, but the next thing to it—a fourpenny piece.

In one second it was in her cold little red-and-blue hand.

'Oh,' she gasped, 'it is true! It is true!'

And then, if you will believe me, she looked straight at the shop directly facing her. And it was a baker's shop, and a cheerful, stout, motherly woman with rosy cheeks was putting into the window a tray of delicious newly baked hot buns, fresh from the oven—large, plump, shiny buns, with currants in them.

It almost made Sara feel faint for a few seconds—the shock, and the sight of the buns, and the delightful odours of warm bread floating up through the baker's cellar window.

She knew she needed not hesitate to use the little piece of money. It had evidently been lying in the mud for some time, and its owner was completely lost in the stream of passing people who crowded and jostled each other all day long.

'But I'll go and ask the baker woman if she has lost anything,' she said to herself, rather faintly. So she crossed the pavement and put her wet foot on the step. As she did so she saw something that made her stop.

It was a little figure more forlorn even than herself—a little figure which was not much more than a bundle of rags, from which small, bare, red, muddy feet peeped out, only because the rags with which their owner was trying to cover them were not long enough. Above the rags appeared a shock head of tangled hair, and a dirty face with big, hollow, hungry eyes.

Sara knew they were hungry eyes the moment she saw them, and she felt a sudden sympathy.

'This,' she said to herself, with a little sigh, 'is one of the populace—and she is hungrier than I am.'

The child—this 'one of the populace'—stared up at Sara, and shuffled herself aside a little, so as to give her room to pass. She was used to being made to give room to everybody. She knew that if a policeman chanced to see her he would tell her to 'move on'.

Sara clutched her little fourpenny piece and hesitated a few seconds. Then she spoke to her.

'Are you hungry?' she asked.

The child shuffled herself and her rags a little more.

'Ain't I jist?' she said in a hoarse voice. 'Jist ain't I?'

'Haven't you had any dinner?' said Sara.

'No dinner'—more hoarsely still and with more shuffling. 'Nor yet no bre'fast—nor yet no supper. No nothin'.'

'Since when?' asked Sara.

'Dunno. Never got nothin' today—nowhere. I've axed an' axed.'

Just to look at her made Sara more hungry and faint. But those queer little thoughts were at work in her brain, and she was talking to herself, though she was sick at heart.

'If I'm a princess,' she was saying—'if I'm a princess—when they were poor and driven from their thrones—they always shared—with the populace—if they met one poorer and hungrier than themselves. They always shared. Buns are a penny each. If it had been sixpence I could have eaten six. It won't be enough for either of us. But it will be better than nothing.'

'Wait a minute,' she said to the beggar child.

She went into the shop. It was warm and smelled deliciously. The woman was just going to put some more hot buns into the window.

'If you please,' said Sara, 'have you lost fourpence—a silver four-pence?' And she held the forlorn little piece of money out to her.

The woman looked at it and then at her—at her intense little face and draggled, once fine clothes.

'Bless us, no!' she answered. 'Did you find it?'

'Yes,' said Sara. 'In the gutter.'

'Keep it, then,' said the woman. 'It may have been there for a week, and goodness knows who lost it. *You* could never find out.'

'I know that,' said Sara, 'but I thought I would ask you.'

'Not many would,' said the woman, looking puzzled and interested and good-natured all at once.

'Do you want to buy something?' she added, as she saw Sara glance at the buns.

'Four buns, if you please,' said Sara. 'Those at a penny each.'

The woman went to the window and put some in a paper bag.

Sara noticed that she put in six.

'I said four, if you please,' she explained. 'I have only fourpence.'

'I'll throw in two for makeweight,' said the woman, with her good-natured look. 'I dare say you can eat them sometime. Aren't you hungry?'

A mist rose before Sara's eyes.

'Yes,' she answered. 'I am very hungry, and I am much obliged to you for your kindness; and'—she was going to add—'there is a child outside who is hungrier than I am.' But just at that moment two or three customers came in at once, and each one seemed in a hurry, so she could only thank the woman again and go out.

The beggar girl was still huddled up in the corner of the step. She looked frightful in her wet and dirty rags. She was staring straight before her with a stupid look of suffering, and Sara saw her suddenly draw the back of her roughened black hand across her eyes to rub away the tears which seemed to have surprised her by forcing their way from under the lids. She was muttering to herself.

Sara opened the paper bag and took out one of the hot buns, which had already warmed her own cold hands a little.

'See,' she said, putting the bun in the ragged lap, 'this is nice and hot. Eat it, and you will not feel so hungry.'

The child started and stared up at her, as if such sudden, amazing good luck almost frightened her; then she snatched up the bun and began to cram it into her mouth with great wolfish bites.

'Oh, my! Oh, my!' Sara heard her say hoarsely, in wild delight. '*Oh, my?*'

Sara took out three more buns and put them down.

The sound in the hoarse, ravenous voice was awful.

'She is hungrier than I am,' she said to herself. 'She's starving.' But her hand trembled when she put down the fourth bun. 'I'm not starving,' she said—and she put down the fifth.

The little ravening London savage was still snatching and devouring when she turned way. She was too ravenous to give thanks, even if she had ever been taught politeness—which she had not. She was only a poor little wild animal.

'Good-bye,' said Sara.

When she reached the other side of the street she looked back. The child had a bun in each hand, and had stopped in the middle of a bite to watch her. Sara gave her a litle nod, and the child, after another stare—a curious lingering stare—jerked her shaggy head in response, and until Sara was out of sight she did not take another bite or even finish the one she had begun.

At that moment the baker-woman looked out of her shop window.

'Well, I never!' she exclaimed. 'If that young 'un hasn't given her buns to a beggar child! It wasn't because she didn't want them, either. Well, well, she looked hungry enough. I'd give something to know what she did it for.'

She stood behind her window for a few moments and pondered. Then her curiosity got the better of her. She went to the door and spoke to the beggar child.

'Who gave you those buns?' she asked her.

The child nodded her head towards Sara's vanishing figure.

'What did she say?' inquired the woman.

'Axed me if I was 'ungry,' replied the hoarse voice.

'What did you say?'

'Said I was jist.'

'And then she came in and got the buns, and gave them to you, did she?'

The child nodded.

'How many?'

'Five.'

The woman thought it over.

'Left just one for herself,' she said in a low voice. 'And she could have eaten the whole six—I saw it in her eyes.'

She looked after the little draggled far-away figure, and felt more disturbed in her usually comfortable mind than she had felt for many a day.

'I wish she hadn't gone so quick,' she said. 'I'm blest if she shouldn't have had a dozen.' Then she turned to the child.

'Are you hungry yet?' she said.

'I'm allus hungry,' was the answer, 'but 't ain't as bad as it was.'

'Come in here,' said the woman, and she held open the shop door.

The child got up and shuffled in. To be invited into a warm place full of bread seemed an incredible thing. She did not know what was going to happen. She did not care, even.

'Get yourself warm,' said the woman, pointing to a fire in the tiny back-room. 'And look here; when you are hard up for a bit of bread, you can come in here and ask for it. I'm blest if I won't give it to you for that young one's sake.'

Sara found some comfort in her remaining bun. At all events, it was very hot, and it was better than nothing. As she walked along she broke off small pieces and ate them slowly to make them last longer.

'Suppose it was a magic bun,' she said, 'and a bite was as much as a whole dinner. I should be over-eating myself if I went on like this.'

It was dark when she reached the square where the Select Seminary was situated. The lights in the houses were all lighted. The blinds were not yet drawn in the windows of the room where she nearly always caught glimpses of members of the Large Family. Frequently at this hour she could see the gentleman she called Mr Montmorency sitting in a big chair, with a small swarm round him, talking, laughing, perching on the arms of his seat or on his knees or leaning against them. This evening the swarm was about him, but he was not seated. On the contrary, there was a good deal of excitement going on. It was evident that a journey was to be taken, and it was Mr Montmorency

209

who was to take it. A brougham stood before the door, and a big portmanteau had been strapped upon it. The children were dancing about, chattering and hanging on to their father. The pretty rosy mother was standing near him, talking as if she was asking final questions. Sara paused a moment to see the little ones lifted up and kissed and the bigger ones bent over and kissed also.

'I wonder if he will stay away long,' she thought. 'The pormanteau is rather big. Oh, dear, how they will miss him! I shall miss him myself—even though he doesn't know I am alive.'

When the door opened she moved away—remembering the sixpence—but she saw the traveller come out and stand against the background of the warmly lighted hall, the older children still hovering about him.

'Will Moscow be covered with snow?' said the little girl Janet. 'Will there be ice everywhere?'

'Shall you drive in a droshky?' cried another. 'Shall you see the Tsar?'

'I will write and tell you all about it,' he answered, laughing. 'And I will send you pictures of mujiks and things. Run into the house. It is a hideous damp night. I would rather stay with you than go to Moscow. Good night! Good night, duckies! God bless you!' And he ran down the steps and jumped into the brougham.

'If you find the little girl, give her our love,' shouted Guy Clarence, jumping up and down on the doormat.

Then they went in and shut the door.

'Did you see,' said Janet to Nora, as they went back to the room—'the little-girl-who-is-not-a-beggar was passing? She looked all cold and wet, and I saw her turn her head over her shoulder and look at us. Mamma says her clothes always look as if they had been given her by someone who was quite rich—someone who only let her have them because they were too shabby to wear. The people at the school always send her out on errands on the horridest days and nights there are.'

Sara crossed the square to Miss Minchin's area steps, feeling faint and shaky.

'I wonder who the girl is,' she thought—'the little girl he is going to look for.'

And she went down the area steps, hugging her basket and finding it very heavy indeed, as the father of the Large Family drove quickly on his way to the station to take the train which was to carry him to Moscow, where he was to make his best efforts to search for the lost little daughter of Captain Crewe.